FORBIDDEN HISTORY

FORBIDDEN HISTORY

Prehistoric Technologies,
Extraterrestrial Intervention, and the
Suppressed Origins of Civilization

Edited by J. Douglas Kenyon

Bear & Company
Rochester, Vermont

Bear & Company
One Park Street
Rochester, Vermont 05767
www.InnerTraditions.com

Bear & Company is a division of Inner Traditions International

Library of Congress Cataloging-in-Publication Data
Forbidden history : prehistoric technologies, extraterrestrial intervention, and the
suppressed origins of civilization / edited by J. Douglas Kenyon.
    p. cm.
  Includes bibliographical references.
  ISBN 1-59143-045-3 (pbk.)
 1. Civilization, Ancient--Extraterrestrial influences. I. Kenyon, J. Douglas.

 CB156.F67 2005
 930--dc22

                                         2005001277

Printed and bound in the United States by Lake Book Manufacturing, Inc.

10 9 8 7 6 5 4

Text design and layout by Rachel Goldenberg
This book was typeset in Sabon, with Avant Garde and Rubber Stamp as the
display typefaces

All pictures reprinted from *Atlantis Rising* magazine unless otherwise noted.

*To the growing number of scientists and scholars willing
to risk their professional prestige, perks, and privileges
for the sake of something as ephemeral as the truth.*

❦

ACKNOWLEDGMENTS

Were it not for *Atlantis Rising*—a bimonthly magazine—and associated projects, this book would not have been possible. All of the resources that for the last ten years have gone into the making of that periodical have also served to create this book. The people who helped to actualize *Atlantis Rising* are the same ones who made *Forbidden History* a reality. And while it is true that this book represents only a small sampling of *Atlantis Rising*'s material it is nevertheless representative of the very best that the magazine has to offer. We are, of course, indebted, not only to the many thoughtful authors who contributed to the content of the current pages of the book, but to the magazine's many other fine writers as well, who though they could not be included here, may yet find their efforts incorporated into future works.

In thanking those who have made this collective endeavor possible (which includes this book, the magazine, the educational videos, and our Web site: AtlantisRising.com), I must first acknowledge my lovely wife, Patricia. Without her loyal support and selfless cooperation, I probably would have spent the last decade in much less productive pursuits. High on the list are also my parents—my late father, John B. Kenyon, D.D., whose own questioning of conventional wisdom catalyzed my thinking at a very early age, and my mother, Bessie, who always backed me in everything I did, in every way she could, with every resource at her command.

Among the stalwart supporters who deserve special thanks are my original financial backers, John Fanuzzi, Gregory Mascari, and Michael Stern, as well as Bob and Judy Colee. A few years later Greg Hedgecock (since deceased), his wife, Dianne, and their son, Cooper, put their shoulders to the wheel and helped to stabilize what was then a somewhat shaky operation. Without the generous help of these extraordinary people, this book would certainly have never come about.

Deserving of special credit here is my partner of many years, Tom Miller, whose brilliant artistic contributions to our early covers helped to set us apart from the competition. Without his participation in so much of the thinking that went into our projects, it is difficult to imagine how things could have unfolded as wonderfully as they did.

Certainly no list of crucial helpers would be complete without Darsi Vanatta, whose diligent and tireless efforts in managing the *Atlantis Rising* office for some years now have kept everything working smoothly and growing at a very healthy pace.

There are many others whom I could also thank, but space here is limited, so I will simply say: You know who you are and you know what your contributions have been. Rest assured that you are not forgotten, nor are your efforts unappreciated. You know how much they mean to me, and how much I thank you for them.

J. Douglas Kenyon, Editor and Publisher
Atlantis Rising Magazine

Contents

PART THREE • **Exploring the Greater Antiquity of Civilization**

PART FOUR • Searching for the Fountainhead

PART FIVE • Ancient High Tech

PART SIX • New Models to Ponder

Introduction

J. Douglas Kenyon

Just a few centuries after what the experts say was the first great labor-saving invention of the ancient world—the wheel—society crossed a major threshold and headed irreversibly toward the modern world. More than anything else, it was the wheel, we are told, that revolutionized primitive society and set the stage for the great achievements that were to follow. The prevailing assumption is that the rise of highly organized society was *unprecedented;* such is the conventional scenario for the dawn of civilization on Earth.

After all, it is argued, if there *had* been an earlier, advanced civilization we would have discovered unmistakable evidence of its existence. Presumably, we would have seen the remains of its highways, and bridges, and electrical wiring. We would have found its plastic bottles, its city dumps, and its CD-ROMs. Those are, after all, the things *we* will leave behind for future archeologists to puzzle over.

But could an ancient civilization have risen to heights similar to our own, yet have traveled a different road? What would we understand of a world that might have employed fundamentally different—though no less effective—techniques to harness the forces of nature? Would we, or could we, comprehend a world capable of, for example, creating and transmitting energy by means other than a power grid, traveling great distances without internal combustion engines, or making highly complex calculations involving earth science and astronomy without electronic computers?

Do we have the grace to recognize and respect achievements other than our own, or must we take the easy way out and resort to crude stereotyping of our mysterious primitive ancestors, dismissing out of hand anything we don't immediately understand? Indeed there are some, including many contributors to this book, who would argue that the evidence of a great but forgotten fountainhead of civilization is overwhelming and needs, at last, to be given its proper due.

Forbidden History, a compilation of essays gathered over time from the

1

magazine *Atlantis Rising*, aims to put forward such evidence, and to propose ideas and theories with regard to the origins of life and the human race itself that may very well be more in accordance with reality than currently prevailing orthodoxy. In proposing these ideas, we hope to pose some interesting and provocative questions.

For example, could today's reigning conception of the limits of prehistoric society be but another in the long line of self-serving conceits to which our ruling elite, if not our flesh, is heir? Take, for instance, the Darwinian/ Uniformitarian view of history, which argues that our world is a very slowly changing place; wherein everything has developed spontaneously, albeit quite gradually, over millions of years, without the help of any external forces—no, God forbid, God!—to interfere in the process. According to this predominant school of thought, the way the world works *now* is the way it has *always* worked.

On the other side, some have tried to argue (without the benefit of much public exposure) that our world today is the product of a series of catastrophes. These "catastrophists" tell us that the story of mankind is one of a never-ending cycle of ascents followed by cataclysmic falls. For more than a century, the uniformitarians have dominated the debate, but this is a circumstance that may be changing.

Probably no one in the past half-century is more directly linked, in the public mind, with the concept of catastrophism than the late Russian-American scientist Immanuel Velikovsky. When Velikovsky's book *Worlds in Collision* was published in 1950, it caused a sensation. His subsequent works, *Earth in Upheaval* and *Ages in Chaos,* further elaborated his theories and expanded the ongoing controversy. Here was a scientist of considerable authority suggesting, among other things, that Earth and Venus might once have collided, leaving behind a vast and puzzling chaotic aftermath that, if we could just decipher its resultant clues correctly, could do much to explain our peculiar history.

For such arguments, Velikovsky was roundly and routinely ridiculed. Nonetheless, many of his predictions have now been verified, and many who initially disagreed with him on many subjects, including the late Carl Sagan, have been forced to concede that, after all and in some ways, Velikovsky may have been on to something.

Very few realize that Velikovsky was a psychoanalyst by profession, an associate of Sigmund Freud and Carl Jung. His insights into the psycho/sociological impacts of cataclysmic events, in my view, were his greatest contribution to a proper understanding of our ancient experience. Sometime in the mid-1980s, I ran across his book *Mankind in Amnesia,* and my own thinking about the condition of humanity on Earth has never been the same. According to Velikovsky, the psychological condition and case history of planet Earth is one of amnesia: We find the planet today in a near-psychotic state, left so by traumatic events of an almost unimaginable magnitude that, thanks to a collective psychological defense mechanism, we cannot bear to remember.

Today, psychiatrists have applied the term post-traumatic stress syndrome to a group of mental disorders that have been known to follow the witnessing of life-threatening events (e.g., military combat, natural disasters, terrorist incidents, serious accidents, and violent personal assaults such as rape). Symptoms of the disorder include depression, anxiety, nightmares, *and amnesia.*

The question that must be asked is whether or not such a diagnosis could be applied to the culture *of an entire planet?* And could a collective unwillingness to explore and define our mysterious past—unconsciously dreading that to do so would open ancient wounds—eventually harden into a systematic repression of the truth? Could it become tyranny? Certainly our reluctance to honestly explore the past has led to many such evils. Over time, this reluctance to consider the truth of our origins has often become codified and institutionalized, culminating in nightmares like the inquisitions of the Middle Ages and the book burnings of Nazi Germany. How often we have watched as a brutal elite, supposedly acting in our name, enforced the collective subconscious wish to keep such threatening—and thus forbidden—knowledge *safely* out of sight? The answer, Velikovsky believed, was, 'all too frequently.'

In many ways, his views were supported by Carl Jung's notion of an innate collective unconscious undergirding all of human awareness. From this vast and mysterious well of shared experience, Jung argued, emerge many of our greatest aspirations and many of our deepest fears. Its influence is recorded in our dreams and in our myths. In the subtext of such narratives, Velikovsky read the tale of a monumental, albeit forgotten, ancient tragedy.

As I reflected on Velikovsky's theories, my own thinking came into sharper focus, for it seemed apparent to me that collectively we have indeed been persuaded to close our eyes to certain realities—to dissociate from them—and that, perversely, compounding the error, we have justified this willful blindness and endowed it with a certain authority, even *nobility.* The strange effect of this has been to turn many moral issues upside down—to make right wrong and wrong right, if you will.

Recall the Church fathers of the Middle Ages and their refusal, because of what they considered to be Galileo's incorrect conclusions, to look through his telescope *for themselve*s. Galileo's notion that the Sun, not Earth, was the center of the solar system was deemed heresy, no matter what the evidence might show to the contrary. In other words, the minds of the authorities had already been made up, and they had no intention of being confused by such minor annoyances as facts.

Does such blindness persist today? Some of us think so. The ruling elite of today may subscribe to a similarly intolerant "religion"—what John Anthony West has sardonically called "the Church of Progress." As Graham Hancock affirmed to *Atlantis Rising* in a recent interview, "The reason we are so screwed up at the beginning of a new century is that we are victims of a planetary amnesia. We have forgotten who we are."

Sadly, the establishments of government and industry and the academic world—along with those who categorically and systematically debunk any and all alternate theories which might undermine the ruling paradigm—today remain determined to thwart any reawakening from the ongoing amnesia.

Often, when it proves difficult to find an adequate rationale to support the misguided choices of our leaders, it is tempting to think in terms of dark conspiracy theories and treacherous hidden agendas. For Velikovsky, though, the explanation for behavior that some might describe as evil and others would view as, at the very least, self-destructive and unenlightened, lies in the classic mechanism of a mind seeking to regain its equilibrium in the aftermath of a near mortal blow.

In the case of amnesia, it's not enough to simply say that a hole has been blown in our memory. The victim of a near fatal trauma is driven, it would appear, by fear—both conscious and unconscious—to exorcise, by whatever means possible, the demons of such a dreadful experience lest he or she be overwhelmed. How else can we get on with our lives, put the past behind us, think about the future? To rid ourselves entirely of the memory of such an episode, however, is not such an easy task. Much more than the record of the trauma itself may be lost in the process. The human identity—what some would call the very soul itself—is often the first casualty. Moreover, what is true on an individual level Velikovsky felt was also true on the collective level.

This process might move more slowly and allow for personal exceptions, but the institutions of society would in time come to reflect and then enforce a deep collective subconscious wish that, for the good of all, certain doors stay closed and certain inconvenient facts stay forgotten—that such history remain a forbidden zone. *And in the meantime, the risk of reenacting the ancient drama grows, as does our need for reliable guidance.*

It is a premise of this book that the map we must follow in order to find our way out of the current dilemma is one that may be drawn from our myths, our legends, and our dreams—from the universal, collective unconscious that Jung talked about. The *real* story of our planet's tragic history, we suspect, can be deduced from these mysterious records.

Read between the lines and Plato's account of Atlantis in the *Timaeus* and the *Critias* is corroborated by the Bible, by the Indian legends of Central America, and by a thousand other ancient myths from every part of the world. Giorgio de Santillana, a professor at M.I.T. and an authority on the history of science, and his co-author, professor of science Hertha von Dechend, hypothesized in their monumental work, *Hamlet's Mill: An Essay Investigating the Origins of Human Knowledge and Its Transmission through Myth,* that an advanced scientific knowledge had been encoded into ancient myth and star lore.

Indeed, the mythology of many ancient societies is filled with stories of cataclysmic destruction of Earth and its inhabitants. We agree with Graham Hancock when he says, "Once one accepts that mythology may have originated in the waking minds of highly advanced people, then one must start listening to what the myths are saying."

What they are saying, we believe, is that great catastrophes have struck Earth and destroyed advanced civilizations (not unlike our own) and, moreover, that such cataclysmic destruction is a recurrent feature in the life of Earth and may very well happen again. Many ancient sources (again, including the Bible), warn of possible cataclysm in a future end time—perhaps in *our* lifetime. If it's true that those who cannot learn from the mistakes of history are doomed to repeat them, these enigmatic messages from our past could very well prove to be something that we can ignore *only at our peril.*

As Hancock points out, we've received a legacy of extraordinary knowledge from our ancestors, and the time has come for us to stop dismissing it. Rather, we must recapture that heritage and learn from it what we can, because it contains vitally important guidance. To prevail in the challenges before us now, we must recover our lost identity. We must remember who we are and where we came from.

We must, at last, be awake.

PART ONE

THE OLD MODELS DON'T WORK: DARWINISM AND CREATIONISM UNDER FIRE

1 Darwin's Demise

On the Futile Search for Missing Links

Will Hart

Charles Darwin was a keen observer of nature and an original thinker. He revolutionized biology. Karl Marx was also an astute observer of human society and an original thinker. He revolutionized economic and political ideology. They were contemporary nineteenth-century giants who cast long shadows and subscribed to the theory of "dialectical materialism"—the viewpoint that matter is the sole subject of change and all change is the product of conflict arising from the internal contradictions inherent in all things. And yet, as much appeal as dialectical materialism had to the intellectuals and working classes of certain countries, by the close of the last century it had failed to pass the test in the real world.

Charles Darwin
(PHOTOGRAPH BY
BENJAMIN CUMMINGS)

Darwinism is beginning to show similar signs of strain and fatigue. It is not just creationists who are sounding the death knell. Darwin was well aware of the weaknesses of his theory. He called the origin of flowering plants "an abominable mystery." That mystery remains unsolved to this day.

As scientists have searched the fossil record assiduously for more than one hundred years for the "missing link" between primitive nonflowering and flowering plants without luck, a host of other trouble spots have flared up. Darwin anticipated problems should there be an absence of transitional fossils (chemically formed duplications of living creatures). At the time, he wrote: "It is the most serious objection that can be urged against the theory."

However, he could not have predicted where additional structural cracks would appear and threaten the very foundation of his theory. Why? Biochemistry was in an embryonic state in Darwin's day. It is doubtful that he could have imagined that the structure of DNA would be discovered in less than one hundred years from the publication of *Origin of Species*.

In a twist of fate, one of the first torpedoes to rip holes in the theory of evolution was unleashed by a biochemist. In *Darwin's Black Box: The Biochemical Challenge to Evolution,* Michael Behe, a biology professor, points to a strange brew bubbling in the test tube. He focuses on five phenomena: blood clotting, cilia, the human immune system, the transport of materials within cells, and the synthesis of nucleotides. He analyzes each phenomenon systemically and arrives at a single startling conclusion: These are systems that are so *irreducibly complex* that no gradual, step-by-step Darwinian route could have led to their creation.

The foundation of Darwin's theory is simple, perhaps even simplistic. Life on Earth has evolved through a series of biological changes as a consequence of random genetic mutations working in conjunction with natural selection. One species gradually changes over time into another. And those species that adapt to changing environmental conditions are best suited to survive and propagate and the weaker die out, producing the most well-known principle of Darwinism—survival of the fittest.

The theory has been taught to children for generations. We have all learned that fish changed into amphibians, amphibians became reptiles, reptiles evolved into birds, and birds changed into animals. However, it is far easier to explain this to schoolchildren—with cute illustrations and pictures of a lineup of apes (beginning with those having slumped shoulders, transitioning to two that are finally standing upright)—than it is to prove.

Darwinism is the only scientific theory taught worldwide that has yet to be proved by the rigorous standards of science. Nevertheless, Darwinists claim that Darwinism is no longer a theory, but rather an established scientific fact. The problem is not a choice between biblical creation and evolution. The issue to resolve boils down to a single question: Has Darwin's theory been proved by the rules of scientific evidence?

Darwin knew that the only way to verify the main tenets of the theory was to search the fossil record. That search has continued since his day. How many paleontologists, geologists, excavators, construction workers, oil- and water-well drillers, archeologists and anthropologists, students and amateur fossil hunters have been digging holes in the ground and discovering fossils from Darwin's day until today? Untold millions.

What evidence has the fossil record revealed concerning Darwin's transitional species? The late Harvard biologist Stephen Jay Gould, the antithesis of a Bible-thumping creationist, acknowledged: "All paleontologists know that the fossil record contains precious little in the way of intermediate forms; transitions between major groups are characteristically lacking."

Notice he didn't say that there is a dearth of fossils—*just* of the ones that are needed to substantiate Darwin's theory. There are plenty of fossils of ancient forms and plenty of newer ones. For example, we find fossils of early and extinct primates, hominids, Neanderthals and *Homo sapiens,* but no fossils of the transition linking ape and man. We find a similar situation with Darwin's dreaded appearance of flowering plants, his Achilles' heel.

Water deposits in the ancient past have left millions of fossils in a vast geologic library. Why do we find representative nonflowering plants from three hundred million years ago and flowering plants from one hundred million years ago still alive today but *no* plants showing the *gradual* process of *mutations* that represent the intermediate species that (should) link the two?

There are no such plants living today, nor are they found in the fossil record. That is Darwin's cross.

This is a serious, even critical issue that needs deep and thorough analysis. In an interview about his penetrating critique, *Facts of Life: Shattering the Myth of Darwinism,* the science journalist Richard Milton describes what made him write the book: "It was the absence of transitional fossils that first made me question Darwin's idea of gradual change. I realized, too, that the procedures used to date rocks were circular. Rocks are used to date fossils; fossils are used to date rocks. From here I began to think the unthinkable: Could Darwinism be scientifically flawed?"

Milton makes it clear that he does not support those who attack Darwin because they have a religious ax to grind: "As a science journalist and writer with a lifelong passion for geology and paleontology—and no religious beliefs to get in the way—I was in a unique position to investigate and report on the state of Darwin's theory in the 1990s," he said. "The result was unambiguous. Darwin doesn't work here any more."

According to Milton, who *had* been a firm Darwinist, when he began to rethink the theory, he became a regular visitor to Great Britain's prestigious

Darwin's exploratory ship, the Beagle, *beached for repairs in New Zealand*

Natural History Museum. He put the best examples that Darwinists had gathered over the years under intense scrutiny. One by one they failed to pass the test. He realized that many scientists around the world had already arrived at the same conclusion. The emperor was as naked as an ape. Why had no one gone public with papers critiquing the theory?

What trained, credentialed scientist earning a living through a university or government position wants to jeopardize a career and earn the disdain of colleagues in the process? Apparently none. Rocking the boat is never popular. The HMS *Beagle* is still afloat and it appears to be buttressed by a Darwinist army that is every bit as dogmatic about its beliefs as are the creationists, who, Darwinists complain, have a religious, nonscientific agenda.

Scientists have dropped hints, however. During a college lecture in 1967, the world-renowned anthropologist Louis B. Leakey was asked about "the missing link." He replied tersely, "There is no *one* link missing—there are *hundreds* of links missing."

Gould eventually wrote a paper proposing a theory to try to explain the lack of transitional species and the sudden appearance of new ones. He called this theory "punctuated equilibrium."

The public is not generally well informed about the *scientific* problems associated with Darwin's theory of evolution. And while the average person is aware that there is a war going on between creationists and evolutionists, that is seen as a rear-guard action, an old battle between science and religion over matters that the Scopes trial settled more than a generation ago. And there is some consternation over "the missing link" between apes and man.

The true believers among Darwinists have long been puzzled by the lack of transitional fossils. The reasoning goes something like this: They must be out there hidden in the record somewhere. How do we know this? Darwin's theory demands it! So the search goes on. But just how long a time and how many expeditions and how many years of research are needed before they finally admit that there must a good reason that the transitional fossils *are not there*?

Critics contend that the reason for the lack of transitional fossils is simple: Darwin's theory fails to meet the rigorous scientific criteria for proof because it is fatally flawed. The main tenets did not predict what has proved to be the outcome of more than a hundred years of research: missing links instead of transitional species.

Darwin knew the flak would come should the fossil record not contain the necessary transitional species.

Geneticists have long known that the vast majority of mutations are either neutral or negative. In other words, mutations are usually mistakes, failures of the DNA to accurately copy information. It would appear that this is not a very reliable primary mechanism and it needs to be, because natural selection is obviously not a dynamic force that could drive the kinds of changes that evolutionists attribute to the theory.

Natural selection operates more like a control mechanism, a feedback system that weeds out poor adaptations and selects successful ones.

The problem with mutation being the driving force is several-fold. As Behe pointed out in his book, life within a cell is just too complex to be the outcome of random mutations. But Darwin didn't have the kind of lab technology that molecular biologists today have at their disposal. Darwin was working with species, not the structure of cells, mitochondria, and DNA. But the mutation theory doesn't work well on other levels, either.

Now we must return to the problem of the sudden appearance of flowering plants. There is a high degree of organization in flowers. Most flowers are specifically designed to accommodate bees and other pollinators. Which came first, the flower or the bee? We'll get to that momentarily; the first question is: How did the alleged primitive nonflowering plant, which had for eons relied on asexual reproduction, suddenly grow the structures required for sexual reproduction?

According to Darwin's theory, it happened when a gymnosperm mutated and then changed over time into a flowering plant. Is that possible? Let's keep a few facts in mind: In flowering plants, the transfer of pollen from the male anther to the female stigma must occur before seed plants can reproduce sexually. The mutation had to start with one plant, somewhere, at some point. There were no insects or animals specifically adapted to pollinate flowers because there were no flowers prior to that time.

Darwin was never able to explain flowering plants like these water lilies.

This is where the idea of combining mutation, natural selection, and gradualism breaks down. When faced with the dilemma of advanced organization and the leap from asexual reproduction to sexual reproduction, Darwinists will say that evolution simply operates *too slowly* for the links to be apparent. That is a non sequitur. If it acts slowly, then there should be a superabundance of fossils demonstrating the existence of the missing links.

Natural selection would not select a gymnosperm (let's say a fern) that suddenly mutated a new structure that required an enormous amount of the plant's energy but had no purpose. In other words, flowerless plants could not have gradually grown the flower parts in a piecemeal fashion over tens of millions of years until a fully functional flower head was formed. That would go against Darwin's own law of natural selection, the survival of the fittest.

The more you isolate the logical steps that had to occur for Darwin's theory to be correct, the more trouble you get into. How would a newly evolved flower propagate without other flowers nearby? Why do we find numerous examples of gymnosperms and angiosperms in the fossil record but no transitional species to demonstrate how mutation and natural selection operated to create flowers?

If Darwinism cannot explain the mechanisms responsible for speciation and how life on this planet evolves, what can? Sir Francis Crick, the codiscover of DNA's double helix structure, proposed the concept of "panspermia," the idea that life was brought to Earth by an advanced civilization from another planet. It is obvious that Crick was not sold on Darwinism. Behe ends his book with an argument for integrating a "theory of intelligent design" into mainstream biology.

Other biologists, like Lynn Margulis, think that Darwinism leans too heavily on the idea that *competition* is the main, driving force behind survival. She points out that *cooperation* is as readily observed and as important, perhaps more important. Nature contains many examples of symbiosis: Flowers need bees and vice versa. Another example is the relationship between mycorrhizal fungi and forest trees. There are bacteria that fix nitrogen for plants. The list goes on. What is a human body but a collection of different kinds of cells and viruses working together to create a complex organism?

The old paradigm is starting to give way to new thinking and new models such as intelligent design and extraterrestrial intervention. Marx and Freud were nineteenth-century pioneers who blazed trails, but so was Newton. Their new paradigms inspired new perspectives and they solved old problems. Still, they had their limits. Their theories were mechanistic and materialistic. Newton's decline came with the introduction of Einstein's theory of relativity. The new paradigm of the laws of physics fit the facts and answered more questions, and that meant it had greater utility. Is Darwin next?

Until a more comprehensive theory of how life originated, changed, and continues to evolve emerges, as Richard Milton put it, "Darwin doesn't work here anymore."

2 Evolution vs. Creation

Is the Debate for Real?

David Lewis

enesis, the biblical story of creation, tells us that God created the universe in six days. He made Adam, the first man, the Bible tells us, from the dust of the earth, an event many Christians believe took place in the Garden of Eden six thousand years ago. Scientists and religious scholars call this scenario "creationism."

Adam and Eve,
by Raphael

In 1859, Charles Darwin came up with another idea. He said man's existence could be explained within the context of material creation alone, through evolution and natural selection—that is, "the survival of the fittest." According to Darwin, man evolved from the apes, an idea distinctly at odds with the biblical scenario.

The debate over human origins has raged ever since. It surfaced recently in Abbotsford, British Columbia, where a school board dominated by Christians requires the teaching of "intelligent design," a form of creationism, along with the theory of evolution. Reports *Maclean's* magazine, "The issue they are debating is a large one . . . arguably the biggest question of them all: how did life begin . . . with a Big Bang or a Big Being?"

Critics of the Abbotsford policy fear the school board would place the Book of Genesis on a par with Darwin's *Origin of Species*. They accuse the board of imposing their religious beliefs on students, while some Christians believe that teaching Darwinism amounts to the same thing, the imposition of a de facto religious belief system.

Recent studies show, however, that adherents to both sides of this wrangle would do well to rethink their positions. A reexamination of old and new

14

research reveals that the creationism-versus-Darwinism debate may be missing the mark entirely.

Richard Thompson and Michael Cremo, coauthors of *Forbidden Archeology* (and its condensed version, *The Hidden History of the Human Race*), have assembled a body of evidence that testifies to the existence of modern man millions of years before his supposed emergence from southern Africa 100,000 years ago.

On "The Mysterious Origins of Man," an NBC documentary that aired in February of 1996, Thompson and Cremo make their case along with other experts. The evidence they reveal suggests man neither evolved

Evolution
(Art by Tom Miller)

from apes nor rose from the dust of the earth just four thousand years before the time of Christ. The implications are profound and may force a reevaluation of the entire issue of human origins.

Narrated by Charlton Heston and drawing on evidence largely ignored by the scientific establishment, "The Mysterious Origins of Man" steps outside the usual Bible-versus-Darwin debate. At issue are human footprints discovered in Texas, side by side with dinosaur tracks; stone tools dating back fifty-five million years; sophisticated maps of unknown antiquity; and evidence of advanced civilization in prehistory.

Based on research assembled as Darwin began to dominate scientific thought at the turn of the nineteenth century, and also upon more recent archeological discoveries, "The Mysterious Origins of Man" exposes a "knowledge filter" within the scientific establishment, a bias that favors accepted dogma while rejecting evidence that does *not* support conventional theory.

As a result, fossil evidence indicating that man is far more ancient than conventional theory allows, and that he did not evolve from apes, has gathered dust for over a century. It has been suppressed, in effect, because it conflicts with an entrenched belief system, the NBC documentary reveals. Moreover, scientists who challenge accepted dogma can find themselves not only on the outside of the debate, but also unemployed.

Thompson, the science investigator Richard Milton, and other experts trace the problem to "speculative leaps" made by researchers too eager to find the missing link in human evolution, the long-sought-after ancestor of both man and apes. "It seems *any* missing link will do," Milton says, regarding the 120-year effort to prove Darwin's theory.

In the case of the so-called pithecanthropus ape-man (aka Java Man, *Homo erectus*), the anthropologist Eugene Dubois found, in Indonesia, a human thighbone and the skullcap of an ape separated by a distance of forty feet. The year was 1891. He pieced the two together, creating the famous Java Man. But many experts say the thighbone and skullcap are unrelated. Shortly before his death, Dubois himself said the skullcap belonged to a large monkey and the thighbone to a man. Yet Java Man remains to this day, to many, evidence of man's descent from the apes, having been featured as such in New York's Museum of Natural History until 1984.

In the case of Piltdown Man, another missing link wannabe, this one "discovered" in England in 1910, the find proved to be a sophisticated fraud perpetrated, in all likelihood, by overly zealous Darwinists. And even the crown jewel of alleged human ancestral fossils, the famous "Lucy," found in Ethiopia in 1974, is indistinguishable from a monkey or an extinct ape, according to many anthropologists.

The physical anthropologist Charles Oxnard and other scientists have drawn a picture of human evolution that is radically at odds with the conventional theory, a fact usually ignored by universities and natural history museums. Oxnard placed the genus *Homo,* to which man belongs, in a far more ancient time period than standard evolutionary theory allows, bringing into question the underpinnings of Darwin's theory. As reported in Cremo and Thompson's *Forbidden Archeology,* Oxnard says, "The conventional notion of human evolution must now be heavily modified or even rejected . . . new concepts must be explored."

What pains other opponents of standard evolutionary theory is its inability to account for how new species and features originate—the supposition that the innumerable aspects of biological life, down to the pores in human skin, and a beetle's legs, and the protective pads on a camel's knees, came about accidentally through natural selection. The notion of intent, or inherent purpose, within creation does not fit in to the Darwinian version of reality.

Life, to a Darwinist, can exist only in the context of absolute materialism: a series of accidental events and chemical reactions that are responsible for everything in the universe. Even common sense seems to take a backseat to scientific dogma. In the case of the human brain, for instance, its advanced capacities (the ability to perform calculus, play the violin, even consciousness itself) cannot be explained by the "survival of the fittest" doctrine alone.

WHAT ABOUT THE BIBLE AND CREATIONISM?

The creationist argument derives from orthodox religious doctrine, rejecting allegorical and metaphorical interpretations of the Book of Genesis. It is a belief system many Christians do not accept literally and which the Bible itself may not support. It also lacks scientific support, in that fossil records reveal that man has existed on Earth for far longer than six thousand years. The six days of creation scenario, moreover, taken literally, bears no resemblance to the time it took for the universe to be born.

The more commonsense notion of intelligent design (creationism without the dogma) strikes a more palatable note, even among some scientists who find it hard to deny that an inherent intelligence exists within the universe. The problem with creationism lies, then, not in the idea of intelligent design, but in its dogmatic and inflexible interpretations of the Bible with regard to the debate over human origins.

NEW GROUND OR ANCIENT WISDOM?

Evidence for extremely ancient human origins will lead many into foreign territory, terrain some would rather avoid. But to others, the standard creationism versus evolution debate was wanting all along. Once looked upon with raised eyebrows, and still facing dogged opposition, the "catastrophist" point of view has made headway of late in the scientific community. This theory holds that sudden disruptions in the continuity of planetary life have taken place, altering the course of evolution. ("Gradualism," on the other hand, a Darwinist tenet that assumes all life evolved slowly and without interruption, has fallen out of favor in some circles.)

Indeed, it has become clear that all sorts of catastrophes have taken place on the globe and in the universe at large. A well-known catastrophist theory proposes that the extinction of the dinosaurs resulted from a huge meteor crashing into the planet with the force of thousands of hydrogen bombs. Other catastrophic theories have to do with drastic changes in climate, seismic upheavals and fluctuations, and even reversals in Earth's magnetic field.

The catastrophism versus gradualism debate, while revealing how little science knows for certain about prehistory, also exposes a distinct prejudice within the scientific community—an antipathy, dating to the time of Darwin, toward anything remotely resembling biblical catastrophes such as the Great Flood, even if the connection has to do only with sudden rather than gradual changes in the course of evolution.

Catastrophism, though, avails another scenario regarding human origins and prehistory. As presented in Graham Hancock's *Fingerprints of the Gods: The Evidence of Earth's Lost Civilization* and in Rand and Rose Flem-Ath's *When the Sky Fell: In Search of Atlantis,* a sudden, catastrophic shifting of the earth's lithosphere, called "crustal displacement," may have occurred at some time in the past. Lent credibility by Albert Einstein, the theory suggests that the earth's outer crust may have suddenly (not gradually, as in continental drift) shifted on the surface of the globe, causing continents to slide into radically different positions.

Drawing on the work of Charles Hapgood, who developed the theory with Einstein's assistance, the Flem-Aths explain that this may be the reason carcasses of hundreds of woolly mammoths, rhinos, and other ancient mammals were found flash-frozen in a "zone of death" across Siberia and northern Canada. Remarkably, the stomachs of these mammals contained warm-weather plants, the implication being that the very ground upon which the animals grazed suddenly shifted from a temperate to an arctic climate. Hapgood and Einstein theorized that a sudden shifting and freezing of the continent of Antarctica, which may have been situated two thousand miles farther north than it is now, could have occurred as a result of crustal displacement.

Ancient maps accurately depicting Antarctica before it was covered in ice also support the idea that the continent was situated in a temperate climate in recent prehistory. Copied from source maps of unknown antiquity, the Piri Ri'is, Oronteus Finaeus, and Mercator maps derive, Graham Hancock and the Flem-Aths propose, from some prehistoric society with the capacity to calculate accurately longitude and chart coastlines, an accomplishment that did not take place in recorded history until the eighteenth century.

As outlined in the Flem-Aths' and Hancock's books, the maps, along with a body of evidence, testify to the existence of a sophisticated prehistoric civilization. Charlton Heston, narrating NBC's "The Mysterious Origins of Man," likens this scenario to Plato's description of the lost continent of Atlantis.

LOST CIVILIZATIONS, THE REAL MISSING LINK?

Examining stonework at ancient cites in Bolivia, Peru, and Egypt, Hancock argues that these megalithic marvels could not have risen from the dust of nomadic hunter-gatherers, which is what conventional science would have us believe. The magnificent city of Tiahuanaco, Bolivia, said by the Bolivian scholar Arthur Poznansky to date to 15,000 B.C.E., emerges as a case in point. Precision stone cuttings performed on immense blocks at Tiahuanaco, and at the other sites, to tolerances of one fiftieth of an inch, and then the transporting of these blocks over long distances, reveal technical capabilities that match or surpass those of modern engineers.

How supposedly primitive people transported these megaliths to the summit of Machu Picchu in Peru, for instance, remains a great mystery and is a feat that conventional science is at a loss to explain. Hancock asserts that even if we accept the later dates most archeologists ascribe to these structures, the knowledge and technical abilities of the builders would had to have been the product of a civilization that evolved over a long period of time, pushing the appearance of civilized man to the predawn of recorded history.

"My view," Hancock says, "is that we are looking at a common influence that touched all of these places, long before recorded history, a remote third-party civilization yet to be identified by historians."

A wide range of natural evidence and recorded human experience points to the existence of such a civilization. Etymology, the study of word origins, postulates that a prehistoric Indo-European language must have existed to account for the deep similarities in the world's languages. Could this have been the language of Hancock's prehistoric civilization?

Hamlet's Mill: An Essay Investigating the Origins of Human Knowledge and Its Transmission through Myth, written by M.I.T. professor of science Giorgio de Santillana and University of Frankfurt professor of science Hertha von Dechend, is a study of how ancient myths depict the procession of the equinoxes. As such, it weighs in on this common-language issue also, testifying to the existence of advanced knowledge proliferated among prehistoric peoples. Discussing myths that originate in the mists of antiquity, and the numerical values and symbology recorded therein, Santillana and von Dechend reveal that the ancients of many cultures shared a sophisticated knowledge of celestial mechanics, knowledge that has been matched only recently, with the help of satellites and computers.

The proliferation of closely related biological species on continents separated by vast oceans, a phenomenon that puzzles Darwinists, can also be explained by the existence of an advanced, seafaring civilization in prehistory. An entire body of evidence, in fact, supports man and civilization having existed at a far earlier date than orthodox science or religion concedes is the case. Could the existence, then, of such a civilization be the *real* missing link in human history?

WHY LIMIT THE DEBATE TO WESTERN MODELS?

The conventional debate over our origins, as we find it characterized in the major media, ignores concepts of human and cosmic origins that are shared by a large portion of the world's population: those of the mystic East. Einstein himself entertained such ideas because they supported his belief in a universal intelligence. More recently, the physicist and Nobel laureate Brian Josephson and others have drawn parallels between Eastern mysticism and modern physics. Fritjof Capra, in *The Tao of Physics,* harmonizes Vedic, Buddhist, and Taoist philosophy with the subtleties of quantum theory.

Albert Einstein (right) with Hindu poet Rabindranath Tagore

The Vedas, in fact, present a scenario similar to the expanding and contracting universe of modern physics, the Great In breath and Out breath of creation, the projection of omnipresent consciousness, Brahman, the essence of which remains intrinsic to all things as creation evolves. Taoism, on the other hand, offers an understanding of conscious reality that closely resembles Heisenberg's "uncertainty principle," wherein perspective, or consciousness, shapes objective reality.

To Einstein, especially in his later years, the idea of consciousness-based reality—the awareness of a universal, conscious presence inseparable from identity and creation—became naturally apparent, as it does now to others in the fields of physics, philosophy, and religion. "As I grow older," Einstein said, "the identification with the here and now [his famous space-time] is slowly lost. One feels dissolved, merged into nature."

The greatest minds, then, of our time and of the greatest antiquity reject Darwin's often unstated premise, his belief in absolute materialism, which holds that all life evolved from primitive matter, accidentally, without purpose or design. At the same time, consciousness-based creation offers an alternative to strict biblical interpretations and the concept of an anthropomorphic creator separate from man and nature.

Establishment science, though, has had a hands-off approach to consciousness, never daring to explore what, by definition, cannot be explained by matter-based beliefs about the origins of life. An article by David Chalmers, in the December 1995 issue of *Scientific American,* "The Puzzle of Conscious Experience," emphasizes the point.

"For many years," Chalmers says, "consciousness was shunned by researchers . . .The prevailing view was that science, which depends on objectivity, could not accommodate something as subjective as consciousness." Chalmers goes on to say that neuroscientists, psychologists, and philosophers are only recently beginning to reject the idea that consciousness cannot be studied. He proposes, while insisting that consciousness is materially based, that "[it] might be explained by a new kind of theory . . . [that] will probably involve new fundamental laws [with] startling consequences for our view of the universe and of ourselves."

The eminent physicist Steven Weinberg, in his book *Dreams of a Final Theory,* puts it another way. He says the goal of physics is to develop a "theory of everything" that will tell us all there is to know about the universe—a law or principle from which the universe derives. So stating, Weinberg exposes the limitations of scientific materialism, while at the same time trying to transcend it, as he butts up against an Absolute, a Logos, if you will, that cannot exist within the context of matter-based creation. The real problem, he admits, is consciousness, because it is beyond what could have derived from material processes alone.

Darwinism, therefore, which depends upon the assumption that *all* existence is matter-based, cannot account for the most human characteristic of all, consciousness, which cannot derive from the process of natural selection in a random, mechanistic creation—the capacity of the human mind being far beyond what is necessary for mere survival. And strict creationism, when pitted against a Darwinism that ignores the origin of consciousness along with other crucial factors, appears to be merely a foil that Darwinists use to make themselves look good.

To understand human origins, then, and to develop a "theory of everything," a true scientist must not only evaluate the tangible evidence presented in *Forbidden Archeology* and in Hancock's *Fingerprints of the Gods,* he also must study consciousness, without which he neglects the most basic capacity of human beings—the ability to think creatively. He would have to experiment in the internal, subjective world, delving into what the scientific establishment considers a forbidden realm. He would have to devote himself, independent of any dogma, to the essence of his own conscious existence, as well as to the study of material creation. Like Einstein, he would see this pursuit as the essential goal of both science and religion, the search for knowledge in its purest sense, or *sciere* in the Latin, from which the word *science* derives. By so doing, science might arrive at a theory of everything.

3 Exposing a Scientific Cover-Up

Forbidden Archeology Coauthor Michael
Cremo Talks about the "Knowledge Filter" and
Other Means for Cooking the Academic Books

J. Douglas Kenyon

In 1966, respected archeologist Virginia Steen-McIntyre and her associates on a U.S. Geological Survey team, working under a grant from the National Science Foundation, were called upon to date a pair of remarkable archeological sites in Mexico. Sophisticated stone tools rivaling the best work of Cro-Magnon man in Europe had been discovered at Hueyatlaco, while somewhat cruder implements had been turned up at nearby El Horno. The sites, it was conjectured, were very ancient, perhaps as old as 20,000 years, which, according to prevailing theories, would place them very close to the dawn of human habitation in the Americas.

Dr. Virginia Steen-McIntyre
(Photograph courtesy of
B.C. Video)

Steen-McIntyre, knowing that if such antiquity could indeed be authenticated her career would be made, set about an exhaustive series of tests. Using four different but well-accepted dating methods, including uranium series and fission track, she determined to get it right. Nevertheless, when the results came in, the original estimates proved to be way off. Way *under,* as it turned out. The actual age of the sites was conclusively demonstrated to be more like a quarter of a million years!

As we might expect, some controversy ensued. Steen-McIntyre's date not only challenged accepted chronologies for human presence in the region, but also contradicted established notions of how long modern humans could have been anywhere on Earth. Nevertheless, the massive reexamination of orthodox theory and the wholesale rewriting of textbooks that one might logically have expected did *not* ensue. What *did* follow was the public ridicule of Steen-McIntyre's

22

work and the vilification of her character. She has not been able to find work in her field since.

More than a century earlier, following the discovery of gold in California's Table Mountain and the subsequent digging of thousands of feet of mining shafts, miners began to bring up hundreds of stone artifacts and even human fossils. Despite their origins in geological strata documented at nine to fifty-five million years in age, California state geologist J. D. Whitney was able subsequently to authenticate many of the finds and to produce an extensive report. The implications of Whitney's evidence have never been properly answered or explained by the scientific establishment, yet the entire episode has been virtually ignored and references to it have vanished from the textbooks.

For decades, miners in South Africa have been turning up—from strata nearly three billion years in age—hundreds of small metallic spheres with encircling parallel grooves. Thus far, the scientific community has failed to take note.

Among scores of such cases cited in Richard Thompson and Michael Cremo's *Forbidden Archeology* (and in its condensed version, *Hidden History of the Human Race*), it is clear that these three examples are by no means uncommon. Suggesting nothing less than a "massive cover-up," Cremo and Thompson believe that when it comes to explaining the origins of the human race on Earth, academic science has cooked the books.

Though the public may believe that all the *real* evidence supports the mainstream theory of evolution—with its familiar timetable for human development (i.e., *Homo sapiens* of the modern type go back only about 100,000 years)—Cremo and Thompson demonstrate that, to the contrary, a virtual mountain of evidence produced by reputable scientists applying standards just as exacting, if not more so, than those of the establishment has been not only ignored but, in many cases, actually suppressed. In every area of research, from paleontology to anthropology and archeology, that which is presented to the public as established and irrefutable fact is indeed nothing more, says Cremo, "than a consensus arrived at by powerful groups of people."

Michael Cremo

Is that consensus justified by the evidence? Cremo and Thompson say no.

Carefully citing all available documentation, the authors produce case after case of contradictory research that has been conducted in the last two centuries. The authors describe astonishing discoveries made, and then go on to discuss the controversies that ensued from those discoveries and the suppression of evidence that invariably followed.

Typical is the case of George Carter, who claimed to have found, at an excavation in San Diego, California, hearths and crude stone tools at levels corresponding to the last interglacial period, some 80,000–90,000 years ago. Even though Carter's work was endorsed by some experts such as the lithic scholar John Witthoft, the establishment scoffed. San Diego State University refused to even look at the evidence in its own backyard and Harvard University publicly defamed Carter in a course entitled "Fantastic Archeology."

What emerges is a picture of an arrogant and bigoted academic elite interested more in the preservation of its own prerogatives and authority than the truth.

Needless to say, the weighty (952-page) volume, *Forbidden Archeology,* has caused more than a little stir. The establishment, as one might expect, is outraged, but it is having a difficult time ignoring the book. The anthropologist Richard Leakey wrote, "Your book is pure humbug and does not deserve to be taken seriously by anyone but a fool."

Richard Leakey

Nevertheless, many prestigious scientific publications, including *The American Journal of Physical Anthropology, Geo Archeology*, and the British *Journal for the History of Science,* have deigned to review the book. While generally critical of its arguments, they have conceded, although grudgingly, that *Forbidden Archeology* is well written and well researched, and some indeed recognize a significant challenge to the prevailing theories.

As William Howells wrote in *Physical Anthropologist,* "To have modern human beings . . . appearing a great deal earlier, in fact at a time when even simple primates did not exist as possible ancestors, would be devastating, not only to the accepted pattern, it would be devastating to the whole theory of evolution, which has been pretty robust up until now."

Yet despite its considerable challenge to the evolutionary edifice, *Forbidden Archeology* chooses not to align itself with the familiar creationist point of view, nor to attempt an alternative theory of its own. The task of presenting his own complex theory—which seeks, Cremo says, to avoid the "false choice" between evolution and creationism usually presented in the media—Cremo has undertaken in another book, entitled

Human Devolution. On the question of human origins, he insists, "We really do have to go back to the drawing board."

As the author told *Atlantis Rising* recently: "*Forbidden Archeology* suggests the real need for an alternative explanation, a new synthesis. In *Human Devolution,* I've gone into that in detail. It's got elements of the Darwinian idea, and elements of the ancient astronaut theory, and elements of the creation-

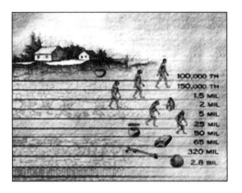

Time line of anomalous artifacts
(IMAGE COURTESY OF B. C. VIDEO)

ist nature, but it's much more complex. I think we've become accustomed to overly simplistic pictures of human origins, whereas the reality is a little more complicated than any advocates of the current ideas are prepared to admit."

Both Cremo and Thompson are members of the Bhaktivedanta Institute—the Science Studies Branch of the International Society for Krishna Consciousness. Cremo and Thompson started their project with the goal of finding evidence to corroborate the ancient Sanskrit writings of India, which relate episodes of human history going back millions of years.

"So we thought," says Cremo, "if there's any truth to those ancient writings, there should be some physical evidence to back it up, but we really didn't find it in the current textbooks." They didn't stop there, though. Over the next eight years, Cremo and Thompson investigated the entire history of archeology and anthropology, delving into *everything* that has been discovered, not just what has been reported in textbooks. What they found was a revelation. "I thought there might be a few little things that have been swept under the rug," said Cremo, "but what I found was truly amazing. There's actually a massive amount of evidence that's been suppressed."

Cremo and Thompson determined to produce a book of irrefutable archeological facts. "The standard used," says Cremo, "[meant] the site had to be identifiable, there had to be good geological evidence on the age of the site, and there had to be some reporting about it, in most cases in the scientific literature." The quality and quantity of the evidence—they hoped—would compel serious examination by professionals in the field, as well as by students and the general public.

Few would deny that they have succeeded in spectacular fashion. Much in demand in alternative science circles, the authors have also found a sympathetic audience among the self-termed sociologists of scientific knowledge, who are very aware of the failure of modern scientific method to present a truly objective picture of reality. The problem, Cremo believes, is both misfeasance and malfeasance. "You can find many cases where it's just an automatic process. It's just human nature that a person will tend to reject things that don't fit in with his particular worldview," he said.

He cites the example of a young paleontologist and expert on ancient whalebones at the Museum of Natural History in San Diego. When asked if he ever saw signs of human marks on any of the bones, the scientist remarked, "I tend to stay away from anything that has to do with humans because it's just too controversial."

Cremo sees the response as an innocent one from someone interested in protecting his career. In other areas, though, he perceives something much more vicious, as in the case of Virginia Steen-McIntyre. "What she found was that she wasn't able to get her report published. She lost the teaching position at the university. She was labeled a publicity seeker and a maverick in her profession. And she really hasn't been able to work as a professional geologist since then."

In other examples Cremo finds even broader signs of deliberate malfeasance. He mentions the activities of the Rockefeller Foundation, which funded Davidson Black's research at Zhoukoudian, in China. Correspondence between Black and his superiors with the foundation shows that research and archeology were part of a far larger biological research project. The following is a quote from that correspondence: ". . . thus we may gain information about our behavior of the sort that can lead to wide and beneficial control." In other words, this research was being funded with the specific goal of control. "Control by *whom*?" Cremo wants to know.

The motive to manipulate is not so difficult to understand. "There's a lot of social power connected with explaining who we are and what we are," Cremo says. "Somebody once said 'Knowledge is power.' You could also say 'Power is knowledge.' Some people have particular power and prestige that enables them to dictate the agenda of our society. I think it's not surprising that they are resistant to any change."

Cremo agrees that scientists today have become a virtual priest class, exercising many of the rights and prerogatives that their forebears in the industrial-scientific revolution sought to wrest from an entrenched religious establishment. "They set the tone and the direction for our civilization on a worldwide basis," he says. "If you want to know something today, you usually don't go to a priest or a spiritually inclined person, you go to one of these people because they've convinced us that our world is a very mechanistic place, and everything can be explained mechanically by the laws of physics and chemistry, which are currently accepted by the establishment."

To Cremo, it seems the scientists have usurped the keys of the kingdom and then failed to live up to their promises. "In many ways the environmental crisis and the political crisis and the crisis in values is *their* doing," he says. "And I think many people are becoming aware that [the scientists] really haven't been able to deliver the kingdom to which they claimed to have the keys. I think many people are starting to see that the worldview they are presenting just doesn't account for everything in human experience."

For Cremo, we are all part of a cosmic hierarchy of beings, a view for which he finds corroboration in world mythologies: "If you look at all of those traditions, when they talk about origins they don't talk about them as something that occurs just on this planet. There are extraterrestrial contacts with gods, demigods, goddesses, angels." And he believes there may be parallels in the modern UFO phenomenon.

The failure of modern science to satisfactorily deal with UFOs, extrasensory perception, and the paranormal provides one of the principle charges against it. "I would have to say that the evidence of such today is very strong," he argues. "It's very difficult to ignore. It's not something that you can just sweep away. If you were to reject all of the evidence for UFOs, abductions, and other kinds of contacts, coming from so many reputable sources, it seems we have to give up accepting any kind of human testimony whatsoever."

One area where orthodoxy has been frequently challenged is in the notion of sudden change brought about by enormous cataclysms, versus the "gradualism" usually conceived of by evolutionists. Even though it has become fashionable to talk of such events, they have been relegated to the very distant past, supposedly before the appearance of man. Yet some individuals, like Immanuel Velikovsky, have argued that many such events have occurred in our past and induced a kind of planetary amnesia from which we still suffer today.

That such catastrophic episodes have occurred and that humanity has suffered from some great forgettings Cremo agrees: "I think there is a kind of amnesia that, when we encounter the actual records of catastrophes, makes us think, oh well, this is just mythology. In other words, I think some knowledge of these catastrophes does survive in ancient writings and cultures and through oral traditions. But because of what you might call some social amnesia, as we encounter those things we are not able to accept them as truth. I also think there's a deliberate attempt on the part of those who are now in control of the world's intellectual life to make us disbelieve and forget the paranormal and related phenomena. I think there's a definite attempt to keep us in a state of forgetfulness about these things."

It's all part of the politics of ideas. Says Cremo, "It's been a struggle that's been going on thousands and thousands of years, and it's still going on."

PART TWO

MAKING THE CASE
FOR CATASTROPHISM:
EARTH CHANGES,
SUDDEN AND GRADUAL

4 In Defense of Catastrophes

Pioneering Geologist Robert Schoch Challenges the Conventional Wisdom on Natural History

William P. Eigles

When the maverick Egyptologist John Anthony West went looking in 1989 for scientific validation that the Great Sphinx of Giza (and possibly other monuments of ancient Egypt) was of a greater antiquity than alleged by orthodox Egyptologists, he found it through the person of Robert M. Schoch, Ph.D., a young but very well-credentialed associate professor of science and mathematics at Boston University. Schoch's specific expertise lay in geology and paleontology, and he possessed just the corpus of scientific knowledge and analytical techniques that West needed to verify the hypothesis, first proposed by the independent archeologist R. A. Schwaller de Lubicz in the 1950s, that the weathering observable on the Sphinx and its rocky enclosure was due to chronic precipitation from the sky rather than long-term exposure to windborne sand.

R. A. Schwaller de Lubicz

Dr. Robert M. Schoch in Egypt

What Schoch found, using accepted geological methodology, is now a matter of public record, popularized in the controversial 1993 television special "The Mystery of the Sphinx," in which he was featured. His findings were that the erosion on the Sphinx and its enclosure incontrovertibly reflects the effects of streaming water, which means that the oldest portions of the ancient statue must date to at least 2,500 years earlier than heretofore posited, or to the period between 7000 and 5000 B.C.E., the last time when large quantities of rain fell in that area of the world.

Schoch's finding was tantamount to setting back the conventionally accepted timetable for the development of human civilization in the Middle East by two and a half millennia—and maybe much more. This propelled the geologist headlong into a vehement debate with the traditional Egyptological establishment, which summarily rejected the overwhelming evidence in favor of his much older date for the Sphinx's construction.

The experience, however, also served to rekindle and amplify a long-standing, if dormant, curiosity in the author to examine the even larger issues of how and why civilizations have come and gone on our planet. As a result of the inquiry thus spurred, Schoch found that his own trained, unquestioning allegiance to the prevailing scientific paradigm of uniformitarianism, which governed his geological fields of interest, began metamorphosing in favor of catastrophism as the theory of choice for explaining past—and perhaps even future—planetary changes of the epochal kind.

This personal intellectual journey informs Schoch's first nontechnical book, *Voices of the Rocks: A Scientist Looks at Catastrophes and Ancient Civilizations,* coauthored with Robert Aquinas McNally, a professional science writer. In it, they survey the evidence and convincingly argue that instead of evolution and cultural change being a gradual process over many millennia (the uniformitarian viewpoint), natural catastrophes such as earthquakes, floods, and extraterrestrially sourced impacts (asteroids, comets, meteorites) have significantly and often abruptly altered the course of human civilization (the catastrophist perspective).

Indeed, research conducted and reported by Schoch and many others strongly suggests that cataclysmic natural events have obliterated civilizations in the past and could well do so again. Schoch admits that he went "screaming and kicking" toward catastrophism, without any prior seeding by professional mentors or university teachers who were closet proponents of the alternate paradigm. But, he says, "I just followed the evidence, and in so doing, it just didn't take me to where I was taught it would. As a scientist, I couldn't dismiss the evidence out of hand, and so another theory was needed to account for it."

In proposing catastrophism as an alternative working model for past events, Schoch's book also sends a clarion call about the need to address various modern environmental issues such as global warming, ozone depletion, and the threat of large terrestrial impacts from outer space, any one of which may portend a disaster of global proportions.

Schoch and McNally begin their book with an overview of the scientific process and, specifically, an examination of how science progresses, including the concept of thought paradigms and how they shift as the world actually changes (or at least human perceptions thereof). By way of example, they note that the ancient worldview of the heavens as being a dangerous place populated by angry gods may not have been mythological fantasy after all, but rather a paradigm using religious language to explain the observation of actual phenomena, such as would occur if and as Earth's orbit carried our planet through a dense meteor stream in space.

After Earth's orbit took it out of that meteor stream and, after time elapsed, this paradigm would eventually become irrelevant and would be superseded by one that reflected the subsequently calmer skies, such as the Earth-centered series of concentric planetary orbital rings later proposed by Aristotle.

The authors claim that the same paradigm-shift phenomenon is at work today concerning geology, the evolution of the species, and human cultural change, with secular catastrophism gaining ascendancy over uniformitarianism. This change is based principally on the abrupt shifts in the fossil records of plant and animal communities in the earth that have been observed by various researchers, indicating relatively rapid mass extinctions of life on the surface of the planet at various points in the past (such as the disappearance of the dinosaurs at the end of the Cretaceous period sixty-five million years ago).

In particular, the work begun in 1980 by the father-son team of Drs. Luis and Walter Alvarez, and repeated by others, identified the presence of higher-than-normal concentrations of iridium in the so-called K-T boundary, the thin demarcation layer of clay between the geological strata of two different, major epochs in Earth's history.

After eliminating volcanic activity as a possible source of this anomaly, the researchers concluded that the only other explanation for such high concentrations of iridium would be an asteroid, or, more precisely, the collision of one with Earth. Confirmation of this theory seemed to appear with the discovery, in 1990, of a large impact crater at Chicxulub in Mexico's Yucatán Peninsula, dated as being of the same vintage as the K-T boundary.

These findings helped give rise to a new model of Earth—and species—change, known as punctuated equilibrium. This theory proposes that our planet's chronology can be likened to a sequence of steady states regularly interrupted by periods of rapid, often radical, change, caused by such catastrophic events as massive volcanic activity, an asteroid impact, and a change in planetary temperature occasioned by various means.

Schoch's personal work in redating the Sphinx to the Neolithic period (which encompasses the 7000–5000 B.C.E. time span, an expanse of time conventionally associated with only very rudimentary societies and building skills), led him to question traditional notions of the linear, uniformly progressive rise of human civilization from approximately 3100 B.C.E. forward, and to postulate the existence of sophisticated cultures far earlier than had been previously supposed.

Countering the claimed absence of evidence for any such notion, he cites some intriguing evidence of technical flint mining from 31,000 B.C.E.; sophisticated Neolithic villages in Egypt dating to 8100 B.C.E.; and, most recently, the astronomically aligned Nabta megalith circle found in the Nubian Desert of the southern Sahara dating to 4500–4000 B.C.E.. Remains of ancient cities elsewhere in the Near East, such as Jericho in Israel from 8300 B.C.E. and Äatal HÅyÅk in Anatolia, Turkey, from the seventh millennium B.C.E., serve to buttress his argument that peoples of even earlier antiquity possessed impressive organizational skills, technical knowledge, and engineering prowess. Additional evidence exists outside of Egypt—in the Americas and Europe—as well: in particular, the astronomically correlated painted imagery discovered on cave walls in Lascaux, France, which has been dated to ca. 15,000 B.C.E.—stunningly earlier still.

Pursuing the thread of inquiry into sophisticated ancient civilizations further led Schoch to confront the reputed existence of the lost continents of Atlantis and Lemuria (or Mu). In his book, he makes short work of Lemuria, dismissing it as pure fantasy after a short review of the associated literature. Reviewing at greater length the accounts of Atlantis proffered by Plato in his dialogues, and the later accounts of the Roman historian Diodorus Siculus, Schoch finds them thoroughly lacking in their ability to help us locate that sunken continent today.

In surveying the list of supposed sites for the sunken landmass, he deftly and methodically disassembles the arguments supporting claims for Atlantis existing in the mid-Atlantic Ocean, on Minoan Crete, or in the South China Sea. With respect to the claim for Atlantis being situated under the ice cap in Antarctica, advanced by such writers as Professor Charles Hapgood, Graham Hancock, and Rand and Rose Flem-Ath, Schoch devotes more time to discounting their shared theory.

Ultimately, Schoch finds no evidence to support the notion of Antarctica being ice-free during the period claimed by Plato for its existence, and notes further that, denuded of the massive weight of its icy covering and surrounded by higher water levels, Antarctica would look a lot different as a geological landmass than has been posited by the modern authors cited.

Last, he marshals evidence that disputes the accuracy of the maps on which these authors rely for their suppositions of advanced cartographic knowledge on the part of prehistoric ancients. In the end, Schoch subscribes to the claim, advanced by Mary Settegast in her book *Plato Prehistorian: 10,000 to 5,000 BC in Myth and Archeology*, that Plato's account refers to the Magdalenians, a western Mediterranean Paleolithic culture that existed and warred chronically in the ninth millennium B.C.E., and whose demise was occasioned by the melting of the glaciers of the last ice age and the probable swamping of their coastal settlements.

Schoch's quest for hard evidence led him to personally explore an underwater cliff cut in a series of immense geometric surfaces that were discovered in 1987 off the coast of Yonaguni, an island in the same Japanese chain that includes Okinawa. The architecture of broad, flat surfaces separated by sheer vertical stone risers appeared to suggest antediluvian human workmanship.

However, after diving the site repeatedly—observing, scraping, and taking samples of the rock—he became convinced that the Yonaguni Monument was a natural formation of bedrock, shaped entirely by natural processes and too imprecise in its shaping and orientation to be the work of human hands. Schoch's scientific training and background also causes him to write off, after some earnest consideration, the recent claims of sentient handiwork for the Face on Mars and other putatively artificial structures in the Cydonia region of the Red Planet.

The potential for pole shifts, tectonic movements, and other Earth-originated catastrophes to change human history is also explored at length by Schoch. Seeking an explanation for the mysteriously widespread demise by fire of scores of settlements in the eastern Mediterranean region outside of Egypt and Mesopotamia at the end of the Bronze Age, around 1200 B.C.E., the author initially considers and then rejects the possibility of volcanic action (there was no known eruption at that time) or a devastating earthquake (none at that time is known to have led to a major conflagration).

While stories of floods of biblical proportion exist in the myths and folklore of cultures all over the world and, together with some scientific evidence, might suggest some watery global destruction in the distant past, they cannot account for the inferno that appeared to engulf the numerous Near Eastern communities extant at the end of the Bronze Age. Schoch also reviews the comings and goings of ice ages and ponders whether forces of nature or Earth's rotation might be responsible for the temperature changes that caused them.

He notes only in passing, but at least with suitable astonishment, the apparent coincidence of a scientifically validated incident of dramatic global warming around 9645 B.C.E. (a rise of fourteen degrees Fahrenheit in fifteen years) with the scientifically postulated scenario of a massive freshwater flood pouring into the Gulf of Mexico at about the same time and coincident with the date that Plato ascribed to the sinking of Atlantis. Although of seemingly great significance, Schoch does not pursue the matter.

Schoch's review also covers the possibility that pole shifts accounted for alterations in the surface conditions on Earth, whether gradual or rapid, actual or only apparent. He examines the work of Dr. Charles Hapgood, who asserted that Earth's crust has slipped over the inner layers and moved the poles at least thrice, by about thirty degrees of latitude, in just the last 80,000 years, with the last movement being completed ca. 10,000 B.C.E. (shades of Atlantis's demise again?). Schoch discounts Hapgood's work, however, on the basis of, among other things, "new and better [paleomagnetic] data" having been collected since the late professor conducted his research.

Schoch also disputes the related "soon-to-be-slipping-polar-ice-cap" thesis of the successful catastrophist author Richard Noone, who wrote *5/5/2000 Ice: The Ultimate Disaster,* asserting that the planetary alignment which occurred on May 5, 2000, would be of very little moment because of its occurrence on the other side of the Sun from Earth.

Still, in seeking an explanation for the so-called Cambrian explosion of wildly diverse and numerous new life-forms over a ten-million-year period more than five hundred million years ago, Schoch is somewhat more sympathetic to the later work of the Cal Tech geologist Joseph Kirschvink and his colleagues, who, using more varied and more reliable data than Hapgood had access to, have proposed that "true polar wander," an entire crustal and mantle displacement of ninety degrees over the earth's core during the Cambrian period, somehow helped make the generation of so many new life-forms possible. Exactly "how" this happened, however, remains a mystery.

Schoch finally turns his attention to the heavens and the possibilities of drastic change owing to impacts on the earth of asteroids, meteorites, and comets (generically called bolides). Since 1957, when scientists finally agreed that the meteor crater in Arizona was the result of an asteroid impact 50,000 years ago, approximately 150 impact craters have been identified around the world, and the number grows annually.

With the discovery in 1993 of the comet known as P/Shoemaker-Levy 9 and the observation of its striking Jupiter in 1994, science was forced to acknowledge the possibility that a comet could indeed, even in contemporary times, collide with a planet and do so with a force sufficient to cause global extinctions.

Whether the Tunguska explosion of 1908, which occurred in Siberia, was the result of a similar impact or that of an asteroid or even an extraterrestrial space vehicle is unknown, but the massive devastation caused by whatever collided with Earth on that fateful day is a sobering portent of what could occur if and when it happens again in or around a highly populated area. Schoch intimates that even a shift in the polar spin axis is possible as a result of such a major collision, if the hypotheses of other researchers are correct.

In any event, two other reputable scientists have cited evidence for a significant bolide impact on Earth circa 10,000 B.C.E. that they claim caused the sudden end of the last ice age and probably led, in turn, to a great flood (Atlantis again?). And in 1996 and 1998, two chains of craters were identified on Earth, chains that can be correlated, in time, with past major extinctions of life on our planet. Whether such phenomena suggest some periodic pattern of destructive hits—for instance, that of an asteroid or comet crossing Earth's orbit on a collision course sometime in the future—is currently a matter of much conjecture and theorizing on the part of scientists. In this vein, Schoch postulates that with respect to the fiery end of the Bronze Age in 1200 B.C.E., a serial stream of hot bolides, fragmenting upon entry into Earth's atmosphere and detonating there with much force and heat, could well account for the widespread devastation recorded for that period.

In terms of the immediate future, in addition to taking steps to preserve the atmospheric ozone layer and counter the environmental trend toward global warming, Schoch advocates protecting our planet against colliding asteroids and comets. According to him, the first action to meet the threat of space-sourced objects would be to create a dedicated system that would locate all objects in space that are in relative proximity to the earth and to determine which ones pose a risk of collision.

The second step would be to find a way to better understand the composition and structure of these objects, information necessary in deciding how to deflect or destroy any threatening object heading our way. And the third activity would be to develop nonnuclear technologies to perform the actual deflection or destruction of these objects should that become necessary, without the attendant risk of collateral harm to human and other terrestrial life.

Schoch believes that we have a sizable window—perhaps until 2200 C.E.—until the next likely swarm of bolides appears and descends on Earth. Of one thing he can be sure: We all hope he's right.

5 Cataclysm 9500 B.C.E.

Two New Works of Immense Scholarship Throw
Orthodox Ice Age Theories into Question and,
in the Process, Corroborate Plato and Many
Other Ancient Sources

David Lewis

In recent prehistory, possibly as late as 9500 B.C.E. (the date ascribed by Plato to the sinking of Atlantis), a profoundly traumatic phenomenon plagued the earth. This event, the result of a distant cosmic explosion, caused severe volcanic eruptions, massive earthquakes, catastrophic flooding, and the upheaval of the world's mountain ranges. Earth's axis may have tilted or its crust may have been violently displaced. Continents rose and sank. Mass extinctions of plants and animals followed, as did a period of eerie global darkness.

The catastrophe struck suddenly, researchers report. Those humans who survived sought refuge in caves and high mountains, the record of their plight preserved to this day in hundreds of ancient deluge/conflagration myths from virtually every cultural tradition. In the last century as well as more recently, scientists gathered the evidence for such a catastrophe, but explained away parts of it through "ice age theory," which is now known to be fundamentally flawed. The rest of the evidence, until now, science has been unable to explain.

No, this is not the synopsis of Hollywood's next disaster extravaganza, nor a rehashing of Immanuel Velikovsky's catastrophe theory, but rather the product of serious research and the subject of two books written by independent experts in the field of recent prehistory. The compelling evidence assembled by these authors reveals the existence of a prehistoric reality that casts orthodox notions about early man into the realm of mere guesswork. The books are *Cataclysm! Compelling Evidence of a Cosmic Catastrophe in 9500 B.C.*, by D. S. Allan and J. B. Delair, and *Earth Under Fire: Humanity's Survival of the Apocalypse*, by Paul LaViolette, Ph.D.

ORTHODOX ASSUMPTIONS

With its long-standing preference for uniformitarianism (the doctrine that nothing sudden occurred in prehistory, but instead only slow evolutionary and geological changes occurred), modern science has discounted what was taken for granted in the last century based on the hard evidence that was uncovered at that time: A global catastrophe occurred recently on Earth. That bias for uniformitarianism, coupled with the dogma of scientific materialism—the presumption that all existence, even consciousness, evolved from matter alone—remains the unproven basis upon which conventional theories of human origins rest.

Ice age theory was born about 180 years ago in connection with studies carried out in the Alps. Geology was then only just being born. Pioneers of the day took most fossil evidence as having resulted from the Great Flood of tradition—*the* benchmark in world history before the birth of modern science—promulgated by Classical writings and religion and tied to beliefs that the world is a mere four thousand to six thousand years old. Geology, however, as a systematic science, found that Earth is millions of years old and that rain-induced flooding could not account for much of the geological devastation that occurred at the time of the mass extinctions. As the scientific movement adopted its uniformitarian dogma, it sought to explain away *all* prehistory in purely materialistic terms, discarding anything that smacked of superstition or *catastrophism*. Scientists of the day, in effect, threw out the baby with the floodwater, adopting prejudices about human origins and past civilizations that dominate to this day.

Within this skewed climate, science ascribed some of the hard evidence of a great cataclysm in recent prehistory to the movement of glaciers, which undoubtedly took place in some areas. But relying on this theory alone necessitated a full-blown ice age, an ice age of greater duration and severity than anything that had come before, to account for burgeoning evidence that something extraordinarily severe had struck the planet and had wiped out most of the world's mammals, uplifted mountain ranges, caused widespread volcanic explosions, carved valleys and fjords, and left massive deposits of stone and gravel strewn across the globe's landmasses.

LETTING THE FACTS SPEAK

To understand more fully the story told by the scientific record, rather than what may be described as the contrived positions of orthodoxy, we spoke with J. B. Delair, a longtime researcher in the field of recent prehistory and coauthor of *Cataclysm! Compelling Evidence of a Cosmic Catastrophe in 9500 B.C.* Delair told us that in his career as a researcher he had come upon many "very strange anomalies," including massive fossil records in "bone caves" where the remains of countless numbers of incompatible prehistoric animals such as saber-toothed tigers, lions, wolves, bison, rhinoceroses, and mammoths were found washed into deep subterranean recesses. These were the remains of animals that perished in recent prehistory all over the world.

Human beings, in many instances, were found in similar conditions, radiocarbon-dated to times consistent with the animal deaths, and from ethnic groups as diverse as European, Eskimo, and Melanesian (as in the case of a find in China). Similar finds have been recorded in India, Brazil, North America, and the Balkans. Geologists have also recorded finding the remains of hundreds of humans who died from *natural* causes in caves, apparently seeking refuge from the catastrophe.

"As a result of this, I wasn't at all happy with some of the explanations," Delair said, "one of these being the ice age, another being the chronology." The key to unlocking the problem of the anomalies proved elusive. But Delair discovered he was not alone in his quest. He received a phone call from Dr. D. S. Allan, a biologist and researcher in the field of Earth severance (shifting landmasses) who shared similar interests, and a partnership was born. Coupling their talents and interdisciplinary backgrounds, they labored for years and found what appears to be the missing link that unlocks the secret of recent prehistory—"global cataclysm."

Allan and Delair discovered that, contrary to scientific dogma, certain events took place very rapidly in Earth's prehistory, such as the shifting of landmasses, as in the case of their own British Isles—which detached from the European mainland just six thousand years ago.

Allan, a Cambridge University doctor of philosophy, versed in physics, chemistry, and biology, had already discovered that many of the same types of plants and animals have existed in different parts of the world when they should not; they are separated by deserts or water. Delair characterized his knowledge of anomalous fossil evidence and Allan's of anomalous biological evidence as "two sides of the same coin . . . bits and pieces of the same puzzle."

After years of work, those pieces would fit together, buttressed by an ignored scientific record that when fully revealed proved stunning. As Delair told us when asked about the implications of his work, "It throws a monkey wrench into almost everything, even evolution. Evolution cannot always be a question of the survival of the fittest. You can have a sudden event that can wipe out the best and worst—the survival of the *luckiest* in those instances," he said.

Using carbon dating, the resources of the British Museum, and those of the Cambridge University library, Delair and Allan established a time frame for the anomalous fossils, which in turn set a time frame for the event that caused their sudden demise.

"The main thing is the dating of the fossils," Delair said. "They are very, very recent in geological parlance, although quite old in human history. The changes they signify are enormous because there are dislocations in entire faunas and floras by thousands of miles. There are also a lot of very abnormal burials. You get sea animals alongside birds and land animals, coal alongside tropical sea urchins, and all sorts of funny things."

CONTRIVED SCIENCE

"It [the ice age] was an invention," Delair stated flatly. In part, it was a reaction to what early geologists and the scientific movement as a whole considered superstition—the flood/conflagration legends. "The original idea of an ice age going back millions of years, ebbing and flowing across the northern and southern hemispheres near the poles, just doesn't stand up to scrutiny, as you can see from our writings. We've drawn upon the literature, which was, in fact, *full* of objections [to ice age notions], on geological and biological grounds."

Many Norwegian fjords, for example, thought to have been carved by ice sheets sliding down from mountains, are open-ended. "There is nowhere for the glaciers to have come down *from*," Delair said. "The fjords were gigantic fissures, filled up with ice at some later time and smoothed by *some* ice action but not *caused* by ice." So-called evidence for an ice age having occurred, moreover, such as striation (grooved or ridged rocks) and erratically strewn boulders—supposedly the result of glacial movements—occurs in parts of the globe where an ice age is known *not* to have taken place.

Research funding that rewards conventional results, Delair told us, is partially responsible for perpetuating erroneous assumptions, along with trying to fit all the evidence into the same worn-out theory, necessitating longer, geographically broader, and more numerous ice ages. Also, Delair notes, fitting together the pieces of this grand puzzle of prehistory requires expertise in a variety of fields. Dr. Allan, what's more, devoted his retirement to this study, a concentration of effort that few, if any, conventionally employed researchers would be able to accomplish.

The picture that Allan, Delair, and others paint, supported by a great deal of field evidence, resembles a catastrophe of mythic proportions. Ice age theory, on the other hand, fails time and again to account for the overwhelming field evidence. The devastation proves to have been so great, in fact, that nothing of earthly origin could have been responsible. Not even a comet or an asteroid, Allan and Delair say, could have wreaked such severe damage. The destructive agent, they tell us, would not necessarily have been very large, but it would have been magnetically powerful, such as an exploding star, a supernova that hurled one or more pieces of its fiery mass our way, upsetting the axes and orbits of various planets through magnetic influence as it moved like a pinball through our solar system for about nine years. The event wreaked horrific trauma upon various planets and caused Earth to convulse, they say, but amounted to nothing more than a minor incident in cosmic terms.

COSMIC EXPLOSIONS

Evidence of a supernova explosion in the form of aluminum 22 (along with other scientific and mythological evidence) found in concentration at the edge of our solar system helped Allan and Delair conclude that a stellar blast probably caused the massive destruction. Iron ore in the earth from 11,000 years ago, its magnetic polarity violently reversed, also testifies to a powerful, extraterrestrial encounter with a magnetically powerful agent at the same time period.

Paul LaViolette, Ph.D., author of *Earth Under Fire: Humanity's Survival of the Apocalypse,* discovered evidence of a different sort of cataclysm—a volley of cosmic waves resulting from an explosion in the galactic core. Entering our solar system, this "galactic superwave" (the most powerful energetic phenomenon in the galaxy) would have interrupted the solar wind's ability to repel most intruding cosmic dust particles, letting the interstellar wind, in effect, have its way with us.

LaViolette, a systems scientist and physicist, found high concentrations of cosmic dust at ice age depths in undisturbed polar ice from Greenland. He determined the amount of cosmic dust in the ice samples by measuring the amount of iridium, a metal that is rare on Earth but abundant in extraterrestrial material. The old uniformitarian assumption was that the rate of cosmic dust depositing in the earth would not have changed over millions of years, but LaViolette found unusually high concentrations in his samples, as well as other evidence of a cosmic visitor during ice age times.

In *Earth Under Fire,* a synthesis of astrophysics and ancient mythical and esoteric traditions, LaViolette details the case for the superwave phenomenon having recently passed through our solar system. He includes in his body of evidence the discovery by NASA's Voyager 2 spacecraft of narrow grooves, like those of a phonograph record, in the rings of Saturn—which, if they were indeed millions of years old, as uniformitarians maintain, would have banded together by now. LaViolette explains how the superwave would have caused the rings to appear as they do, while Allan and Delair describe how a super-nova "chunk" would have disrupted the orbital paths and axial rotations of neighboring planets. Some researchers stated, even before the Voyager visit, that Saturn's rings may be a mere 10,000 to 20,000 years old, within the time period LaViolette, Allan, and Delair say the cataclysm took place.

Within months of the event, LaViolette says, a shroud of cosmic dust would have caused severe climatic changes on Earth, periods of darkness, severe cold and then extreme heat, massive flooding, and incendiary temperatures as the dust interacted with the Sun, "causing it to go into an active, flaring state," LaViolette said. "If you could imagine the worst solar storm that's ever occurred and beef that up a thousand or hundred thousand times—that would be going on continuously. . . . And then you have the possibility that a flare event could engulf the earth."

Dr. Paul LaViolette
(Photograph by
Patricia Kenyon)

WHAT THE ANCIENTS KNEW

LaViolette builds a scientific and mythological foundation for cataclysm as a cyclical event, a recurrence of galactic core explosions in 26,000-year cycles—a period that relates to the precession of the equinoxes. This is the duration of one Great Year, recognized by the ancient Greeks, Zoroastrians, and Chinese. Hindu scriptures recognize the same cycle, a succession of declining and advancing ages that seem to relate to our solar system's orbit around the galactic core. This is the apparent astrological focus of the "Central Sun" of existence, *Brahma*, conscious experience of which results in transcendental ecstasy and liberation from cycles of mortal suffering, or *karma*.

"The galactic core explosion cycle is another important cycle that Earth must reckon with," LaViolette says, citing numerous ancient traditions, many of which reveal that advanced astronomical knowledge, and therefore advanced human beings, existed in precataclysmic times.

The zodiac, in fact, LaViolette says, probably came down to us as a cryptogram—a time capsule—designed to alert us to the ongoing emanations from the galactic core, and the sphinx and pyramids of the Giza plateau stand as an astronomical memorial to the great catastrophe. The figures of the zodiac, Delair told us, appear in most catastrophe myths. And the universality of this time capsule's message, the knowledge of cosmic cycles, is difficult to ignore.

LaViolette and others find it encoded in numerous myths, in cultural and mystical traditions, and in the world's megalithic architecture (see *The Orion Mystery: Unlocking the Secrets of the Pyramids,* by Robert Bauval; *Fingerprints of the Gods: The Evidence of Earth's Lost Civilization,* by Graham Hancock; and *The Message of the Sphinx: A Quest for the Hidden Legacy of Mankind,* by Graham Hancock and Robert Bauval). As these commentators point out, the ancient myths speak universally of a seafaring people who seem to have been the guardians of advanced knowledge. Their universal message, apparently passed down from a forgotten precataclysmic world, urges human progress, and harmony with the source of all creation.

Almost unavoidably, then, LaViolette, Allan and Delair, Hancock, and Bauval (as well as Thompson and Cremo in their book *Forbidden Archeology*) reveal that recent prehistory was not at all what modern science, burdened by its prejudices, has assumed. A past cloaked in mystery comes objectively to light. This accumulated rich, diverse body of work, interdisciplinary in nature, is filled not only with ancient lore but also with hard evidence that supports timeless traditions, the result of it being that the way mankind sees itself must profoundly change.

6 The Case for the Flood

Exposing the Scientific Myth of the Ice Age

Peter Bros

hose people who are not satisfied with the paradigms supported by the scientific establishment regarding the creation of the universe are naturally interested in Plato's story of Atlantis, a prehistoric civilization destroyed in a flood. We are all aware of the degree of opposition the story creates in the scientific community. Atlantis is up there with flying saucers and free energy devices as targets for the professional skeptics (who are organized to perpetuate entrenched scientific dogma), because it raises the specter of an actual source for the thousands of seemingly impossible megalithic remains, including the pyramids, that dot the surface of the earth.

Graham Hancock, in his book *Underworld: The Mysterious Origins of Civilization,* visits the remains of a prehistoric, worldwide civilization using the monuments it left behind. He posits that this worldwide culture was brought to an end by superfloods. Robert M. Schoch, Ph.D. contends in *Voyages of the Pyramid Builders: The True Origins of the Pyramids from Lost Egypt to Ancient America* that the geological, linguistic, and geographical evidence associated with the worldwide megalithic monuments demonstrates the actual existence of such a prototype civilization, a civilization that was dispersed around the globe by rising sea levels caused by a flurry of comets.

While the edges of evidence appear to support the notion of Atlantis as a worldwide civilization lost in a catastrophic flood, many authors have sought out Atlantis in specific locales because the scientific establishment unknowingly cast its lot against a prehistorical civilization before the evidence began showing up. It did so by enforcing the eighteenth-century rule of reason which stipulated that God could not be used as an explanation for physical reality, thereby rejecting out of hand the possible validity of all biblical accounts and, in the case of a worldwide prehistoric society, the possibility that a flood of biblical proportions destroyed all but the megalithic evidence for that civilization.

Making the world of science safe against Bible-thumpers became the overriding goal of nineteenth-century science. Pierre-Simon de Laplace had barely finished banishing God as the source of Newton's perpetual motion of the solar system (by creating his swirling mass of gas out of whole cloth) before evidence for the worldwide flood described in the Bible began to accumulate. Science, at this time, was unaware that accounts of a universal flood appear around the globe, the universal flood being a part of the myths and traditions of more than five hundred widely separated cultures.

As explorers started to bring home descriptions of the world from afar, science was horrified to see a picture emerging of a planet scarred by massive movements of water, generally from the northwest to the southeast, over its surface. The northwestern sides of whole mountains were scored as if they had been subjected to fast-moving waters containing gravel and boulders. Floodwater was unmistakably the source of the scoring because science could see the same effect from fast-moving rivers. Furthermore, those same sides of the mountains were also home to massive buildups of drift materials, detritus presumably left behind by receding waters. Again, this was an effect that mimicked natural actions in the real world. These drift deposits even contained the remains of animals, including the woolly mammoth.

More horrifying to nineteenth-century scientists than the evidence of water damage and silting were the gigantic boulders exposed to public view all over the European countryside in places where they clearly didn't belong. These oversized rocks, many weighing thousands of tons, could have been moved only by massive floodwaters carrying them along and then depositing them when the waters receded. The movement of these rocks by the floodwaters would have been, in part, responsible for the aforementioned mountainside scouring.

What to do with these discoveries that constituted irrefutable evidence of a worldwide flood? If science had been true to the evidence and concluded that the evidence had, in fact, resulted from a worldwide flood, religious crazies would have filled the pulpits and newspapers with cries that the biblical story of the flood, and thus the entire Bible, had been scientifically confirmed: not a desirable result.

The only thing science had going for it was the lack of an apparent *source* for the floodwaters. Arguments that its waters had originated from the visible seabeds and ocean floors of the moon were easily squelched by referring to Newton's theory of gravitation, which holds that gravity is proportional to matter. All the matter in the Moon that has ever been there appears still to be there. Thus, there could have been no lessening of the gravity and thus no way for the Moon's apparent seas and oceans to have escaped its gravity and move the quarter of a million miles across space, in response to the earth's stronger gravity, and produce a worldwide flood.

Science, however, is an enterprise that turns beliefs into facts, and it accomplishes this feat so well that its myths become more real than actual facts. It takes hypotheses, mere notions, and crafts a methodology designed to do the impossible—to turn those notions into facts. Science holds that hypotheses that predict facts that are later found are as good as fact.

The scientific landscape is littered with hypotheses that have been accepted as scientific fact even though the term *scientific fact* is an admission that proven hypotheses are not facts. There is nothing that can be done to turn an idea into a fact. The scientific process merely accepts theories as scientific fact so long as they have not been disproved. Of course, what we have when we accept as fact ideas that have never been disproved are a bunch of ideas that have never been disproved. Laplace's swirling mass of gas, light as water waves, the oxygen/carbon dioxide cycle, the electron, even Newton's mass/gravity are scientific facts, ideas capable of neither proof nor disproof.

The task that faced science when it was confronted with the incontrovertible evidence of a worldwide flood was to create a scientific fact that would provide a substitute for the already existing evidence left behind by the actual flood. In the early 1820s, a Swiss engineer, Ignaz Venetz, focused on the remains of woolly mammoths found in the drifts, pointing out that as the same animals were being found in the frozen Siberian wastes, the area in which the drifts were found must have at one time been covered with ice. A chorus of experts joined in, positing the slow descent of glaciers from the north, a process that, because it visualized the inexorable creep of ice over eons, deftly captured the spirit of uniformitarianism, Charles Lyell's theory, published in the 1830s, which maintains that geologic processes occur *gradually* rather than catastrophically. Lyell's own reconstruction of the earth's history, focusing on the layers of sediment left as the floodwaters receded, pictured the sediments as deposited over eons so they could be used to produce a fictitious dating system for the earth to counter the biblical creation story.

Charles Lyell
(Photograph by
G. Stodart)

A decade later, the Swiss naturalist Louis Agassiz consolidated the speculations of Venetz and his chorus of approving voices by enthroning himself as the inventor of the ice age. Agassiz's creation, for scientific and public consumption, was a distinct reversal of the scientific process. Instead of taking an idea and using unknown facts to prove it to be a scientific fact, Agassiz took disparate facts that led inexorably to an uncomfortable conclusion—

Louis Agassiz

a worldwide flood—and then created an idea—the ice age—that could be used in place of the uncomfortable (flood) idea. And then he exclaimed his ice age theory to be scientific fact!

Because no methodology can prove an *idea*, ideas have to be accepted or rejected on the basis of the evidence they explain. The glacier theory did not explain why the scoring, labeled striations that supported glacier theory appeared only on *one* side of the mountains or why the drifts, called *moraines* to tie them to glacier theory, contained the remains of animals that were found *only* in equatorial regions, insects that were found *only* in the southern hemisphere, and birds that were native to Asia. The glacier theory did not explain why the giant boulders, named *erratics* to accommodate glacier theory, were found in desert regions where no glacier could possibly go.

But these discrepancies were small potatoes compared to the scientific reality of glaciers themselves. Glacier theory simply ignored the basic facts of glacier movement. Glaciers are flows of ice that, like rivers, respond to gravity. Glaciers do not climb hills and they do not travel across level land. However, because scientific facts are merely notions, ideas that cannot be disproved, those who present strong visual confirmation of their truthfulness are always both widely and wildly accepted. Even though glaciers could not have carried the erratics the thousands of miles required to reach (and cover) the European countryside, the fact that the North Pole was north, which was "up there" on the globe, was more than ample scientific proof that gravity could cause the glaciers to inch "down" over the sides of the globe.

Pierre-Simon de Laplace

No one proposed that ice fields covered the southern half of the planet because that would require the glaciers to defy gravity and travel "up" the sides of the globe from the South Pole.

Such is the stuff upon which empirical science bases its notions of reality.

Like Laplace's swirling mass of gas, which was proposed four decades before Agassiz's ice age and provided the template for turning theories about existing facts into scientific facts, the ice age is no more than a *proposition*, a *possible* explanation for the reality that we see. Science saw the evidence of the flood described in the Bible and created the ice age to avoid the appearance of verifying an event described in the Bible.

Once the ice age was accepted as a reality, the only problem that science encountered was its need to produce a model that would explain how the earth could undergo vast temperature variations, a task at which it has failed so far. In the meantime, subsequent discoveries continued to verify the existence of a worldwide flood and mirrored the hundreds of newly encountered myths and traditions attesting to the flood's actuality. The very drifts that contained the bones of the woolly mammoths that gave rise to the idea of the ice age contained, along with the remains of exotic animals, insects and birds that had *never* lived in the same location and vegetation that could *never* have been local to where the drifts were found. There was no way to explain this admixture of life by glacial movements.

It was as if all the creatures, all the trees, all the vegetation of the earth had been caught up in flowing whirlpools, mixed together, and then deposited wherever the water settled. In addition to the drifts at the northwest bases of mountain chains, these jumbles of diverse life-forms were also found in drifts that filled isolated valleys and made up entire islands in the Arctic whose boneyards contained not only the remains of animals from warmer climes, but also uncountable tree trunks extirpated with their roots intact—trees that could have grown only below the Arctic treeline.

Science did not rush to proclaim the existence of a warm age!

Instead, as soon as the ice age became a scientific fact, the fossil remains of life that had been found in the drifts, including the woolly mammoth that gave rise to the myth of the ice age, disappeared from scientific discourse and the newly named moraines became a simple admixture of sand and rock. When the same admixture of bones and plant life was found stuffed deep in caves, a process that could have occurred *only* if it had been carried into the small cracks and crevices by the recession of massive floodwaters, the caves were deemed an anomaly that explained nothing, and the evidence was allowed to be mined into nonexistence.

Then came evidence that the scattered islands of the Pacific had once been home to a civilization that had stretched from the shores of Asia to the coast of South America. Plato's accounts of a lost civilization in the *Timaeus* and *Critias* had always been the subject of debate, but the debate had not arisen because of physical evidence on the face of the earth. The pyramids, impossible structures, had always existed, but there was never a context in which to place them until the discoveries of ancient cities in the Pacific and then in Central and South America started coming to light.

Similarities among the various megalithic societies being uncovered led to the application of the word *diffusion* to describe the way culture passed from one group of people to another. With cultural diffusion again pointing clearly to an antediluvian civilization, the scientific establishment reacted with archeology's first rule: the ironclad law that cultural transfers could not extend beyond the shores of the oceans. At the same time, a social movement was forged that was designed to preserve the dignity of indigenous populations in the face of the encroachment of modern technology.

In the United States, the late-nineteenth-century job of establishing that native populations had never been influenced by foreign contact fell to Major John Wesley Powell, who was the creator and director of the Bureau of Ethnology at the Smithsonian; a founder and president of the politically influential Cosmos Club; a founder and president of the Anthropological Society of Washington; one of the earliest members of the Biological Society of Washington; an organizer of the Geological Society of Washington; a founder of both the National Geographic Society and the Geological Society of America; and president of the American Association for the Advancement of Science.

During the nineteenth century, evidence of both European presence and the existence of a prehistoric civilization was being uncovered all over North America, primarily in the mounds that dotted the countryside east of the Rockies. Powell sent out his ethnology emissaries to systematically destroy the mounds and any evidence they contained that pointed to nonnative origins, thereby successfully eradicating the history of the North American continent.

Powell's prestige and fanaticism, together with the law against cultural diffusionism, translated into a worldwide rule of science that megalithic structures, no matter where found, were the product of whatever local inhabitants happened to live around the megaliths at the time of their discovery. Thus the world was taught that the pyramids sprang from the hands of hunter-gatherers who had discovered farming on the shores of the Nile, the massive megalithic complexes in the Americas were the product of the ancestors of the natives Cortez had quickly defeated, and the megalithic monuments dotting the islands of the Pacific were built by the natives' ancestors who had set aside their fishing spears long enough to craft cities out of fitted slabs of fifty-ton rocks!

There was no room in the past for a megalithic society, a worldwide, antediluvian civilization that would easily explain both the physical remains of such a civilization and the flood that brought that civilization to an end. The past was dominated by an ice age created to explain the evidence for the flood that destroyed the worldwide civilization.

Today, we are stuck with the scientific fact, the myth, that ice can creep down from the North Pole and cover Europe and North America. Once the scientific community has accepted a theory as fact, any evidence is acceptable so long as it is cast to support the theory and no evidence is sufficient to disprove the theory. Without opposition, the theory becomes part of the founding principles of whole new fields of inquiry. There can, then, be no Agassiz speaking into a void created by an overwhelming desire to discredit an event described in the Bible, nor a Powell powerful enough to undo the damage done by Powell.

This is because there is no longer a steward overseeing the entire field, given that the field itself is now fractured into dozens of disciplines whose disciples can all take responsibility for claiming the theory to be wrong. If and when people in the individual fields who have adopted the scientific fact of the ice age attempt to challenge the theory, they are charged with operating out of their area of competence.

The ice age is more real than the striated rock, the moraine-buried mountains, and the erratics it was crafted to explain, a nonexistent vision that is more a visible fixture of the landscape than the landscape itself.

But the discoveries of flood evidence keep coming. The breathtaking ruins of a submerged city off Yonaguni Island in Japan have produced a storm of controversy, which has been drowned out by the cries of rage against the later discovery of the remains of a huge underwater city lying off the western tip of Cuba just east of the Yucatán. Before critics could scream themselves hoarse at this discovery, another startling find, of a sunken city in India's Bay of Cambay, sent establishment delusionists like the Harvard archeologist Richard Meadows scrambling for an international commission to gain control of the nature of the knowledge permitted to come out of these finds.

Any researcher attempting to come to grips with the emerging facts of the past is faced with the scientifically unassailable reality of the ice age in trying to explain the facts and, by acknowledging the ice age, ends up further distorting our view of reality. Some seize on the "crustal displacement" theory suggested by Charles Hapgood and fleshed out by the Flem-Aths, the notion that parts of the earth that are now at the poles were farther toward the equator, speculating that such an event would have caused massive movements of the world's oceans. Others favor the idea that giant comets or meteors caused the earth to tilt on its axis, thus displacing the oceans. Still others believe the encroachment of black holes caused the oceans to heave. The most effective proponent of a worldwide civilization, Graham Hancock, perceives that the melting ice sheets created massive water dams in accordance with ice age theory proposed by the late professor Cesare Emiliani. These dams, Hancock posits, broke and produced the superfloods that inundated what became the underwater cities.

Because these explanations accord reality to the scientific myth of the ice age and do not explain where the waters of the flood came from—the waters whose weight submerged the landmasses of the Pacific and the Atlantic, forcing up mountain peaks at their margins—I prefer to look elsewhere than the earth for the source of the floodwaters. The most obvious source, of course, would be the Moon, whose seabeds, outlined on its surface, have long been recognized by their names as being the remnants of seas and oceans.

Let us speculate for a moment and say that the scientific fact of gravity, rather than being the static result of mass, is the dynamic product of what the matter is doing—that is, cooling. This is a conclusion that is supported by the fact that the measurement of the product of cooling, the electromagnetic emissions such as light, is identical to the measurement of gravity, and both diminish inversely with the square of their distance. Given this, the Moon, being smaller than Earth, would have cooled off first, lessening its gravitational field and allowing the still-hot Earth, with its still-strong gravitational field, to attract the Moon's oceans across space.

Attempting to disagree with the nature of the static gravity that causes the masses of ice to slip slowly down the sides of the planet, in our view, is a bigger sin than claiming that the billion pounds of copper mined in upper Michigan during the Mediterranean Bronze Age produced the Bronze Age. Gravity is a property rather than a dynamic process, and North American copper could not have crossed the ocean. We're faced with a scientific process that turns ideas into facts that, once accorded consensus reality, are beyond challenge because with no evidence for their validity, there can be no evidence for their invalidity.

The ice age was crafted out of whole cloth to counter the possibility that evidence turning up all over the world could be used to support biblical interpretations of the world. No one wants to go back to the days of feudal science, when decisions about reality were filtered through belief systems designed to provide for our salvation. However, we have created a scientific system that enshrines off-the-cuff ideas of men who lived before we knew about the atom, electricity, or even that some stars were galaxies—in short, we are allowing our views of reality to be controlled by the unverifiable notions of dead men who knew relatively nothing.

Because the project of science is no longer unified, but is instead splintered among a thousand different disciplines, these embedded ideas creep into diverse disciplines unchallenged, and in doing so become unchallenge-able. If we don't consciously challenge basic assumptions at every step of the way, those of us involved in seeking explanations for the actual reality of our existence—in this case the evidence for a worldwide antediluvian civ-ilization—will find ourselves trapped in the very paradigm we are attempt-ing to penetrate.

7 The Martyrdom of Immanuel Velikovsky

As Catastrophists Gain Ground, an Early Hero
Gets Some Long Overdue Credit

John Kettler

We may not realize it, but we're going through the death throes of a fundamental geological doctrine, a doctrine called uniformitarianism, which holds that the geological processes we see today are the same ones that have always existed, and that while changes *do* occur, the process is gradual, unfolding over eons.

Right. Try selling that one to your children. They've been steeped in classes, through TV and movies, in an altogether more radical view of how things work, geologically speaking. That model is called catastrophism and is exemplified by the now famous "asteroid that wiped out the dinosaurs." Yes, we're talking about the Chicxylub crater in the Yucatán and an asteroid strike some sixty-five million years ago.

In 1950, this was the rankest sort of scientific heresy. The chief heretic was a man named Immanuel Velikovsky, a man who made vast contributions to a variety of disciplines, but who today is all but unknown, even to many who benefit directly from his pioneering work.

Immanuel Velikovsky was a Russian Jew, born June 10, 1895, in Vitebsk. He mastered several languages as a child and graduated from gymnasium (high school) in 1913 with a gold medal, having performed exceptionally well in Russian and mathematics. He then left Russia for a time, traveled to Europe and Palestine, and took natural sciences (premed) courses at the University of Edinburgh. He returned to what was then czarist Russia before World War I started and enrolled in the University of Moscow. Somehow he was not swept up in either the slaughter on the Eastern Front or the civil war when the Bolsheviks came to power in 1917, and he emerged with a medical degree in 1921 and also a strong background in history and law.

Shortly thereafter, he moved to Vienna, where Cupid's arrow found him, resulting in his marriage to Elisheva Kramer, a young violinist. While

Moses and the Seventh Plague of Egypt
(ART BY JOHN MARTIN)

in Vienna, he edited the *Scripta Universitatis,* a major academic work to which Albert Einstein contributed the mathematical–physical science section. He also studied psychoanalysis under Sigmund Freud's pupil Wilhelm Stekel and studied the working of the brain in Zurich.

By 1924, Velikovsky and his wife were living in Palestine, where he practiced psychoanalysis. He continued his academic editing work by taking on the *Scripta Academica Hierosolymitana,* a major Jewish piece of scholarship. The year 1930 saw his first original contribution in the form of a paper that argued that epileptics are characterized by pathological, distinctive encephalogram patterns. A portion of his writings appeared in Freud's *Imago.* It was Freud's *Moses and Monotheism,* though, that would plant the fateful seed that led Immanuel Velikovsky from the quiet pursuits of healing minds and organizing great thoughts to worldwide fame, ten years of academic ostracism, and a subsequent lifetime of vilification and scorn.

The "seed" was a nagging wondering whether Freud's hero, the monotheist iconoclast pharaoh Akhnaton, might be the real-life model for Oedipus, the legendary individual whose strange desires and worse acts were said by the Freudians to underlie the psychology of all young men. Velikovsky later argued in *Oedipus and Akhnaton* that Akhnaton was indeed the real-life model for the tragic and legendary Oedipus. In 1939 Velikovsky went on sabbatical for a year, and took his family with him to the United States only weeks before World War II began. He spent the next eight months doing research in the great libraries of New York.

April 1940 brought another key question to the fore of Velikovsky's questing mind, a mind well trained in ancient history and steeped in the Hebrew faith. Was there any evidence in Egyptian records of the great catastrophes that were depicted in the Bible as preceding the Exodus?

Velikovsky went looking and came up with what is known as the Papyrus Ipuwer, a set of lamentations by an Egyptian sage by the name of Ipuwer that describe a series of disasters that befell his beloved country, disasters that matched those described in the book of Exodus, the source of the well-known description that first appeared in the King James version of "hail and burning hail" that destroyed Egypt's crops.

This rather amazing bombardment is the result of human interference, you see. The King James version of the Bible dates back to the 1600s, and it wasn't until the middle to late 1700s that a scientific concept for *meteorite* even existed. Thus, when the translators encountered the Hebrew *barad* (stone) in early manuscripts, they elected to render it as "hail." Velikovsky noticed description after description in myths and legends and historical accounts of "burning pitch" falling from the heavens, and from this he proceeded to develop deep insights into the nature and structure of Venus (more on this later).

The discovery of the Papyrus Ipuwer launched Velikovsky on nothing less than an attempt to reconcile the conflicting Hebrew and Egyptian chronologies, an effort that eventually led to academic war with Egyptologists, archeologists, and ancient historians when he published *Ages in Chaos* (revised chronology) in 1952 and *Earth in Upheaval* (wherein he presented geological and paleontological evidence for *Worlds in Collision*) in 1955. A titanic clash with the full force of astronomers, cosmologists, experts in celestial mechanics, and academicians ensued when Velikovsky presumed to upset their tidy model of an orderly, highly stable cosmos by publishing his bombshell, *Worlds in Collision*, in 1950.

The key idea from which the book arose came about in October 1940 when Velikovsky, reading the Book of Joshua, noticed that a shower of meteorites preceded the Sun's "standing still." This made him wonder whether this might be a description not of a local event but of a global one. He went looking for evidence in history and archeology and also in the myths, legends, and repressed memories of all humanity, his psychoanalytical training standing him in excellent stead here. What he found indicated to him that the planet Venus had been the major player in a series of global cataclysms recorded all over the world. It also made him wonder whether Venus could be related to the upheavals preceding the Exodus.

For ten years Velikovsky, now a permanent resident of the United States, continued to research his two manuscripts, meanwhile trying to find a publisher for *Worlds in Collision*. Two dozen rejections later, the Macmillan Company, a major publisher of academic textbooks, agreed to take on his book. The scientists who wrote Macmillan's books and the academics who bought them applied blatant pressure tactics in an attempt to prevent Macmillan from publishing the book, but Macmillan was not dissuaded.

And yet by the time that *Worlds in Collision* had become Macmillan's number one best seller, the pressure had become so great that Macmillan ended up transferring the book to its competitor Doubleday. At Doubleday, the book went on to enjoy worldwide success, success that was aided considerably by a public backlash against the pressure tactics.

INTERNATIONALLY FAMOUS; SCIENTIFICALLY DAMNED

Worlds in Collision was a bomb detonated in the china shop of astronomy, whose tidy model of the stable solar system in no way provided for planets departing their orbits and wreaking worldwide havoc even once, let alone several times. In briefest form, Velikovsky's argument was that Venus hadn't always been a planet. Instead, he posited, it had been ejected as a comet from the body of Jupiter and had a highly eccentric orbit that had either caused it to collide directly with Earth or had several times brought it close enough to Earth to trigger cataclysms that laid waste to entire kingdoms all around the globe before "settling down." The arguments in the book also maintain that there were records of this having occurred within historical times.

Consider why the controversy regarding the book's publication erupted. It was 1950, and the United States, having triumphed in World War II, was enjoying incredible prosperity and optimism. The people, perhaps reacting to all the chaos and horror of the recently ended war and the perceived rising menace of global Communism (Soviets had suddenly gotten the bomb in 1949), largely closed ranks, went back to work, and resumed their lives or started new ones. Emphasis was on patriotism, conformity, and consumption. How ironic, then, that the public (in its backlash against the book's suppression) turned out to be more open-minded than what were presumed to be the open minds of academe and science. That's how it was, though.

Reader's Digest, that citadel of American conservatism, said of Velikovsky's seminal work: "Fascinating as a tale by Jules Verne, yet documented with a scholarship worthy of Darwin." The *New York Herald-Tribune* called it "A stupendous panorama of terrestrial and human histories," and *Pageant* beautifully summarized the public reaction by saying: "Nothing in recent years has so excited the public imagination." The above are all review excerpts taken from the back cover of the Dell paperback edition, in its eleventh printing by 1973, the date of the writer's copy. The Dell paperback first went into print in 1967, some seventeen years after *Worlds in Collision* was first published in hardcover.

The scientific and academic reaction to the book was generally presaged by the extortion, practiced prior to and after publication, against the Macmillan Company. As the book began to garner public and—in some circles even scientific—interest and acclaim, all pretense of genteel discussion went by the boards. Out came the mailed fists, the naked threats, and oceans of mud and offal. The attacks targeted three main groups: the public, the scientific and academic community, and Immanuel Velikovsky himself. Nor were such niceties as actually reading the book before denouncing it and its author employed.

Even before the Macmillan Company published the book, the renowned astronomer Harlow Shapley arranged multiple intellectual well poisonings in a learned journal, by an astronomer, a geologist, and an archeologist, not one of whom had read the book. This was a pattern used over and over again.

Shapley and his minions also engineered the sacking of the veteran senior editor (twenty-five years at the Macmillan Company) who had accepted *Worlds in Collision* for publication. Shapley was also responsible for the director of the famous Hayden Planetarium being fired for the high crime of proposing to mount a display at the planetarium on Velikovsky's unique cosmological theory. Meanwhile, Velikovsky was systematically attacked in the scientific journals via distortion, lies, misrepresentation, claims of incompetence, and ad hominem attacks, while there never seemed to be space in which he could reply in order to defend himself.

Interestingly, one of Velikovsky's attackers was the astronomer Donald Menzel, since identified through the UFO researcher Stanton Friedman's digging to be a highly cleared disinformation specialist during World War II. Donald Menzel was a major UFO debunker, but his name is one of those on the famous/notorious TOP SECRET (Codeword) MJ-12 document, where he is listed as composing part of the super-covert investigative team for the July 1947 Roswell crash, alleged technology from which was discussed in an *Atlantis Rising* magazine article entitled "The Fight for Alien Technology: Jack Shulman Remains Undaunted by Mounting Threats."

Let's look now at some of Velikovsky's then shocking claims, and see whether he got anything right. (Velikovsky's claims are in bold.)

Venus is hot.

Correct. Velikovsky argued that Venus was incandescent in historical times and would therefore still be hot. Venusian cloud temperature measurements in 1950 showed temperatures well below freezing day and night. In 1962, NASA's Mariner II satellite showed the surface temperature to be 800 degrees Fahrenheit, more than enough to melt lead. Surface probes later determined the true value to be about 1,000 degrees Fahrenheit.

A large comet was in collision with Earth.

Correct. Even before the famous Chicxylub story became public knowledge, researchers had found, in August 1950, rich deposits of meteoric nickel in the red clay of ocean bottoms and in March 1959 had found a layer of deep sea white ash, deposited in a "cometary collision" or "the fiery end of bodies of cosmic origin."

Some cometary tails and also some meteorites contain hydrocarbons.

Correct. By 1951, spectral analysis disclosed hydrocarbons in comet tails. By 1959, hydrocarbons in meteorites were found to be composed of many of the same waxes and compounds found here on Earth.

Evidence of petroleum hydrocarbons will be found on the Moon.

Correct. Samples brought back by the Apollo XI mission had evidence of organic matter in the form of aromatic hydrocarbons.

Jupiter emits radio noises.

Velikovsky made this claim at Princeton in 1953. Eighteen months later, two scientists from the Carnegie Institute announced receiving strong radio signals from Jupiter, then considered a cold body enshrouded in thousands of miles of ice. By 1960, two Cal Tech scientists had found that Jupiter had a radiation belt around it that was emitting 1,014 times more radio energy than Earth's Van Allen belt.

Quite a few "lucky guesses" and "coincidences," wouldn't you say?

Let's now turn to Velikovsky's single greatest "crime," which not only put him in the soup but also kept him there: his interdisciplinary investigations.

VELIKOVSKY: INTERDISCIPLINARY SCIENTIFIC HERETIC

Dr. Lynn Rose, writing in *Pensée: Velikovsky Reconsidered,* in an article entitled "The Censorship of Velikovsky's Interdisciplinary Synthesis," noted an automatic tendency toward uniformitarianism in all the scientific disciplines. This condition was born of a profound ignorance concerning evidence of catastrophism found by other disciplines, leading to the ignoring or rejecting of such evidence within any particular discipline.

As Dr. Rose put it: "Each isolated discipline tends to remain unaware of the catastrophic data hidden away as skeletons in the closets of other disciplines. Velikovsky has removed those skeletons from various closets and has been rattling them loudly for all to hear. His suggestion is that when one looks at all the evidence without restricting oneself to the limited number of 'facts' usually considered by one group of specialists, it becomes possible to make a strong case for catastrophism."

Immanuel Velikovsky

To say Velikovsky's skeletal music was unwelcome to many would be putting it mildly. Said Dean B. McLaughlin, professor of astronomy at the University of Michigan, in his May 20, 1950, letter of protest and threat to the Macmillan Company (as quoted by Dr. Rose): "The claim of universal efficacy is the unmistakable mark of the quack . . . There is specialization within specialties . . . But no man today can hope to correct the mistakes in more than a small subfield of science. And yet Velikovsky claims to be able to dispute the basic principles of several sciences! These are indeed delusions of grandeur!"

Does this explain in part why Velikovsky was essentially crucified, then ostracized, by most of the scientific community?

Does this explain why he was harangued ad nauseum at his "day in court" twenty-four years after *Worlds in Collision* was published? This "day in court" took the form of a special meeting of the American Association for the Advancement of Science, held in San Francisco on February 25, 1974. It was arranged by Carl Sagan and had been promised to be a fair forum. Instead, it turned into a snide dismissal of Velikovsky, an unprincipled, many-on-one attack on a slow-speaking, seventy-nine-year-old man deluged with objections and assertions and given near zero time to respond. Velikovsky endured two sessions of this abuse, which lasted seven hours, and while he managed to score some good points, to many who participated in this rigged event he came across poorly. Nor was a key paper by Albert Michelson (of speed of light measurement fame), which supported Velikovsky's arguments, allowed to be read before reporters left to file their stories.

The stunning findings of planetary probes ended Velikovsky's college exile and overloaded his schedule. Velikovsky died, still researching, in 1979, leaving us a rich published and unpublished body of work.

⑧ The Perils of Planetary Amnesia

As Evidence of Ancient Cataclysm Mounts, the Legacy of a Rejected Genius Is Reconsidered

Steve Parsons

At one time, Immanuel Velikovsky was known and respected as a world-class scholar. After studying at Edinburgh, Moscow, Zurich, Berlin, and Vienna, Velikovsky earned a reputation as an accomplished psychoanalyst and enjoyed close ties to Albert Einstein and Freud's first pupil, Wilhelm Stekel.

But with the 1950 publication by the Macmillan Company of his best-selling book *Worlds in Collision,* Velikovsky's reputation in the halls of science plummeted all the way to the basement. His stature as a researcher and scholar would not recover for the rest of his life. Overnight, Velikovsky became *persona non grata* on college campuses across the nation, and his work was vilified by mainstream astronomers.

How did this Russian-born Jewish scholar, educated at the world's most respected centers of learning, bring such a firestorm of criticism upon himself? What caused powerful men of science to denounce Velikovsky as a liar and charlatan on the basis of hearsay, swearing never to read his popular book? Why have respected professionals lost their jobs for committing the crime of recommending an open investigation of Velikovsky's conclusions?

After examining the ancient records of cultures around the world, Velikovsky made three unusual claims in *Worlds in Collision.* He postulated that (1) the planet Venus moved on a highly irregular course, passing very close to Earth within human history, (2) electromagnetic and electrostatic forces operate on a planetary scale, powerful enough to affect the motions and activity of planets, and (3) the planet Venus took the form of an immense comet in the ancient sky, inspiring great awe and fear in the hearts of our distant ancestors.

Velikovsky's conclusions were controversial, but this alone cannot explain the intensity of the response from the halls of academe. Controversy alone cannot explain why, over many years, the popular Carl Sagan mounted a personal campaign to discredit Velikovsky. Normally, the marketplace of ideas will accommodate a broad range of thought, from the weird to the boring, but not this time.

The sheer novelty of Velikovsky's work cannot explain why Dr. Harlow Shapley, director of the Harvard Observatory, along with ranking astronomer Fred Whipple and other powerful scientists, would force Macmillan to cease publication and fire its own editor, James Putnam, even though *Worlds in Collision* had soared to the top of the best-seller lists. Some have speculated that only the power of truth touching the raw nerve of mass denial could cause grown men to go ballistic like this.

Only a deeply buried trauma in the mass consciousness could erupt with such irrational fury. In the case of the "Velikovsky affair," the organized, frantic defense of entrenched belief produced one of the most pathological episodes in the history of science. Had Immanuel Velikovsky penetrated the veil of "planetary amnesia"?

As a psychoanalyst, Velikovsky was well qualified to recognize pathology in human behavior. In a later book, *Mankind in Amnesia,* he claims that the ancient sages exhibited a frightened state of mind, haunted by a particular fear based on terrible events their ancestors had experienced when the world was ripped apart by monstrous natural forces. He describes the means by which this deepest of collective traumas was gradually buried and forgotten over the years, but not eliminated.

Aristotle's cosmology, which dominated scholastic thinking for two thousand years, acted with surprising precision to suppress all lingering fears of planetary disorder. Then in the 1800s, modern science agreed that the solar system, Earth, and all forms of life on Earth had *absolutely never* passed through any kind of wild or disorderly phase in the past. This idea, known as uniformitarianism, became established dogma in science. The tide of human thought has successfully driven the memory from conscious awareness, but the evidence indicates it is still alive in the collective human psyche.

Velikovsky understood our tendency to suppress trauma but also to express and repeat trauma in peculiar ways. For example, the early wars of conquest were deliberately conducted as a ritual exercise to reenact the havoc and destruction brought by the planetary gods of old.

In today's world, we barely recognize our own violence and certainly don't associate it with ancient roots. That's the nature of buried trauma. One doesn't see one's own shadow.

Immanuel Velikovsky initially believed that the checks and balances of science would encourage others to examine his conclusions and perform their own investigations along the same lines. Unfortunately, however, by the time he passed away, in 1979, he had come to believe that his ideas would never be taken seriously by mainstream science. Though the early seventies saw a renewal of public interest in Velikovsky's work, the doors of science have remained tightly shut on it to this day. Only the most highly motivated individuals with independent financial support have been able to continue the research where Velikovsky left off.

Interestingly, recent findings by the space program have confirmed much of what Velikovsky said. Consider the following Venusian puzzles.

Venus spins in a direction opposite that of the other planets and its temperature of 1,000 degrees Fahrenheit is much hotter than expected for an object in its orbital position. The chemistry of Venus violates the established theory of planet formation. The upper atmosphere of Venus is marked by extreme, faster-than-rotation winds and the calm, lower atmosphere displays continuous lightning discharges. The body of the planet is covered with 100,000 volcanoes that have completely resurfaced the planet in recent geological time.

And finally, the traditional theory cannot account for the invisible remnant of a cometlike tail extending forty-five million kilometers into space. The Venusian tail was detected by the Earth-orbiting SOHO satellite and reported in the June 1997 issue of *New Scientist*. The Venusian puzzles make sense, it can be argued, if we believe what ancient people actually *said* about Venus. They said that Venus was a comet. They called Venus the long-haired star, the bearded star, and the witch star. They said Venus took the form of the goddess in both her beautiful aspect and her terrible aspect, that she was a fierce dragon who attacked the world. A newly arriving body that has not yet achieved thermal and electrical equilibrium with its environment could present such a display in the sky.

Apparently Velikovsky opened the door to our buried collective memories by regarding the testimony of ancient peoples as credible evidence for unusual natural events in our past.

His journey began when he studied the Egyptian and Hebrew accounts of the disasters and wonders that accompanied the Old Testament Exodus, dated at approximately 1500 B.C.E. He discovered close parallels in the historical writings of other cultures, suggesting that the same sequence of catastrophes beset the entire globe and was experienced by all people simultaneously.

In 1950, science was not yet ready to accept the testimony of ancient peoples as credible evidence for unusual planetary events. The physical sciences would not tolerate an intrusion by an outsider who drew conclusions that crossed academic boundaries. But nearly fifty years later, science has opened the door a crack.

Two innovative theorists in the scientific establishment have recently published a book bearing a distinctive Velikovskian tone. Dr. Victor Clube, dean of the department of astrophysics at Oxford, together with his colleague, Dr. William Napier, has developed a thesis of cometary catastrophe that draws upon mythical themes as primary evidence. Though Clube and Napier's cometary visitor was not a planet, the story is surprisingly close to that of *Worlds in Collision*.

Other innovative theorists have thrown themselves even more wholeheartedly into this line of research. The comparative mythologist David Talbott and the physicist Wallace Thornhill independently recognized the power of Velikovsky's discoveries and have followed up with forty-five years of combined research of their own.

OPENING THE MIND TO THE ELECTRIC UNIVERSE

By breaking from the pack and looking at observed facts with fresh eyes, Wallace Thornhill has become convinced that planets and stars function in an electrically dynamic environment. The Venusian tail, discovered last year, retains its ropelike or filamentary structure across forty-five million kilometers because it is a current carrying plasma. These plasma structures, Birkeland currents, are well known to plasma physicists but remain unrecognized by astronomers. The very existence of Birkeland currents in the solar system demonstrates the existence of a flow of electric current in the plasma that fills the solar system. And this opens up a whole new way of seeing things.

Thornhill says that stars do not produce all of their light and heat by thermonuclear processes. Instead, our Sun and all other stars resemble great spheres of lightning. These spheres receive energy externally rather than from nuclear fusion at their core, he says. The accepted theory that stars produce energy by nuclear fusion suits the mind-set of the atomic era but does not conform to actual observations.

Sadly, the general public has no way of knowing that the behavior of our Sun does not fit the conventional theory. We observe a lack of neutrinos; temperature reductions rather than gains as one approaches the surface; accelerated solar wind; strange rotation behavior and holes in the surface that reveal a cooler, rather than hotter, interior.

"You have to observe what nature actually does," he says, "not what you *think* it should do." Thornhill's empirical approach does allow ancient human testimony to count as credible evidence. Fables, legends, and myths don't prove Thornhill's ideas, but they provide clues.

For instance, the mythical gods hurled great thunderbolts at each other

Ancient catastrophes
(Art courtesy of the Kronia Group)

when they battled in the heavens. The flashing thunderbolt was their weapon of choice. And the earliest written records of the ancient sages and stargazers confirm that the gods who battled in the sky were named with the same names as our most familiar planets.

If (1) the mythical gods were the planets, and if (2) the planets moved so close to each other in the sky that they exchanged colossal electrical bolts, and if (3) this took place within human memory, then where are the scars and the craters?

Actually, the scars of colossal electric strikes literally cover the Moon and most of the planets. These scars are fresh and abundant, just waiting to be studied from a new perspective. Specific patterns in these scars bear a remarkable similarity to the patterns left behind by natural lightning strikes and arcs produced in laboratories on Earth.

Planetary geologists speculate that the long, tapering "sinuous rilles" found on the moon and Mars, which travel both uphill and downhill for hundreds of kilometers, are collapsed lava tubes or dry riverbeds or cracks in the crust. But conventional experts are grasping at straws on this one. The electrical signature is unmistakable.

Such hard evidence is dangerous to science. What if Thornhill's claims are taken seriously? What if the glass collected from the bottom of small craters of the moon and brought back by the astronauts were really heated and melted by electrical discharge rather than meteor impact? What if the Valles Marineris was actually caused by a giant thunderbolt that ripped across the face of Mars, leaving a gaping chasm that could swallow a *thousand* Grand Canyons?

Wallace Thornhill
(Photograph by
Patricia Kenyon)

If thousands of marks and scars on the planets were caused by powerful electrical discharges—the thunderbolts of the gods—then astronomy is left with more than egg on its face. We're talking about an omelet!

Fortunately for Thornhill, he has not suffered persecution for his unusual views, at least not yet. Perhaps this is because the views of this unassuming Aussie have not received much exposure. But that will change soon.

UNLOCKING AMNESIA THROUGH MYTH

David Talbott has already found himself the subject of a ninety-minute documentary, titled "Remembering the End of the World." Unlike Thornhill's work in the physical sciences, Talbott's work rests upon unusual and unexpected patterns found in human memory. And what a memory!

Imagine a global event of extreme drama, experienced by the entire human race, involving great wonders in the sky. Imagine the intensity of the experience and its memory to be so great as to alter the course of human development. For the first time ever, entire nations began to erect grand monuments to the gods and perform passionate rituals in a futile effort to relive the earlier experience, to magically restore life to the way it was before the great collapse.

At the dawn of civilization, perhaps five thousand years ago, says Talbott, every dimension of civilized life pointed to the earlier time when things were better, when heaven was close to Earth, before the gods went away. The arts, the songs, the stories, the architecture, the religious beliefs, the military affairs, and the meaning of words and symbols all provide us with lasting evidence of what people experienced then. And according to Talbott, people used every device known to keep alive the memory of a glory that once was. That glory and its violent collapse involved catastrophic displays in the heavens as planets moved close to Earth and appeared huge in the sky.

But just as the fabled gods had gone away, the memory of the golden time would eventually go away. The memory of the violent collapse of the golden time would also go away, but its scars would not. Those scars of massive collective trauma, of doomsday, dwell within every human being alive today and powerfully affect how we relate to the world and to each other.

Velikovsky understood the way by which an individual suppresses the painful memory of trauma in the psyche. He reasoned that the entire human race has collectively suppressed the trauma of its expulsion from the womb-like golden time. Yet that suppressed trauma keeps expressing itself as human violence and alienation.

David Talbott
(PHOTOGRAPH BY
PATRICIA KENYON)

We accept the background pain as a normal state of existence, because that's what everyone has always felt, going back as far as anybody can remember. But Velikovsky would say that this state is not "normal." We collectively suffer a distorted view of life because of this greatest of all traumas, when the Time of Perfect Virtue (as the Chinese call it) came to a cold and bitter end.

Talbott has extended Velikovsky's work by showing, in exquisite detail, the way that Saturn, Jupiter, Mars, and Venus were intimately tied to human experience during primordial times. These planets traveled very close to Earth, actually assuming a stable and symmetrical, colinear configuration immediately prior to the myth-making epoch. The "Age of the Gods," according to Talbott's astonishing story, harkens both to the stable/peaceful period and to the violent/dramatic period when the colinear configuration destabilized and collapsed completely.

Throughout the world, people have drawn images and symbols bearing a distinctive crescent. Laypeople and experts alike always assume that the crescent represents the Moon. Sometimes the crescent has been drawn with a star in its center, but think about it. No star will ever be seen within the crescent of the Moon, as the body of the moon occupies that space. And no orb sits squarely in front of the Moon that we see today.

Talbott could speak for hours on this symbol alone to show that we are confronting an image whose imprint is far deeper in human consciousness and far more awesome than our familiar Moon. In fact, Talbott found no astronomical records of a moon prior to about 500 B.C.E., even though the people of early times were nearly obsessed with observing the activity in the sky.

The crescent was cast by our Sun on Saturn when Saturn occupied the pole position in the sky so close as to subtend up to 20 degrees of arc or more. The small orb in the center was Venus in her dormant phase. Venus appeared as a shining star when in her radiant phase.

Wallace Thornhill's understanding of plasma-discharge phenomena allows even the nontechnical mind to visualize the way a young Venus might have produced the radiating luminous streamers found in ancient representations of the planet.

Using research methods borrowed from Velikovsky, Talbott examined the mythology of every major culture in the world. Since mythical stories become more locally embellished with the passage of time, he traced the stories back to their oldest and purest forms. This led him to the earliest writings from the cradle of civilization in the Middle East and ancient Egypt.

The great pyramids, according to Talbott, are filled with human writings that describe a world that we do not see today, a sky that we do not see today. That's why the meaning of the hieroglyphs bewilders our best experts. *These inscriptions don't answer to our world.* This is an important clue.

With support from Thornhill and a growing number of accomplished scholars, David Talbott is mounting a heresy even more radical than Velikovsky's. He claims, with complete assurance, that Venus, Mars, Saturn, and Jupiter traveled very close to Earth within human memory. He says that together these planets presented a stupendous form in the sky, at times peaceful and at times violent.

The people alive during this "Age of the Gods" felt a deep kinship with these familiar forms. That's why the battles of the gods in the sky and the departure of these gods caused such confusion and trauma. The emotional climate for those people might have resembled that of innocent children whose reliable and loving parents suddenly turned into capricious tyrants before finally abandoning them. For the first time, people began to experience the illusion of separation and all forms of human violence. The rest is history.

9 Thunderbolts of the Gods

Does Growing Evidence of an Electric Universe
Reveal Previously Hidden Meaning in
Ancient Mythology?

Mel and Amy Acheson

Who would have guessed that the myths of ancient cultures could throw new light on the mysterious surface features of planets and moons? Or give new meaning to current work in artificial-lightning laboratories? If the mythologist David Talbott, of Portland, Oregon, and the physicist Wallace Thornhill, of Canberra, Australia, are correct, then ancient myths and symbols are a key to an expanded and holistic understanding of both history and the physical universe.

Yet in our age, world mythology seems a most unlikely source of discovery. Until recently, mythologists sought to explain the ancient stories with references to events in everyday life: to the seasons, to the power of a storm, to phases of the Moon, or to movements of the Sun. But their efforts have produced a morass of contradictions, reinforcing the popular belief that myth is fiction pure and simple—anything but a dependable guide to the past.

COMPARATIVE MYTHOLOGY

In contrast, David Talbott, inspired by Immanuel Velikovsky's theory of interplanetary upheaval, developed a method for comparing the myths of far-flung cultures. His objective was to discover whether reliable memories were embedded in the different stories. This method is similar to the reasoning of attorneys in a court of law, questioning witnesses who may be lying, or incompetent, or remembering incorrectly. When statements from independent witnesses converge on unique details, they tend to corroborate each other, even if the witnesses are not reliable in other things they say. Similarly, according to Talbott, there are hundreds of common themes in world mythology in which different words and different symbols point to the same remembered events. The more peculiar the points of convergence, the more unreasonable it is to dismiss them.

When allowed to speak for themselves, these universal memories tell a coherent and detailed story, Talbott claims. But it is a story that seems preposterous from today's worldview: According to Talbott, what the ancients worshipped and feared as powerful *gods* were *planets* positioned extremely close to Earth. This close congregation of planets appeared as huge powers in the sky. Their instabilities and unpredictable movements gave rise to one of the most common themes of myth—the wars of the gods. In these dramatic stories, the gods pounded each other with cosmic lightning while fire and stone descended on Earth.

THE WEAPON OF THE GODS

In ancient traditions, few images are more vividly presented than the thunderbolts of the planetary gods, Talbott notes. Consider the gas-giant Jupiter, whom the Greeks remembered as the ruler Zeus, the victor in the celestial clash of the Titans. "Jupiter is just a little speck of light in our sky, but ancient peoples recalled the *god* Jupiter as a towering form in the heavens, wielding lightning as his weapon of choice. What does this mean? If the gods were planets, then the thunderbolts of the gods were nothing less than interplanetary lightning discharges."

The lightning-bearer Zeus, Greek god of the planet Jupiter

In Hesiod's *Theogony,* we read of Zeus, "From Heaven and from Olympus he came immediately, hurling his lightning: the bolts flew thick and fast from his strong hand together with thunder and lightning, whirling an awesome flame . . ."

When the dragon Typhon attacked the world, there was "thunder and lightning, and . . . fire from the monster, and the scorching winds and blazing thunderbolt." Destroyed by a lightning bolt from Zeus, the world-threatening dragon came to be known as the "thunderstricken." Indeed, it is remarkable how many mythical figures are struck down by lightning.

In Classical myth alone, these figures include Enceladus, Mimas, Menoetius, Aristodemus and Capaneus, Idas, Iasion, and Asclepius. "The biggest mistake a scholar can make," Talbott says, "is to look for terrestrial explanations. The earliest forms of these stories are cosmic. The gods, the great heroes, and the thunderbolts that fly between them are celestial through and through." Hebrew tradition has remembered well the lightning of the gods. Psalm 77 proclaims: "The voice of thy thunder was in the heaven: the lightnings lightened the world: the Earth trembled and shook." From India, the *Mahabharata* and *Ramayana* relate that lightning of the gods filled the heavens like a rain of fiery arrows. From ancient Egypt, Babylon, Scandinavia, China, and the Americas, myths and legends describe conflagrations attributed to thunderbolts from the gods.

These stories of cosmic battles provide much of the content of the myths we know today. Talbott writes: "If we've failed to recognize the celestial players, it's because the planets which inspired these stories have receded to pinpoints of light. In modern times, we see no interplanetary lightning arcing between them."

But Talbott reminds us that if there is anything to these global memories, the physical evidence should be massive. This amounts to a call for objective investigation of the surface features of planets and moons, to see if the telltale markers of interplanetary discharges might be present.

ELECTRICITY AND ASTRONOMY

Unbeknownst to Talbott, the Australian physicist Wallace Thornhill had been pursuing just such an investigation. Thornhill had discovered Velikovsky's books shortly before starting his university career. "I was the only physics undergraduate to haunt the anthropology shelves of the university library," he says. "The result was a strong conviction that Velikovsky had presented a case that required further study." But his next discovery was the reluctance, even hostility, of scientists to question the assumptions underlying their theories.

One of those assumptions that Thornhill questioned was the insignificance of electrical phenomena on astronomical scales. The Nobel laureate Hannes Alfven, a pioneering investigator of the properties of plasmas in electrical discharges such as lightning, had admonished theoretical physicists that their models were wrong. Real plasmas didn't behave the way mathematical deductions predicted. They are not superconductors, Thornhill explains, nor can they be treated as a gas, as is implicit, for example, in the term *solar wind*. Electrical currents flow in them, pinching into long filaments and then braiding themselves into ropelike structures. These long, twisted filaments are visible in solar prominences, galactic jets, and comet tails. They were detected as "stringy things" in the forty-million-kilometer-long tail of Venus last year.

Following the suggestion of Ralph Juergens, an electrical engineer who studied Alfven's work, Thornhill began to amass evidence showing that most features now being photographed on planets, satellites, and asteroids are scars of plasma discharges: interplanetary lightning.

"By scaling up electrical effects seen on Earth and in the laboratory, I can provide stunning support for the ancient imagery of a different sky and hence the likelihood that planets and moons *did* move in close proximity in the recent past," he claims. "An electrical model provides a simple mechanism for re-ordering a chaotic planetary system in a very short time and maintaining that stability."

One of the laboratory effects is produced by moving a high-voltage pointed rod just above the surface of a powder-covered insulator placed on a grounded metal plate. The spark forms characteristic patterns in the powder. A long, narrow main channel of fairly uniform width will have a narrower, more sinuous channel engraved along its center. Tributary channels run parallel to the main channel for a distance, then they rejoin it almost perpendicularly.

Thornhill points out that these same features are seen on a larger scale in lightning strikes to Earth, such as on golf courses. Trenches of constant width are created, with narrower furrows snaking down their centers. The soil blasted from the trench is deposited along both sides. Secondary channels may run parallel to the main channel, and tributary channels join at right angles.

PLANETARY PLASMA EFFECTS

Thornhill describes how the same effects are repeated on a planetary scale in features called sinuous rilles. Long, uniformly narrow channels snake across the surface, often with levees of material deposited along each side.

The more sinuous inner channels often have chains of small, circular craters precisely centered along their axes, or the craters overlap to produce fluted walls. There is generally no sign of rubble from collapsed roofs, as would be expected if the conventional "lava tube" explanation for rilles on the Moon were correct. Nor is there

Hyginus Rille on the Moon.
Neither water nor lava produces channels
punctuated by circular pits, but this is a
common feature of discharge channels,
according to Wallace Thornhill.
(NASA PHOTOGRAPH)

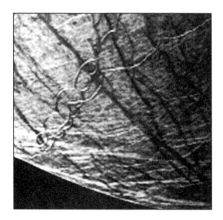

The characteristic "corkscrew" form of a plasma filament arcing across the surface of Europa, one of the moons of Jupiter
(NASA PHOTOGRAPH)

evidence of the outwash that would result if the channels had been formed by water, as has been proposed for rilles on Mars.

Furthermore, the rilles run uphill and down, Thornhill points out, following an electrical potential rather than the gravitational potential, as water and lava do. Where rilles intersect, the younger channel and its levees continue uninterrupted across the older as though the older channel weren't there. This is especially obvious on Europa, where the levees are often darker than the surrounding terrain. They are also darker than the central channel, which creates a problem for the accepted explanation that they are darker material welling up through cracks in the ice. Thornhill surmises that the electrical forces of the arc altered the chemical or, possibly, the nuclear, composition of the debris.

Particularly remarkable is the series of *looping* rilles on Europa. Ice cracking in loops is unheard of, but the characteristic corkscrew form of a plasma filament arcing across the surface easily explains it.

Thornhill also notes the similarities of craters on the planets and moons to those created in the laboratory. Both tend to be perfectly circular because an electrical arc always strikes perpendicular to a surface. Walls are nearly vertical and floors are nearly flat as the circular motion of the arc machines out the crater. Impact and explosion craters, by contrast, tend to have a bowl shape: Instead of being lifted from the surface, excavated material undergoes shock displacement, shattering and flowing in a manner similar to that of a fluid for the duration of the shock.

Another common feature of electrically generated craters, Thornhill explains, is terracing along the sides, sometimes corkscrewing down to the floor, following the rotary motion of the arc. The Moon and Mars both provide many examples of terraced and corkscrew craters.

Central peaks tend to be symmetrical and steep-sided, similar to the central "nipple" left by plasma machining as the rotary corkscrewing motion of the arc cuts out the material around it. Thornhill contrasts this with the irregular mass of the so-called rebound peak in a lab-produced impact or explosion crater. In a number of craters on the Moon, the central peak connects to the surrounding terrain with an "isthmus," just as in a plasma-machined crater when the arc is quenched before completing a full rotation.

A telling characteristic of electrical origin, Thornhill says, is a crater centered on the rim of another crater. This is a common sight on the Moon and some planets. It's an expected effect of the arc jumping to or striking the highest elevations.

Lightning crater with rilles on Mars's moon Phobos
(NASA PHOTOGRAPH)

Finally, many volcanoes are more likely scaled-up versions of fulgamites, Thornhill claims. Fulgamites are blisters of material raised on lightning arrestors during a strike. Typically, a fulgamite has a steep, fluted outer edge and a crater at the top, formed as the more diffuse discharge that raised the fulgamite pinches down to a narrow arc. The most impressive example is Olympus Mons on Mars, six hundred kilometers across and twenty-four kilometers high. A six-stroke crater was machined into the top as the arc narrowed and jumped to high spots on each successive rim.

THE LIGHTNING-SCARRED GOD

The possibility that human memories could explain some of the great surprises of the space age does *not* come as a surprise to Talbott. As an example, he describes the ancient Scarface Motif.

A theme that occurs in many cultures is that of the warrior-god who, at a time of upheaval, receives a gaping wound or scar on his forehead, face, or thigh. At first sight, this is hardly surprising, because warriors and wounds *do* go together. However, this is not the story just of *a warrior,* but of the celestial *archetype* of warriors—the god whom human warriors celebrated as their inspiration on the battlefield. In early astronomies, this warrior archetype is identified with a specific planet—Mars.

It was said of the Greek Mars, named Ares, that this celestial warrior received a deep gash, as in his encounter with Diomedes; then the god lets loose the howl of a thousand warriors and rushes to Zeus to bemoan his gaping wound. An alternative Greek name for Mars was Heracles, and this god too suffered a harsh wound, in his thigh.

The Blackfoot Indians do not appear to have preserved any astronomical associations with their legendary warrior Scarface. Nor do the Aztecs appear to have remembered any planetary connection for their famous scarred god Tlaloc. But Talbott insists that a comparative approach can demonstrate the common roots of such mythical themes.

Is it possible, then, that the "wounding" of Mars refers to an actual event? "I remember looking at one of the first Mariner photographs of Mars," Talbott recalls. "It displayed a stupendous chasm cutting across the face of the planet. Even from a considerable distance, the chasm looked like a scar." Astronomers christened it Valles Marineris—its size was such that it would swallow a thousand Grand Canyons and more. "At that moment I realized that of all the planets and moons in our solar system, Mars alone bore the likeness of the warrior-god's wound."

This comparative method can also account for numerous details that the experts have missed. Most dramatic is the connection between the Scarface theme and the lightning of the gods. Talbott gives as an example the god Enceladus, struck down by a thunderbolt of Zeus. The god was remembered as "the lightning-scarred god." Enceladus appears to be a counterpart of the monster Typhon, the "thunderstruck" god. Both can be identified as the terrible aspect of the celestial warrior, according to Talbott, for it was in his "man-slaying" rampage that Ares received his wound.

Talbott was the first to connect the highly visible scarring of the Aztec Tlaloc to lightning. "That's entirely due to the fact that the experts have not looked at the worldwide theme," he tells us. Tlaloc was, in fact, directly linked to lightning, and it was through lightning that he dispatched souls to the Aztec heaven. In Aztec mythology there is a special afterlife world reserved for people who are killed by lightning. It is ruled by Tlaloc and is called Tlalocan.

"Could something as massive as Valles Marineris have been carved by interplanetary lightning?" Talbott wondered. As it turned out, he had the opportunity to pose that very question to Wallace Thornhill.

THE LIGHTNING-SCARRED PLANET

Thornhill and Talbott met nearly a decade after the first images of Valles Marineris were returned. Talbott summarized his investigation of the lightning-scarred god theme. "Could Valles Marineris have been caused by a thunderbolt?" he asked.

Thornhill replied, "It couldn't have been anything else."

At four thousand kilometers long, seven hundred kilometers across in places, and up to six kilometers deep, it's comparable to scaling up the Grand Canyon to stretch from New York to Los Angeles. Approximately two million cubic kilometers of the Martian surface was removed with no comparable debris field apparent.

"Valles Marineris was created within minutes by a giant electric arc sweeping across the surface of Mars," Thornhill claims. "The rock and soil were lifted into space. Some of it fell back around the planet to create the great, strewn fields of boulders seen by both Viking Landers and Pathfinder."

He points to the steep, scalloped walls of the canyon and the central ridges as typical of plasma machining. The side gullies often terminate in circular alcoves and are left hanging with no debris apron in the main channel. They tend to join at right angles. Smaller channels and crater chains run parallel to the main channels. "The arc probably began in the east in the region of chaotic terrain," Thornhill speculates. "It then swept westward, forming the great parallel canyons. It finally terminated in the huge rilles of Noctis Labyrinthus."

Thornhill has published a CD entitled *The Electric Universe,* which describes these and other electrical phenomena on an astronomical scale. He cites the research of Talbott that demonstrates that ancient peoples witnessed an age when these now quiescent energies were dominant.

All the planets associated with the deities of myth are covered with scars that are best explained as plasma-discharge features. The craters, volcanoes, and canyons, when examined in detail, show essential differences from terrestrial counterparts. Yet those anomalous features *do* correspond with the features of lightning scars. Talbott's prediction that the reconstructed themes of myth should be verified in massive physical evidence on the planets gains support with every image returned by space probes.

Valles Marineris bears the most striking correspondence with the mythical warrior-god's wound. This mighty chasm represents the confluence of two worldviews: the dramatic, historical worldview of mythology and the objective, physical worldview of science. If Talbott and Thornhill are correct, the accepted understanding of both myth and science must be rebuilt on a new foundation that will support both the historical past and the electrical future.

PART THREE

EXPLORING THE GREATER
ANTIQUITY OF CIVILIZATION

10 The Enigma of India's Origins

The Dating of New Discoveries in the Gulf of Cambay Upsets the Orthodox Scenario for the Dawn of Civilization

David Lewis

With three quarters of the planet covered by water, it's been said we know more about the surface of Venus than about that which lies beneath the sea. Yet this may be changing. The discovery of what may be a lost city off the coast of western Cuba startled the archeological world in the spring of 2001. Reports from Havana spoke of massive stone blocks stacked at a depth of 2,100 feet in perpendicular and circular formations, some resembling pyramids. Researchers in a miniature submarine described the area as an urban development, with structures that may once have been roads and bridges.

Because a prediluvian "lost city" does not fit into the accepted paradigm of prehistory, the halls of orthodoxy remain silent on the matter—at least for now. And while those halls still stand, other recent discoveries have begun to seriously erode their foundations. Finding the ruins of an ancient, submerged civilization raises more questions than it answers and causes more problems than it solves. How did the land and its structures sink? What could have prompted such a large-scale cataclysm? When did civilization on Earth actually begin? What do we *really* know about the ancient past and human origins? And how does the establishment of science, so fixed in its doctrines, grapple with the potential demise of its most cherished presumptions?

If the lost city of the Caribbean wasn't enough, about the same time an equally startling discovery occurred twenty-five miles off the coast of Gujurat, India. The discovery took place in that part of the Arabian Sea known as the Gulf of Cambay. India's National Institute of Ocean Technology (NIOT) turned up some amazing sonar images from the gulf's depths while scanning for pollution levels. Using equipment that penetrates the sea floor, marine experts discovered a pattern of distinct, man-made formations across a five-mile stretch of seabed.

According to reports published worldwide, NIOT's sonar-imaging technology detected what appeared to be the stone pillars and collapsed walls of at least two cities. The site was described as part of an ancient river valley civilization not unlike the River Saraswati of the *Rig Veda,* thought to be mythical but—according to recent independent findings by Indian scientists—has been proved to have flowed to Gujurat. Divers at the Gulf of Cambay site later retrieved from depths of 120 feet two thousand man-made artifacts, including pottery, jewelry, sculpture, human bones, and evidence of writing, according to *The Times of London.*

1. 2. 3.

4. 5.

1. *Inscribed pottery from the Gulf of Cambay.*
2. *Artifact from the Gulf of Cambay. Small asymmetrical cylindrical object with hollowed middle.* (PHOTOGRAPH BY SANTHA FAIIA)
3. *Artifact from the Gulf of Cambay. Possible carving of a deer or other animal appears symmetrically on both sides of object.* (PHOTOGRAPH BY SANTHA FAIIA)
4. *Group of four objects from the Gulf of Cambay.* (PHOTOGRAPH BY SANTHA FAIIA)
5. *Artifact from the Gulf of Cambay. Stone slab suggested by NIOT to be engraved with archaic script or other deliberate marking or symbols.* (PHOTOGRAPH BY SANTHA FAIIA)

"Underwater structures that have been found along the Gulf of Cambay, Gujarat, indicate an ancient township that could date back anywhere before or during the Harappan civilization," Science and Technology Minister Murli Manohar Joshi told the world at a press conference in May 2001.

Joshi's initial guess was that the five-mile-long site was four thousand to six thousand years old and had been submerged by an extremely powerful earthquake. But in January 2002, carbon dating revealed that an artifact from the site was astonishingly ancient, between 8,500 and 9,500 years old (the oldest known civilization in the world by thousands of years). This was a time when, according to orthodox archeological standards, India should have been peopled with primitive hunter-gatherers and a few settlements, not the inhabitants of a lost civilization.

The author and underwater researcher Graham Hancock described buildings at the site as being hundreds of feet in length, with drains running along the streets. "If the case is made [for the age of the underwater cities], then it means that the foundations are out of the bottom of archeology," Hancock said.

The scope and sophistication of the site dismantles the specific belief that civilization began five thousand years ago in Sumeria, according to Hancock, even as the alternative scholarship movement, of which he is a central figure, in general challenges orthodox views about human origins. In the orthodox (Darwinist) view, life, and then human beings, emerged extremely slowly from highly improbable accidental causes over a period of time necessitated by laws of probability.

The theoretical four-billion-year age of the planet was determined *not* by scientific or geologic evidence, according to the science writer Richard Milton (author of *Facts of Life: Shattering the Myth of Darwinism*), but by estimating how long it *should* have taken for accidental life to have occurred, given the extreme *improbability* of life having occurred at all through random, material causes.

Civilization followed, according to the scenario, after the theoretical "out-of-Africa" migration (about 100,000 years ago), fairly recently in prehistory. Evidence of extremely ancient civilizations, or of severe cataclysmic disruptions (those resembling mythical events that may have shaped the ancient world), throws a wrench into the conventional machinery. Discoveries that reveal civilizations having existed several thousand years earlier than previously thought are greeted with disbelief, consternation, silence. Evidence, then, of modern man having lived, say, 250,000 years ago in South America is considered preposterous and heretical, although the evidence for it exists.

Other views, modern and ancient, portray life as having emerged by more mysterious means, not by a series of astronomically improbable accidents, not through a biblical creationist scenario, but by virtue of some other unknown agency. This other, unknown agency, an all-pervasive life force more in keeping with *The Tao of Physics* than *Origin of Species,* is such as that evidenced in Eastern healing disciplines and codified impressionistically in the world's mythologies.

In this latter view, the idea that prehistoric civilizations existed needs not be rejected due to a presumption that life evolved from material causes alone over an arbitrary time line necessitated by improbability. Tradition in India has always held, in fact, that Indian culture predates all understanding, being virtually timeless, stretching into the mists of antiquity from whence sprang the gods and myth—the non-space/non-time reality of modern theoretical physics.

As we shall see, certain *mythical* traditions maintain that the landmass of ancient India greatly exceeded its present size, and even that it stretched from Australia to Madagascar, perhaps as an archipelago. As with the archeological discovery of Troy, once thought to be a myth, it must be recognized that at least some of India's supposedly mythical traditions are rooted in historical fact. This leads to the idea of an "Asian Atlantis," which may seem fantastic, but early geologists believed such a continent existed. The notion may again be gaining credence after the discoveries in the Gulf of Cambay and given NIOT's intention to investigate other submerged archeological sites off Mahabalipuram and Poompuhar in Tamil Nadu.

Current conceptions of Western scholars conflict with traditional Indian beliefs about such things, but that wasn't always the case. In the mid to late nineteenth century, when scientific ideas about human origins had begun to take shape in Europe, early geologists and archeologists accepted the idea of a biblical flood, lost continents (for which they found much evidence), and a landmass in the Indian Ocean—the great Southern Continent of the British naturalist Alfred Russell Wallace.

Even today, mainstream science believes such landmasses as Gondwanaland and Pangaea existed, although they are relegated to the extremely ancient epochs of 180 to 200 million years ago, in keeping with beliefs about the age of the planet necessitated by an admittedly improbable evolutionary process. And consider the South Asian traditions that mimic the findings of the early geologists, those who say an inhabited continent existed across what are now the Indian Ocean, the Arabian Sea, and the Bay of Bengal. These traditions live to this day in the lore of southern India, Sri Lanka, and the islands of the Andaman Sea.

"In a former age," an ancient Sri Lankan text states, "the citadel of Rawana (Lord of Lanka), 25 palaces and 400,000 streets were swallowed by the sea."

The submerged landmass, according to one ancient account, rested between Tuticoreen on the southwest Indian coast and Manaar in Sri Lanka. This submerged landmass was not a landmass of the size envisioned by the early geologists, but—if it actually existed—a submerged portion of the Indian subcontinent just the same.

Another cultural tradition, cited in Allan and Delair's *Cataclysm! Compelling Evidence of a Cosmic Catastrophe in 9500 B.C.*, that of the Selungs of the Mergui Archipelago off southern Burma, also speaks of a sunken landmass: ". . . formerly [the] country was of continental dimensions, but the daughter of an evil spirit threw many rocks into the sea . . . the waters rose and swallowed up the land. . . . Everything alive perished, except what was able to save itself on one island that remained above the waters."

One of the Tamil epics of southern India, the *Silappadhikaram,* frequently mentions a vast tract of land called Kumara Nadu, also known as Kumari Kandam, stretching far beyond India's present-day coasts. Ancient south Indian commentators wrote in detail of a prehistoric "Tamil Sangham," a spiritual academy situated in that ancient land. They wrote also of the submersion of two rivers, the Kumari and the Pahroli, in the middle of the continent, and of a country dotted with mountain ranges, animals, vegetation, and forty-nine provinces. This Pandya kingdom, according to tradition, reigned from 30,000 B.C.E. to 16,500 B.C.E. At least one branch of modern-day south Indian mystics claims a direct lineage from those extraordinarily ancient times, when their spiritual progenitors were said to have achieved extremely long lives through yogic techniques.

And India's epic poem the *Mahabharata,* dated by non-Westernized Indian scholars to five thousand years before Christ, contains references to its hero, Rama, gazing from India's present-day west coast into a vast landmass now occupied by the Arabian Sea, an account supported by the recent underwater discoveries. Less celebrated Indian texts even mention advanced technology, in the form of aircraft used to transport the society's elite and wage war.

The writings describe these aircraft in detail and at great length, puzzling scholars and historians. The great Indian epics, what's more, vividly describe militaristic devastation that can be equated only with nuclear war. Was there, at one time, not just an ancient civilization in India, but an *advanced* ancient civilization?

Flying machines . . . lost continents . . . are these mythical tales of mythical lands or do these ancient references provide us with a historical record long forgotten and then dismissed by Western science as fantasy?

To answer that question, we must look at the history of scholarship as it pertains to India. Since the nineteenth century, Western scholars have dismissed the historical significance of the cultural traditions of ancient peoples, those of southern Asia included. With a decidedly ethnocentric bias, the experts reinterpreted history as it was taught in the East. Having found, for example, that root words of India's ancient Sanskrit turn up almost universally in the world's major languages, Western scholars devised an ethnocentric scheme to explain the phenomenon—one that modern Indian intellectuals have come to accept.

A previous European people must have once existed, the scholars imagined—an Indo-European race upon which the world, including India, drew for its linguistic roots and genetic stock. The scholars also expropriated the Aryans of ancient India to flesh out this scenario. This Aryan race, they told us, derived from Europe and then invaded the Indus Valley in the north of India—making Sanskrit and Vedic culture relatively young and a product, rather than a progenitor, of Western civilization.

The "Aryan invasion" theory has since fallen into disrepute. James Schaffer, of Case Western University, a noted archeologist specializing in ancient India, had this to say on the matter. "The archeological record and ancient oral and literate traditions of south Asia are now converging."

In other words, India's mythology is being proved historically accurate. Schaffer then wrote. "A few scholars have proposed that there is nothing in the 'literature' firmly placing the Indo-Aryans outside of south Asia, and now the archeological record is confirming this. . . . We reject most strongly the simplistic historical interpretations [of Western scholars], which date back to the eighteenth century. . . . These still prevailing interpretations are significantly diminished by European ethnocentrism, colonialism, racism . . ."

Southern India, a land whose cultural roots are said by some to stretch into an even more profound antiquity than do those of the north, suffered a similar fate. Speakers of a proto-Dravidian language, the forerunner of a family of languages spoken in the south—and some say of Sanskrit itself—entered India from the northwest, the Western scholars insist. Both invasion theories were necessitated by Western beliefs, at first about the Garden of Eden theory of origins and then, with the arrival of the Darwinists, beliefs about the widely held out-of-Africa theory.

But the Aryan invasion theory has been debunked. No skeletal evidence shows any difference between the supposed invaders and the indigenous peoples of India. And satellite imagery now shows that the ancient Harrapan civilization of the Indus Valley, and Mohenjo-Daro, probably declined and disappeared due to climatic changes, the drying up of the *mythical* Saraswati River, rather than to the descent of imaginary invaders. The demise of the Aryan invasion theory, though, and the recently discovered underwater ruins open a Pandora's box for orthodox scholars regarding the past—not just India's past, but that of the human race. If Sanskrit predates the world's other languages, and if ancient civilizations existed where there are now seas, how can prehistory be explained in modern Western terms?

And how much of the actual history of India is still obscured by ethnocentricism, colonialism, or scientific materialism? The demise of the Aryan invasion theory may represent only the tip of the iceberg of misconceptions about the age and nature of ancient India, her culture, her people, and her accomplishments.

It has long been claimed that Mother India was born in a time before all myth began, when *rishis,* men of great wisdom and phenomenal spiritual attainment, walked on Earth. This ancient India dates to the times out of which the epic poems the *Ramayana,* the *Mahabharata,* and the ancient traditions of Tamil Nadu in the south grew. The Tamil Nadu was a land whose culture is said by some to predate that of the north, having once existed as part of Kumari Kandam and dating to a staggering 30,000 B.C.E.

A great deluge inundated Kumari Kandam, obscure texts of the Siddhanta tradition of Tamil Nadu reportedly say. This is a notion echoed in the writings of Colonel James Churchward and W. S. Cervé, both of whom claim knowledge of texts, Indian and Tibetan, respectively, that speak of a long-lost continent situated in the East.

While continental drift theory presumes the extremely slow and uniform movement of landmasses over many hundreds of millions of years, a great deal of evidence exists that Earth's surface changed rapidly and violently in recent prehistory. A great sudden extinction of mammals and plants took place on the planet around the end of the last ice age, perhaps as recently as 12,000 years ago. Hundreds of mammal and plant species disappeared from the face of the earth, many of the carcasses having been driven by flooding into deep caverns and charred piles the world over. Modern science has been unable to adequately explain this event, and unwilling to consider what seems obvious, based on the evidence.

D. S. Allan and J. B. Delair, in *Cataclysm! Compelling Evidence of a Cosmic Catastrophe in 9500* B.C., amass a formidable quantity of *known* evidence corroborating the flood/conflagration legends stored in the world's mythological record. If we suspend belief in the textbook accounts of prehistory, Allan and Delair fill the void in a convincing way, replacing gradualist doctrines that involve extremely slow glacial movements (which are supposed to have accounted for the great extinction) with what seems to have been, upon a review of the evidence, a worldwide, phenomenal disaster that submerged landmasses and ruptured Earth's crust.

Much of the evidence centers on southern Asia. Records gathered by the Swedish survey ship *Albatross* in 1947 reveal a vast plateau of hardened lava for at least several hundred miles southeast of Sri Lanka. The lava, evidence of a severe rupture in Earth's crust, fills most of the now submerged valleys that once existed there. The immense eruption that gave off the lava may have coincided with the downfall of Wallace's Southern Continent (aka Kumari Kandam), for which much zoological and botanical evidence exists that would give such a landmass a recent date, according to Allan and Delair, not the 180 million years that orthodoxy ascribes to such a continent. The lost cities of the Gulf of Cambay may have suffered a similar fate, at the same time or as a result of unstable tectonic conditions resulting from the initial disturbance—an asteroid, perhaps, or a displacement of Earth's crust—that caused the recent extinction and destruction of the ancient cities.

Among the troves of evidence compiled by early geologists and resurrected by Allan and Delair are Asian bone caves filled with diverse species of recent prehistoric animals *from around the world*. These carcasses could have been driven to their final resting places only by vast amounts of water moving across the globe. In light of Allan and Delair's work, other evidence such as India's Deccan trap, a vast triangular plain of lava several thousand feet thick covering 250,000 square miles, and the Indo-Gangetic trough, a gigantic crack in Earth's surface stretching from Sumatra through India to the Persian Gulf, can be interpreted as evidence of a cataclysm that ruptured Earth's crust, submerged various landmasses, and caused the great extinction.

Other titillating fragments of anomalous evidence suggest a pervasive if not advanced seafaring or even airborne culture having once existed in ancient India—for example, the identical nature of the Indus Valley script to that found at Easter Island on the other side of the Pacific Ocean. Initial reports suggest, it should be noted, that the script found recently in the Gulf of Cambay resembles the Indus Valley script. According to certain south Indian researchers, the indecipherable scripts are written in a proto-Tamil language, which would link the culture of distant Easter Island and its famous megalithic statues with ancient southern India, Kumari Kandam—an idea echoed in the lore of Easter Islanders about a lost continent to the West from which their people originated.

With the recent advent of underwater archeology, records of the past are being rewritten. More research is needed, as well as more expeditions into treacherous waters and the depths of the world's oceans; but more than ever, textbook scenarios of prehistory are drowning of their own weight while scenes of a more glorious past rise to the surface via acoustic imaging. Past being prologue, those images are of interest not to academics alone, but to all who would solve the mystery of human origins.

11

Pushing Back the Portals of Civilization

For John Anthony West, the Quest for Evidence of Advanced Prehistoric Civilization Is Bearing New Fruit

J. Douglas Kenyon

"**J**ust as an athlete's ego is bound up in winning and he feels miserable at losing the Super Bowl," chuckles John Anthony West, "the egos of scholars and scientists are tied up in being right. They don't have much money and much fame and there's no glamour in it, and when someone comes along, like me, from out of left field they react like scalded cats."

Tormenting the reigning breed of cats remains a favorite source of amusement to this self-appointed scourge of the "Church of Progress." For West, the modern Western version of civilization, with "its hydrogen bombs and striped toothpaste," is no match for its long-buried predecessors (both historic and otherwise), and scholars who disrespect the legacy of our ancient forebears West considers to be, at the very least, "idiotic."

When the saga of *Atlantis Rising* magazine began in November 1994, our cover story, "Getting Answers from the Sphinx," featured the brewing storm surrounding research by West and the Boston University geologist Robert M. Schoch, Ph.D., indicating that the Sphinx of Giza was rain-weathered and thus thousands of years older than had been maintained by the Egyptological establishment. The controversy has hardly subsided.

Since that time, the writers Graham Hancock and Robert Bauval have joined the fray with enormous internationally best-selling books underscoring West's contentions and adding their own concerning the astronomical purposes of the Giza monuments. And while all four remain *persona non grata* among most professional Egyptologists, their ideas—publicized worldwide in numerous media accounts—have achieved an unprecedented notoriety and forced the establishment to break from its standard practice of simply ignoring impudent notions and actually, on occasion, to argue the merits of them.

The result has not been particularly encouraging to the Church of

John Anthony West at the Sphinx
(PHOTOGRAPH BY PATRICIA KENYON)

Progress. The September 16, 2002 Fox TV/ National Geographic special entitled "Opening the Lost Tombs: Live from Egypt" aired live from Giza in prime time was but the latest of many broadcasts to give major time to the heretical views of West, Schoch, Hancock, and Bauval. Despite all efforts of the debunkers, support for their notions continues to snowball.

At the heart of the controversy are the mysteries surrounding the birth of civilization. Did we, as the academic establishment insists, emerge from the Stone Age about five thousand years ago and only then begin the slow and painful ascent to our present "lofty" heights? Or was there, in remotest antiquity, a fountainhead of civilization that rose to levels of sophistication equal if not superior to our own, and yet which vanished so completely that hardly a trace of it remains?

If the latter is true and can be proved, the implications are profound indeed, if not earthshaking. That West and Schoch may be producing the first scientifically irrefutable evidence for the existence of that progenitor culture could be one of the most important scholarly achievements of our time, and one that could rain convincingly on the parade of the Church of Progress.

Atlantis Rising talked with John West about his ongoing struggle with the establishment and new evidence he has accumulated to buttress and perhaps clinch his case for the existence of a sophisticated prehistoric civilization. He also talked about his debt to an obscure Alsatian archeologist whose contribution to our understanding of ancient Egypt is only beginning to be appreciated.

THE LEGACY OF SCHWALLER DE LUBICZ

The master plan to understanding the wisdom of ancient Egypt is already in place, West believes, but does *not,* as you might expect, come from within the precincts of the Egyptological establishment. The massive work of R. A. Schwaller de Lubicz, assembled during an exhaustive study of the Temple at Luxor from 1937 to 1952, amounts to nothing less than "a unified field theory" of the philosophy and science of ancient Egypt. Schwaller de Lubicz is best known for his comprehensive, seminal work on ancient Egypt entitled *The Temple of Man*. He founded the "symbolist" school of Egyptology, of which West is currently the most outspoken proponent. West's book, *Serpent in the Sky*, remains the most complete commentary in English on Schwaller de Lubicz's work.

Schwaller de Lubicz was looking for evidence of ancient insight into the principles of harmony and proportion. In particular he was looking for knowledge of the Golden Section (a ratio mathematically expressed as 1 plus the square root of 5 over 2), which has been credited to the Greeks but not the Egyptians. Using measurements that were then in the process of determination by a French team of architects and archeologists, Schwaller de Lubicz was able to demonstrate that, indeed, the Golden Section was applied at Luxor and with a complexity and sophistication never achieved by the Greeks.

Here was irrefutable evidence of advanced mathematical development existing more than a thousand years before Pythagoras. "Obviously this didn't spring out of nowhere," says West. "New Kingdom Egypt (Luxor was built by Amenhotep III in the fourteenth century B.C.E.) is in the tradition of Middle and Old Kingdom Egypt, so by extension, Schwaller de Lubicz pretty much proved that Egypt understood harmony and proportion from the reputed very beginnings of its existence, back to 3000 B.C.E. or a bit earlier." All of which suggests the likelihood of still older developments, coinciding nicely with the theories of West and Schoch about the age of the Sphinx, which, interestingly, were based upon a casual observation by Schwaller de Lubicz that the Sphinx had been weathered by water.

"Egypt was in *no* way a kind of magnificent dry run for Greece, which in turn gave rise to our brilliant civilization," says West. "The Greeks themselves acknowledged the greater fount and source of the wisdom that came later. In other words, civilization has been on a downhill slide since ancient Egypt. In fact, ancient Egypt itself was on a downhill trip from its very beginnings because, strangely enough, it reached its absolute peak—the height of its prowess and sophistication—fairly early in the Old Kingdom around 2500 B.C.E. . . . and pretty much everything thereafter was a lesser accomplishment, even the fabulous temples of the New Kingdom."

"But, . . . " the question has always persisted, "if there was an advanced civilization in prehistory, where are the artifacts?" That is a question that John West has long sought to answer, and with the discoveries at the Sphinx he has made a significant first step.

But the undeniable physical remains of that mother culture, he insists, are in no way limited to the Sphinx. Several sites, potentially as compelling, provide evidence that thousands of years before the oldest acknowledged remnants of the so-called Old Kingdom, Egypt was host to a highly developed civilization. One previously unnoticed site West now believes might well make his case.

SECRETS OF THE RED PYRAMID

Usually attributed to the fourth-dynasty pharaoh Snefru, the Red Pyramid of Dahshur is part of a military reservation and was until recently closed to the public. A near equal in total volume to the Great Pyramid (credited to Snefru's son Cheops), the Red Pyramid (so named for its pink granite) slopes a bit more gently. Fairly accessible now, it offers visitors the opportunity to climb a steep staircase on the northern face and then descend the 138 steps of a long, sloping corridor to the first of two high-gabled chambers that, though horizontal, resemble the grand gallery of the Great Pyramid.

At the end of the second chamber are wooden steps, provided by the Egyptian antiquities department, leading to still a third gabled chamber, which, rising to a height of fifty feet, is at right angles to the first two. Standing on a wooden balcony, the visitor is able to look down into a kind a pit surrounded by a jumble of worked stones. No sign of a burial of any kind has ever been found in the Red Pyramid.

When this writer first looked at that place, several points seemed obvious. The stones in the pit were clearly of a different type from those of the structure above. Moreover, while the pyramid had been built with great precision, the arrangement of the pit was chaotic. And even though the stones were doubtless cut artificially, their edges had been rounded in a way that suggested water weathering. I remarked to West that I thought the place must be part of a much older site, over which the Red Pyramid had been built, possibly to memorialize a sacred spot. Whatever weathering had occurred clearly had been brought to a halt by the sheltering pyramid. In making these observations, I thought I was doing no more than stating the obvious, but to my amazement, John West became very excited. "I think you're absolutely right," he exclaimed. "I don't see any other possible explanation."

As it turned out, this was not the first time he had wondered about the meaning of that chamber. "I'd been into that Red Pyramid half a dozen times since it reopened a couple of years ago," he recalled, "puzzling over this strange, so-called burial chamber, which didn't look as though it had been plundered . . ."

(Top) Burial Chamber beneath the Red Pyramid of Dahshur
(PHOTOGRAPH BY J. DOUGLAS KENYON)

(Middle) Red Pyramid Burial Chamber. Note the line between
Old Kingdom masonry above and the older structure below.
(PHOTOGRAPH BY COOPER HEDGECOCK)

(Bottom) Ancient weathered masonry in the
Burial Chamber beneath the Red Pyramid
(PHOTOGRAPH BY J. DOUGLAS KENYON)

John West continues, "Why is it in that state of disarray? It looks as though it's been taken apart, but then it *doesn't* look as though it's been taken apart. Not once did it occur to me that, hey, this was once *outside*—not *inside*. Yes, these are old, deeply weathered stones. The trick now is to get the geologists over there and see just what kind of stones they are."

The experts, like Schoch, West believes, will also find ways of dating the place. Currently West is of the opinion that the stones are hard limestone, and very old indeed. "I think it was a sacred spot to the very ancient Egyptians," he said, "and they built the whole Red Pyramid around it."

Throughout the rest of our tour, West referred again and again to what he said he felt was a "truly important discovery," even dubbing the chamber Kenyon's Cavern, and adding that he felt the place might serve, as nothing had yet, to "clinch" his case.

"The opposition is always saying," complains West, "how can the Sphinx be the only evidence of this earlier civilization? Well, it isn't. But then they go selectively deaf when I start pointing out the other pieces of evidence." Before the discovery in the Red Pyramid, he looked at the Mastaba Fields, southwest of the Sphinx, where a structure once served as the tomb of Khentkaus, the queen of Menkaure—the builder, it is said, of the third and smallest Giza pyramid. The ruined southwest corner of the structure reveals that the 4,500-year-old repair covers blocks that are obviously much older and which bear the same telltale signs of water weathering that caused all the furor at the nearby Sphinx.

And there are other anomalies, "The two-stage construction of the Khafre pyramid (the Greek historian Herodotus is our only source for the attribution)—the giant blocks on the bottom and on the paving, the slabs around the base— are absolutely out of sync with the other Old Kingdom masonry that constitutes that pyramid. The same applies to the Menkaure pyramid.

Corner of tomb of Khentkaus; Old Kingdom masonry reveals older, weathered masonry beneath.
(Photograph by J. Douglas Kenyon)

The Osirion at Abydos
(PHOTOGRAPH BY J. DOUGLAS KENYON)

And there's the deeply weathered shaft east of the midpoint of the Saqqara pyramid."

He also sees strange inconsistencies between the valley temple near the Sphinx and other constructions supposedly by Chephren. Moreover, West believes that the so-called Osirion at Abydos, with its massive undecorated granite blocks, is certainly much older and of a style completely alien to the neighboring temple of Osiris built by Seti I in the New Kingdom: "To attribute these two temples to the same builder is like saying the builders of the Chartres cathedral also built the Empire State Building." West is hopeful that the many feet of Nile silt strata that once covered the Oseirion, and which still surround it, will eventually be carbon-dated and that this will put the matter to rest.

West's evidence is not confined to architecture. In the Cairo Museum, for instance, is a small vase associated with the dawn of the Old Kingdom. Made from the hardest of diorite, the precision of its form and its perfectly hollowed interior are impossible to explain in terms of any known tooling techniques of the time. It could be much older, as could many similar vases that have been discovered.

And, of course, there are the pyramid texts carved into the walls of fifth and sixth dynasty pyramids. The consensus among experts is that the texts were copied from much older sources. Just how much older is the question. On that same trip to Egypt, West was accompanied by Clesson H. Harvey, a physicist and linguist who has spent the better part of forty years translating the pyramid texts. The texts, Harvey believes, reveal that the Egyptian religion originates not millennia, but rather tens of millennia before the Old Kingdom. West thinks Harvey is on the right track.

Despite the weight of the evidence, though, West is not expecting established Egyptology to give ground quickly. "It's very similar to the Church of the Middle Ages and its rejection of Galileo's heliocentric solar system. The centrality of humanity in God's scheme wasn't something they were prepared to give up easily. . . . Now, the idea of a much more ancient source of civilization is a very hard thing for Egyptologists to acknowledge. And it's not just that civilization is older—but that it was sophisticated and capable of producing technological feats that we can't reproduce."

TOWARD A PROPER EGYPTOLOGY

When it comes to proposing a suitable course for Egyptology, West is not ungenerous with his advice. Ph.D.'s in the field, he feels, would be better earned on challenges more meaningful than inventorying Tutankhamen's underwear. In fact, he can reel off dozens of suitable projects for more enlightened research. He would, for example, like to see the kind of meticulous architectural studies that Schwaller de Lubicz did on the temple of Luxor done elsewhere.

Studies of that type, he feels, should be applied to certain temples to determine the harmonics, proportions, measures, and so on. "The temples have been surveyed, but nobody's looked at their geometric breakdowns—how they grow from the core sanctuary into the finalized temple. It's through that kind of study that you would come to understand the esoteric doctrine, mathematical, geometric, harmonic, et cetera, attached to each of the gods or principles."

West also believes that a study of gestures in temple art would yield much insight. Another possible line of research has to do with the systematic effacements on temple walls. He has observed that the careful selection, in many temples, of certain images to efface indicates not the work of later religious fanatics, but indeed the carefully considered actions of Egyptian priests who saw one era ending and another dawning and were taking the appropriate measures.

So far, though, there appears to be no rush to pick up his gauntlet. Yet, if the present surge of interest in what he and Schwaller de Lubicz might call "a return to the source" continues, an emerging generation of scholars, equipped with new information and deeper insight, may soon venture into terrain where few of their predecessors have dared to go.

12 New Studies Confirm Very Old Sphinx

Orthodox Protests Notwithstanding,
Evidence for the Schoch/West Thesis Is Growing

Robert M. Schoch, Ph.D.

For the past ten years, I have been working closely with John Anthony West on the redating of the Great Sphinx of Giza. The traditional date for the statue is circa 2500 B.C.E., but based on my geological analysis, I am convinced that the oldest portions of the Sphinx date back to at least circa 5000 B.C.E. (and John West believes that it may be considerably older still). Such a chronology, however, goes against not just Classical Egyptology, but also many long-held assumptions concerning the dating and origin of early civilizations. I cannot recall how many times I have been told by erstwhile university colleagues that such an early date for the Sphinx is simply impossible because humans were technologically and socially incapable of such feats that long ago. Yet, I must follow where the evidence leads.

My research into the age of the Great Sphinx led me to ultimately question many aspects of the "traditional" scientific worldview that, to this day, permeates most of academe. I got to a point where there were so many new ideas buzzing around in my head that I felt I had to organize them on paper, and this led me to coauthor the book *Voices of the Rocks: A Scientist Looks at Catastrophes and Ancient Civilizations* with Robert Aquinas McNally, in 1999.

The manuscript for *Voices of the Rocks* was completed in August 1998. Since that time I have learned of two independent geological studies of the Great Sphinx and its age. These studies go a long way toward both supporting my analysis and conclusions and rebutting the inadequate counterarguments of the critics.

In both cases they corroborate the primary conclusions of my original studies of the Great Sphinx, namely that the Sphinx and the Sphinx enclosure show evidence of significant precipitation-induced weathering and erosion (degradation), and the core body of the Sphinx and the oldest portions of the Sphinx temple predate the pharaohs Khafre (ca. 2500 B.C.E.) and

Khufu (Khufu, or Cheops, a predecessor of Khafre, reigned about 2551–2528 B.C.E.).

The first study was undertaken by the geologist David Coxill and published in an article entitled "The Riddle of the Sphinx" in *Inscription: Journal of Ancient Egypt*. After confirming my observations on the weathering and erosion of the Sphinx, and pointing out that other explanations do not work, Coxill clearly states: "This [the data and analysis he covers in the preceding portions of his paper] implies that the Sphinx is at least 5,000 years old and pre-dates dynastic times."

Coxill then discusses very briefly the seismic work that Thomas Dobecki and I pursued and my estimate of an initial date of 5000 to 7000 B.C.E. for the earliest parts of the Sphinx based on the seismic data. He neither supports nor refutes this portion of my work, but simply writes: "Absolute dates for the sculpturing of the Sphinx should be taken with extreme caution and therefore dates should be as conservative as possible—until more conclusive evidence comes to light."

I can understand that he could take this stance, although perhaps I feel more comfortable with, and confident in, the seismic analysis we did. Coxill, in the next paragraph of his paper, continues: "Nevertheless, it [the Sphinx] is clearly older than the traditional date for the origins of the Sphinx—in the reign of Khafre, 2520–2490 B.C.E."

Bottom line: Coxill agrees with the heart of my analysis and likewise concludes that the oldest portions of the Sphinx date to before dynastic times—that is, prior to circa 3000 B.C.E.

Another geologist, Colin Reader (who holds a degree in geological engineering from London University), has also pursued a meticulous study of weathering and erosion (degradation) features on the body of the Sphinx and in the Sphinx enclosure. This he has combined with a detailed analysis of the ancient hydrology of the Giza plateau, which has been published as a article entitled "A Geomorphological Study of the Giza Necropolis, with Implications for the Development of the Site" in *Archaeometry*. Like Coxill, Reader points out the problems and weaknesses in the arguments of my opponents.

Reader notes that there is "a marked increase in the intensity of the degradation [that is, weathering and erosion] towards the west [western end] of the Sphinx enclosure." Reader continues, "In my opinion, the only mechanism that can fully explain this increase in intensity is the action of rainfall run-off discharging into the Sphinx enclosure from the higher plateau in the north and west. . . . However, large quarries worked during the reign of Khufu [as noted above, a predecessor of Khafre, the "traditional" builder of the Sphinx] and located immediately up-slope, will have prevented any significant run-off reaching the Sphinx."

Thus Reader concludes that "when considered in terms of the hydrology of the site, the distribution of degradation within the Sphinx enclosure indicates that the excavation of the Sphinx pre-dates Khufu's early fourth dynasty development at Giza."

Interestingly, Reader also concludes that the so-called Khafre's causeway (running from the area of the Sphinx, Sphinx temple, and Khafre Valley temple up to the mortuary temple on the eastern side of the Khafre pyramid), part of Khafre's mortuary temple (which Reader refers to as the "Proto-mortuary temple"), and the Sphinx temple predate the reign of Khufu.

I have come out strongly in favor of not only an older Sphinx, but also a contemporaneous (thus older) Sphinx temple (at least the limestone core being older than the fourth dynasty). Independently of Reader, John Anthony West and I have also concluded that part of Khafre's mortuary temple predates Khafre, but I had not published this conclusion or spoken of it at length in public, as I wanted to collect more corroborative evidence first. Reader has now come to the same conclusion concerning Khafre's mortuary temple. I am pleased to see his confirmation. I believe that there was much more human activity at Giza in pre–Old Kingdom times than has previously been recognized. I even suspect that the second, or Khafre pyramid, may actually sit on top of an older site or structure.

According to the Egyptologists John Baines and Jaromír Málek and as discussed in their book *Atlas of Ancient Egypt,* the Khafre pyramid in ancient times was referred to as the Great Pyramid while the Khufu pyramid (referred to in modern times as the Great Pyramid) was known in antiquity as "The Pyramid Which Is the Place of Sunrise and Sunset." Does the ancient designation of the Great Pyramid for the Khafre pyramid indicate that the site, if not the pyramid itself, was of supreme importance and predated many other developments and structures on the Giza plateau?

Reader tentatively dates the "excavation of the Sphinx" and the construction of the Sphinx temple, proto-mortuary temple, and Khafre's causeway to "sometime in the latter half of the Early Dynastic Period" (that is, circa 2800 to 2600 B.C.E.) on the basis of "the known use of stone in ancient Egyptian architecture." I believe that Reader's estimated date for the excavation of the earliest portions of the Sphinx is later than the evidence indicates. I would make three general points:

1. In my opinion, the nature and degree of weathering and erosion (degradation) on the Sphinx and in the Sphinx enclosure is much different

from what would be expected if the Sphinx had not been carved until 2800 B.C.E., or even 3000 B.C.E. Also, mudbrick mastabas on the Saqqara plateau, dated to circa 2800 B.C.E., show no evidence of significant rain weathering, indicating just how dry the climate has been for the last five thousand years. I continue to believe that the erosional features on the Sphinx and in the Sphinx enclosure indicate a date much earlier than 3000 or 2800 B.C.E.

In my opinion, it strains credibility to believe that the amount, type, and degree of precipitation-induced erosion seen in the Sphinx enclosure was produced in only a few centuries. Reader points out, as I have previously, that even the Egyptologist Zahi Hawass (one of the most ardent "opponents" when it comes to my redating of the Sphinx) contends that some of the weathering and erosion (interpreted as precipitation-induced by Reader, Coxill and me) on the body of the Sphinx was covered over and repaired during Old Kingdom times—thus we can safely assume that the initial core body of the Sphinx was carved out much earlier.

2. Reader never addresses the seismic work that we pursued around the Sphinx, which is in part the basis I used to calibrate a crude estimate for the age of the earliest excavations in the Sphinx enclosure. In my opinion, the date estimate based on our seismic work is compatible with the type and amount of erosion and weathering seen in the Sphinx enclosure and also nicely correlates with the known paleoclimatic history of the Giza plateau. Some of my critics have suggested that our seismic studies simply recorded subsurface layers of rock rather than weathering per se.

Here I would point out that the differential weathering pattern that we recorded in the subsurface cuts across the dip of the rock layers and parallels the floor of the enclosure (as is to be expected of weathering). Furthermore, the dramatically shallower depth of the low-velocity layer immediately behind the rump of the Sphinx is totally incompatible with the notion that the seismic data simply records original bedding in the limestone.

3. I do not find dating the Sphinx on the basis of "the known use of stone in ancient Egyptian architecture" convincing. I would point out that massive stonework constructions were being carried out millennia earlier than circa 2800 B.C.E. in other parts of the Mediterranean (for instance, at Jericho, in Palestine). Even in Egypt, it is now acknowledged that megalithic structures were being erected at Nabta (west of Abu Simbel in Upper Egypt by the fifth millennium B.C.E.) and the predynastic "Libyan palette" (circa 3100–3000 B.C.E.), now housed in the Cairo Museum, records fortified cities (which may well have included architectural stonework) along the western edge of the Nile delta at a very early date. I find it quite con-

ceivable that architectural stonework was being pursued at Giza prior to 2800 or 3000 B.C.E.

Bottom line as far as I am concerned: Reader is one more geologist who has corroborated my basic observations and conclusion: The oldest portions of the Sphinx date back to a period well before circa 2500 B.C.E..

It is not only concerning the age of the Sphinx that there have been significant developments since the original publication of *Voices of the Rocks*. In June 1999, I participated in an amazing conference organized by Professor Emilio Spedicato of the University of Bergamo entitled "New Scenarios for the Solar System Evolution and Consequences in History of Earth and Man, at which I was invited to speak on the age of the Sphinx.

A number of scientists and researchers attended this conference, representing many "alternative," "heretical," and "catastrophic" viewpoints. In particular, the University of Vienna geologist Professor Alexander Tollmann discussed the work pursued by him in conjunction with his late wife, Edith Tollmann. The Tollmanns accumulated a mass of evidence supporting cometary impacts with Earth at the end of the last ice age, between some 13,000 and 9,500 years ago (between circa 11,000 and 7500 B.C.E.).

Another important researcher attending the "New Scenarios" conference was Dr. Mike Baillie, a dendrochronologist (one who studies tree rings) at the Queen's University in Belfast. Further supporting themes developed in *Voices of the Rocks,* Baillie has documented a series of "narrowest-ring events" in the Irish oak tree–ring chronology at the following dates: 3195 B.C.E., 2345 B.C.E., 1628 B.C.E., 1159 B.C.E., 207 B.C.E., and 540 C.E.

As Baillie pointed out, these dates mark major environmental downturns and also the general time periods of major disruptions and changes in the history of human civilizations. Baillie also noted that some or all of these dates may be associated with cometary activity influencing Earth. Indeed, I believe that these dates, along with the date of 1178 C.E. elucidated by Professor Spedicato, may all represent periods of more or less intense cometary impacts somewhere on our planet. Also note that these dates appear to follow a roughly five-hundred- to one-thousand-year cycle.

Looking at each of these dates in turn, we can make a few casual observations and speculations:

3195 B.C.E.: Possibly this marks the final end of the "Sphinx culture" (a time that the Great Sphinx and other very ancient megalithic monuments were built), which, due to its collapse and the resulting cultural vacuum, paved the way for the dynastic culture of Egypt and other Mediterranean civilizations and the development of writing as we know it.

2345 B.C.E.: The early Bronze Age crisis.

1628 B.C.E.: The end of the Middle Kingdom in Egypt; dynastic changes in China.

1159 B.C.E.: The end of the Bronze Age.

207 B.C.E.: Social disruption in China and the Far East; the decline of various Hellenistic empires in the circum-Mediterranean region that cleared the way for the dominance of the Roman Empire.

540 C.E.: Collapse of the traditional Roman Empire, which ended the ancient world and set off the Dark Ages.

1178 C.E.: Social unrest and turmoil, particularly in the Pacific region and Asia (including the rise of the Mongols under Genghis Khan).

Based on the pattern above, I will not be surprised if our planet experiences another major cometary encounter during the twenty-first or early-twenty-second century. This predicated future event may have already been foreshadowed by the 1908 extraterrestrial impact (I believe it was cometary in origin) in the Tunguska region of Siberia.

Extraterrestrial events have recently been acknowledged as also playing a major role in the development of human culture in the very distant past. The March 3, 2000, issue of *Science* magazine includes an article on stone tools from southern China dated to approximately 800,000 years ago. What is particularly interesting about these tools is their association with tektites, glassy fragments of molten rock that resulted from a meteorite impact (the result of a comet or asteroid colliding with our planet). It seems that the impact scorched the landscape, dramatically altered the local environment, exposed the rocks from which the stone tools were ultimately manufactured, and paved the way for early human innovation. In the devastation of the impact and its aftermath, new opportunities for cultural development arose.

Clearly the evidence continues to accumulate that extraterrestrial and, in particular, cometary events have directly influenced the course of human civilization. I stand by the ideas presented, and themes discussed, in *Voices of the Rocks*. More than ever, I believe we must learn from the past even as we prepare for the future. Let us hope that we learn in time.

13 R. A. Schwaller de Lubicz's Magnum Opus

The Keys to Understanding the Wisdom of the Ancients Have Been Preserved

Joseph Ray, Ph.D.

From time to time, significant events occur unbeknownst to virtually everyone. Great discoveries, formidable inventions, and even profound legacies have been delivered to humanity in relative obscurity and sometimes against its unconscious collective will. Such an event occurred in late 1998 with the publication of R. A. Schwaller de Lubicz's greatest work, *The Temple of Man.*

The Temple of Man is an accomplishment of truly Herculean proportions. Nothing written in the past two hundred years, with the exception of only one book, even approaches it in enormity of purpose, scope, subject matter, majesty, and profundity. It is also physically enormous, as well as beautiful, and to read it properly is a year's commitment. To comprehend it and finally to understand it may require additional years of effort, rereading, pondering, and, most significantly, *revelation.*

One needs to learn to read this book and then immerse oneself in it. Were one to do this, and assuming diligence, sincerity, determination, and some ingenuity by the reader, the outcome toward which all human life is aimed, the evolution of consciousness, is ensured. "Consciousness cannot evolve unconsciously," said G. I. Gurdjieff. His great work, *Beelzebub's Tales to His Grandson,* conveys much of the occult and profound teachings set forth in *The Temple of Man,* requires similar effort, and can exert a similar effect upon the reader.

Essential in both is the reader's open-mindedness and state of receptivity, produced by consciously suspending mental reactions until the teachers (the ancient sages whose mode of thought is being transmitted) have completed their work and the transcribers of this knowledge, the authors, have exhausted their understanding.

Every man who attempts to fathom the profound expresses himself about it uniquely. This includes his turns of phrase, the ordering of his thoughts, and the very manner in which he thinks (by hops, leaps and bounds, one rung at a time, or in a direct line). To become his student, which is to say to place oneself in a state of maximum sensitivity to the ideas he expresses, one must familiarize oneself with his turns of phrase and mode of expression. To the extent that one becomes able to think, reason, and ponder in a fashion similar to one's teacher, a psychological fusion can occur. This fusion, by a sort of inner "resonance" in the reader-student, metaphorically speaking shakes loose the embedded knowledge from its innate repository, the "Intelligence of the Heart" and a fresh understanding emerges.

The more subtle, oblique, and ineffable knowledge is, the less suited is the cerebral intelligence to it and the more it will react against it. "Knowledge (or even elements of the knowledge) cannot be conveyed through writing alone; the symbolism of the image is indispensable," Schwaller de Lubicz says. The "symbolique," then, is "the concrete image of a *synthesis* that cannot be expressed in time . . ." and it is these *images* that evoke the synthesis. It may sound awkward, but the process is straightforward. True symbols appeal to the Intelligence of the Heart, where they draw knowledge from it. Ordinary language and the thought expressed in it, the currencies of cerebral intelligence, are ill suited to this knowledge and always distort it.

However, not only the pharaonic mode of thought but its mode of perception, as well, differed from our own. We are, says Schwaller de Lubicz, the victims of our own "mechanistic mentality" and as such suffer from a materialistic misunderstanding of nature. (It is worth noting that, ever since Schwaller de Lubicz's time, materialism has further extended its grip on human thought. Today, despite inaccuracy and verbal inefficiency, practically everything is described in terms of "amount"—e.g., a "fair amount" of: knowledge, accuracy, time, skill, speed, and/or any psychological resource. Not everything is quantity or volume!)

To become adept in the pharaonic mode requires effort, suffering, and experiment. Two shorter works by Schwaller de Lubicz, *Nature Word* and *The Temple in Man*, are desirable precursors to *The Temple of Man*, either new or in rereading. Casual readers need not be deterred either, for they may discover themselves being hooked by the beauty, interconnectedness, and depth of these extraordinary teachings of the ancient sages. This knowledge is for those willing to struggle, and Schwaller de Lubicz warns against concluding "that the ancients meant to say something that we understand; rather one should try to find out why they expressed themselves thus."

The Temple of Man is not a straightforward presentation of ancient teachings. Nor is it Schwaller de Lubicz's own path, recounted in somewhat objectified form but based upon his personal discoveries and illuminations. It is both and much more. Schwaller de Lubicz assimilated what the ancients

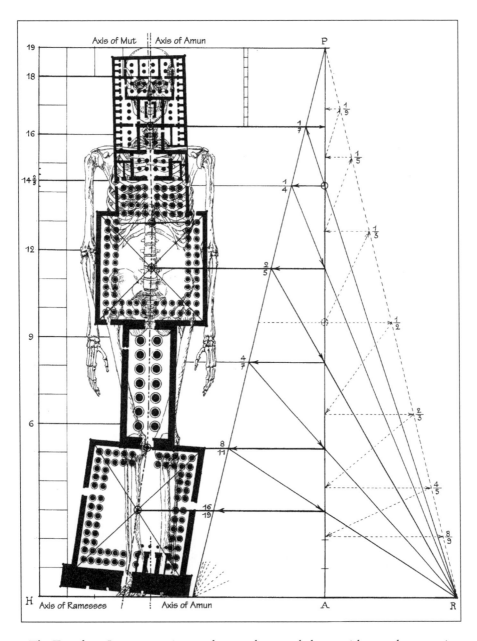

The Temple at Luxor superimposed over a human skeleton with sacred geometric proportions demonstrated by R. A. Schwaller de Lubicz

taught: He allowed himself to be *affected* (impacted emotionally) by the symbolic language transcribed into the Temple of Luxor. This language transcends ordinary language, is vital and not dead, and thus is the only means of transmitting the ineffable to future humanity free of distortion.

The Temple of Luxor is a pedagogical device, built to embody and encode knowledge through the use of a variety of subtle cues (e.g., the rep-

Temple at Luxor

resentation of an incorrect anatomical detail such as two left hands, a missing detail present on the other side of a wall). Painstakingly, the ancients integrated occult knowledge into visual, auditory, conceptual, and architectural symbolic expressions. In so doing, they specifically intended to bypass cerebral intelligence.

Their goal was to evoke from the student the sublime, evanescent knowledge they knew to be embedded in the student's Intelligence of the Heart. This *true* education, involving experience, emotional impact, and work (action), causes the student to *become* the knowledge, as opposed to remembering something. As Gurdjieff said, "A man is what he knows."

True education is an end in itself, yet is also a means of consciousness evolution, for it incorporates its own form of suffering. *The Temple of Man* can teach the reader by means of Schwaller de Lubicz's experience rendered as his understanding. Our experience will be less rich, but understanding can develop because the ideas themselves vivify.

How will the "scholars" within the Egyptological establishment react to this seminal work? A handful may peruse it; many will avoid (i.e., feign ignorance of) *The Temple of Man*. Some may describe the work as a concoction of Schwaller de Lubicz's fertile imagination. In this regard, it needs to be stated: No mere mortal ever, in history or in the future, could have an intelligence so vast, an imagination so fecund, and an integrative capacity so complete as to have made up, somehow or other, the contents of *The Temple of Man*.

It proves itself in its very unimaginability. Moreover, many of the teachings and unifying conceptions in it can be found in sources entirely independent of ancient Egyptian thought. Consider the "science of correspondences"—knowledge that underlies the ancients' selection of symbols.

Swedenborg, who lived during the eighteenth century and never visited Egypt, wrote at length on the subject of "correspondences," and it became the title of one of his books. A section of *Heaven and Hell* is devoted to the subject. "The most ancient people, who were celestial men, thought from correspondence itself, as the angels do"; "The whole natural world corresponds to the spiritual world . . ."; "the knowledge of correspondences is now wholly lost."

Indeed, the seminal Anthropocosmic principle, upon which correspondence depends and that underlies pharaonic teaching, is considered extensively by Swedenborg, who described the universe as "The Grand Man" and humanity as this in miniature. Schwaller de Lubicz uses the phrase "Colossus of the Universe" as he confirms and amplifies all that Swedenborg told us in 1758.

The Temple of Man is organized into six parts. It contains forty-four chapters and is presented in two large volumes. Chapter 27 onward concerns the particular architecture of the Temple of Luxor: These chapters contain 101 plates and about a third of the book's three hundred figures.

These latter chapters include commentaries on the plates and their subject matter. Occasionally, the style of presentation varies, as required by the topic. The earlier chapters form a basis for many of the later discussions. Some are difficult and some possibly are of lesser interest. When I felt that rereading a chapter would facilitate the growth of my understanding of it, I did so immediately. One must not be deterred by an apparent opacity of the text and the ideas therein that may be beyond present comprehension: Mental alchemy can and will occur.

Schwaller de Lubicz warns that "effort" is required. This effort is a form of suffering. And the ancient sages stated clearly that suffering is the engine for the evolution of consciousness: "It is suffering that causes the widening of consciousness," where suffering "is understood as a profound experience brought about by the conflict of consciousness, not as sorrow." Acquiring just some of the pharaonic mentality is suffering itself as the modern, "mechanistic mentality presents a formidable barrier," in Schwaller de Lubicz's words. He describes the nature of cerebral intelligence, ordinary thought, as constrictive and "centripetal."

Indeed, most of us live within the cage of ordinary consciousness established and maintained by the cerebral intelligence. Conversely, pharaonic mentality, the "noncerebral" Intelligence of the Heart, is expansive, synthetic (as opposed to analytic), intuitive, noncomparative, direct, and innate, and thus evoked. Getting there is one's personal death and life story: Suffer gladly.

Schwaller de Lubicz wrote *The Temple of Man* ". . . first to show the means of expression used by the ancients to transmit knowledge," and ". . . second, to present an outline of the doctrine of the Anthropocosmos, the guide to the way of thinking of the sages." To fulfill this goal required the consideration and discussion of subjects seldom seen in occult, esoteric, or spiritual writings: Anthropocosmos, Pharaonic Calculation, Cosmic Principle of Volume, The Covered Temple, The Head, Crossing, The Knees, Receiving and Giving are examples.

One must acquire a good feeling for Elements, Consciousness, and Irreducible Magnitudes, as well as Symbolique, to begin to fully appreciate all of these latter chapters. This may take some time. As mentioned, however, even casual readers—that is, nonstudents—will find wise statements everywhere, conjectures verified now by time (this book is more than forty years old), and remarkable insights: The pages contain much spiritual food, some of which may be ingested raw.

"The Anthropocosmic doctrine [holds that] each plant and animal species represents a stage in the evolution of consciousness . . ." Man is a microcosm of the macrocosm. "Thus the Universe is incarnate in man and is nothing but potential Man, Anthropocosmos." In this system, creation and generation are central; the forces of genesis and the moment of expansion are the subject matter.

Humanity, by the way, procreates but creates nothing. In applauding our pseudo-understanding of life because we genetically engineer a plant, clone a sheep, or grow a human pinna (ear) on a mouse's back, we succumb to pride and self-delusion, our great foibles.

Were modern humanity not so disordered in life, out of touch with nature, and imbalanced as well, gaining pharaonic insights would still be difficult. But we have developed the "cult of convenience" to a high order and live by another modern principle, that of "something for nothing." Inasmuch as, in the spiritual realm, payment is a principle, such a worldview further amplifies the impediments toward pharaonic mentality.

Those who have seen, generally, the hollowness of modern thought must be at pains to discover its effects in themselves, so invidious is its process. The

The Amun Temple at Luxor

need to be surrounded by people, sound, activity, even noise, arises in the psychological consciousness of the cerebral intelligence, which subsists on stimulation. Says Schwaller de Lubicz, most modern people (as of the 1950s) could not have "stood" the serenity that prevailed in ancient Egypt.

Schwaller de Lubicz tells us that, in order to grasp the essence of the Anthropocosmic teaching, we need to reestablish in our minds a proper notion of the term *symbol*. A symbol is not merely "any letter or image that is substituted for the development of an idea." Instead, a symbol is "a summarizing representation, which is commonly called a synthesis." This process "feels" like something, often exhilaration.

The ancients selected these symbols knowing virtually everything about the natural counterpart (the correspondent) from gestation to its death. Mental caution is necessary, however, and the tendency to "fix," by definition, the essence of the symbolic representation must be avoided. The qualities of a symbol are many and varied and not to be linguistically rigidified any more than molten lava. The symbol is alive, vital, and dynamic, because Anthropocosmic doctrine is a vitalist philosophy.

"To explain the Symbol is to kill it . . ." and, indeed, the landscape of academic Egyptology is everywhere strewn with the carcasses of dead, unheard symbols. "Rational thinkers" believe we've passed beyond simplistic thinking. Rather, in the last two millennia, we have fallen into it.

The Hypostyle Hall at Luxor

Many concepts of modern thought are defined and understood differently in *The Temple of Man*—so many, in fact, that scientists, academics, and people generally, having unconsciously espoused a mechanical rationalism, will be *forced* to reject these ideas out of hand. "Cause and effect are not separated by any time." There exists a "principle of the (present moment), mystical in character, that modern science ignores," says Schwaller de Lubicz.

These and other similar statements cannot be reconciled with the current and opposing worldview. But one may examine the modern socio-scientific-technological state of the world in light of these ideas and, from so doing, draw tentative conclusions concerning the relative merit of the ancients' teachings.

The history of science demonstrates that we seldom build upon the great discoveries of preceding generations of scientists. Few physicists today know Kepler's laws of planetary motion; even fewer mathematicians appreciate that his unconventional use of the fractional notation of powers (e.g., X2/3 power) and the unique position he accorded the number 5 (which led to this) were a part of pharaonic mathematics thousands of years earlier. Modern science is as "pouring from the empty into the void," to quote Gurdjieff. Modern science, Schwaller de Lubicz says, is founded upon incorrect premises. We know *kinetic* energy, not *vital* energy, and we tamper with forces, powers, and processes we do not and cannot now understand: We *are* the Sorcerer's Apprentice.

Cerebral intelligence is based upon the sensory information conveyed to it by the major sensory systems. These are understood by the ancients in terms of both their natural, exoteric function (to provide the brain with information) and their esoteric, spiritual function. One cannot but be amazed, again, at the subtlety of the insights they conveyed. For example, "the faculty of discernment, located in the olfactory bulb, is the seat of judgment in man . . ."

Well, the olfactory bulb is a so-called primitive structure of the brain with no direct connections to the cortex, the "advanced" gray matter. Nevertheless, apparently in deference to its unique anatomical characteristics, the ancients accorded olfaction one of the three secret sanctuaries in the head of the Luxor temple, Room V.

The moral sense, sexuality, and the physiological distribution of vital energy are combined in the relevant symbol, the cobra. Here in Room V of the temple is located "conscience." Goodness has a spiritual fragrance (a fact noted by Swedenborg, who mentioned that the ancient Egyptians were the *last* to fully understand the science of correspondences).

Subtlety is all the more difficult to acknowledge and recognize when what is taught conflicts diametrically with what people already believe. Ironically, we seldom have evidence that appears to contradict the ancients' teachings, which typically go beyond our accepted facts.

Schwaller de Lubicz includes a lengthy discussion of the Edwin Smith Surgical Papyrus. This papyrus (from Luxor in 1862) was translated after 1920 by the renowned Egyptologist J. H. Breasted. The effort convinced him of the elevated status of ancient Egyptian science and mathematics (as it did others) but apparently modern Egyptologists remain uninfluenced by his writing. An extensive anatomical dictionary of the skull, head, and throat (also in hieroglyphics) enables the reader to comprehend the many cases of head injury described in the papyrus. Despite the ancients' lack of a really good source of head injury cases (e.g., automobile accidents), their knowledge of clinical neuroanatomy was detailed and correct, without the benefit of EEGs, CAT scans, and magnetic resonance imaging.

The ancients described a human as comprising three interdependent beings, each having its own body and organs. Of course, all were essential and important. However, the head was especially so, for it was the seat of the spiritual being. There, the blood was spiritualized, infused with vital energy prior to coursing through the corporeal and sexual bodies. These bodies, vivified by the spiritual being, live a lifetime without knowing it in a state of ignorance or self-delusion.

Modern humanity has struck an iceberg of its own making. Those forces we have tampered with and let loose, but which we do not understand, threaten our annihilation. We have a role in cosmic metabolism but are unable to fulfill it. We must cease fiddling while our planet burns, cease occupying ourselves with liposuction, with killing birds to kill insects, with poisoning the soil to kill weeds, with polluting air and water. Any sane person can see our way of "life" has become unnatural, a condition the ancients foresaw.

Everyone's consciousness needs to expand, to evolve: We need to become aware of a great deal that, right now, escapes us. This can occur by choice—the price is some suffering. "And now that the temple of Luxor has shown us the way to follow, let us begin to explore the deeper meaning of the teaching of the pharaonic sages," wrote Schwaller de Lubicz. We shall discover along the way what a trivial price we are asked to pay.

14 Fingerprinting the Gods

A Bestselling Author Is Making a
Convincing Case for a Great
but Officially Forgotten Civilization

J. Douglas Kenyon

lthough few people would question the popularity of the movie *Raiders of the Lost Ark,* no academic worth his salt ever dared to say the movie was more than a Hollywood fantasy, either. So when the respected British author Graham Hancock announced to the world in 1992 that he had actually tracked the legendary Ark of the Covenant of Old Testament fame to a modern-day resting place in Ethiopia, serious eyebrows everywhere twitched upward. Nevertheless, objective readers of his monumental volume *The Sign and the Seal* on both sides of the Atlantic soon realized that Hancock's case, incredible though it seemed, was not to be easily dismissed. The exhaustively researched work went on to enjoy widespread critical acclaim and to become a best seller in both America and the United Kingdom as well as the subject of several television specials.

Hancock's writing and journalistic skills had been honed during stints as a war correspondent in Africa for *The Economist* and *The London Sunday Times.* Winner of an honorable mention for the H. L. Mencken Award (*The Lords of Poverty,* 1990), he also authored *African Ark: Peoples of the Horn,* and *Ethiopia: The Challenge of Hunger.* In *The Sign and the Seal,* Hancock was credited by *The Guardian* with having "invented a new genre—an intellectual whodunit by a do-it-yourself sleuth . . ."

Apparently, though, the success of *The Sign and the Seal* only whetted the writer's appetite for establishment chagrin. His subsequent book, *Fingerprints of the Gods: The Evidence of Earth's Lost Civilization,* sought nothing less than to overthrow the cherished doctrine taught in classrooms worldwide, that civilization was born roughly five thousand years ago.

Anything earlier, we have been told, was strictly primitive. In one of the most comprehensive efforts on the subject ever—more than six hundred pages of meticulous research—Hancock presents breakthrough evidence of a forgotten epoch in human history that preceded, by thousands of years, the presently acknowledged cradles of civilization in Egypt, Mesopotamia, and the Far East. Moreover, he argues, this same lost culture was not only highly advanced but also technologically proficient, and was destroyed more than 12,000 years ago by the global cataclysm that brought the ice age to its sudden and dramatic conclusion.

Kirkus Reviews called *Fingerprints of the Gods* "a fancy piece of historical sleuthing—breathless but intriguing, and entertaining and sturdy enough to give a long pause for thought."

Graham Hancock
at the Great Pyramid
(PHOTOGRAPH BY CHRISTOPHER DUNN)

Graham Hancock discussed *Fingerprints of the Gods* with *Atlantis Rising,* wherein he indicated that the book was enjoying the kind of favorable media attention that helped to make *The Sign and the Seal* an American hit. Interviewers, Hancock felt, were generally positive and open to his ideas. Though the reception among academics had been something less than cordial, that was to be expected.

"One of the reasons the book is so long," he explained, "is that I've really tried to document everything very thoroughly so that the academics have to deal with the evidence rather than me as an individual, or with what—they like to think—are rather vague, wishy-washy ideas. I've tried to nail it all down to hard fact as far as possible."

Nailing down the facts took Hancock on a worldwide odyssey that included stops in Peru, Mexico, and Egypt. Among the many intriguing mysteries that the author was determined to investigate fully were:

- Ancient maps showing precise knowledge of the actual coastline of Antarctica, notwithstanding the fact that the location has been buried under thousands of feet of ice for many millennia.
- Stone-building technology—beyond our present capacity to duplicate—in Central and South America, as well as Egypt.
- Sophisticated archaeoastronomical alignments at ancient sites all over the world.
- Evidence of comprehensive ancient knowledge of the 25,776-year precession of the equinoxes (unmistakably encoded into ancient mythology and building sites, even though the phenomenon would have

taken, at a minimum, many generations of systematic observation to detect, and which conventional scholarship tells us was not discovered until the Greek philosopher Hipparchus in about 150 B.C.E.).
- Water erosion of the Great Sphinx dating it to before the coming of desert conditions to the Giza plateau (as researched by the American scholar John Anthony West and the geologist Robert M. Schoch, Ph.D.).
- Evidence that the monuments of the Giza plateau were built in alignment with the belt of Orion at circa 10,500 B.C.E. (as demonstrated by the Belgian engineer Robert Bauval).

Unfettered as he is by the constraints under which many so-called specialists operate, Hancock sees himself uniquely qualified to undertake such a far-reaching study. "One of the problems with academics, and particularly academic historians," he says, "is they have a very narrow focus. And as a result, they are very myopic."

Hancock is downright contemptuous of organized Egyptology, which he places in the particularly short-sighted category. "There's a rigid paradigm of Egyptian history," he complains, "that seems to function as a kind of filter on knowledge and which stops Egyptologists, as a profession, from being even the remotest bit open to any other possibilities at all." In Hancock's view, Egyptologists tend to behave like priests in a very narrow religion, dogmatically and irrationally, if not superstitiously. "A few hundred years ago they would have burned people like me and John West at the stake," he says, laughing.

Rudolph Gantenbrink and his robot camera

Such illogical zealotry, Hancock fears, stands in the way of the public's right to know about what could be one of the most significant discoveries ever made in the Great Pyramid. In 1993, the German inventor Rudolph Gantenbrink sent a robot with a television camera up a narrow shaft from the Queen's Chamber and discovered what appeared to be a door with iron handles. That door, Hancock suspects, might lead to the legendary Hall of Records of the ancient Egyptians. But whatever is behind it, he feels it must be properly investigated.

So far, though, there has been no official action, at least not a public one. Citing episodes personally witnessed, he protests, "You have Egyptologists saying 'There is no point in looking to see if there's anything behind that slab'—they call it a slab, they won't call it a door—'because we know there's not another chamber inside the Great Pyramid.'" The attitude infuriates Hancock: "I wonder how they know that about this six-million-ton monument that has room for three thousand chambers the same size as the King's Chamber. How do they have the temerity and the nerve to suggest that there's no point in looking?"

The tantalizing promise of that door has led Hancock to speculate that the builders may have purposely arranged things to require technology of ultimate explorers. "Nobody could get in there unless he had a certain level of technology," he says. And he points out that even one hundred years ago, we didn't have the means to do it. In the last twenty years the technology has been developed and now the shaft has been explored, "and lo and behold, at the end is a door with handles. It's like an invitation—an invitation to come on in and look inside when you're ready."

Hancock is far from sanguine about official intentions: "If that door ever does get open, probably there will be no public access at all to what happens." He would like to see an international team present, but suspects that instead "what we're going to get is a narrow, elite group of Egyptologists who will strictly control information about what happens." In fact, he thinks it's possible that they've even been in there already. The Queen's Chamber was suspiciously closed for more than nine months after Gantenbrink made his discovery.

"The story was given out that they were cleaning the graffiti off the walls, but the graffiti were never cleaned off. I wonder what they were doing in there for those nine months. There's what really makes me angry, that this narrow group of scholars control knowledge of what is, at the end of the day, the legacy of the whole of mankind."

Gantenbrink's door is not the only beckoning portal on the Giza plateau. Hancock is equally interested in the chamber that John Anthony West and Robert M. Schoch, Ph.D., in the course of investigating the weathering of the Sphinx, detected by seismic methods, beneath the Sphinx's paws. Either location might prove to be the site of the "Hall of Records." In both cases, the authorities have resisted all efforts at further investigation.

Hancock believes the entire Giza site was constructed after the crust of the earth had stabilized following a 30-degree crustal displacement that destroyed most of the high civilization then standing. According to Rand and Rose Flem-Ath's *When the Sky Fell: In Search of Atlantis,* upon which Hancock relies, that displacement had moved an entire continent from temperate zones to the South Pole, where it was soon buried under mountains of ice. This, he believes, is the real story of the end of Plato's Atlantis, but the

"A" word is not mentioned until very late in his book. "I see no point in giving a hostile establishment a stick to beat me with," he says. "It's purely a matter of tactics."

The Giza complex was built, Hancock speculates, as part of an effort to remap and reorient civilization. For that reason he believes the 10,500 B.C.E. date (demonstrated by Bauval) to be especially important. "The pyramids are a part of saying this is where it stopped. That's why the perfect alignment, for example, to due north, of the Great Pyramid is extremely interesting, because they obviously would have had a *new* north at that time."

Despite a determination to stick with the hard evidence, Hancock is not uncomfortable with the knowledge that his work is serving to corroborate the claims of many intuitives and mystics. On the contrary, he believes that "the [clairvoyant ability] of human beings is another one of those latent faculties that modern rational science simply refuses to recognize. I think we're a much more mysterious species than we give ourselves credit for. Our whole cultural conditioning is to deny those elements of intuition and mystery in ourselves. But all the indications are that these are, in fact, vital faculties in human beings, and I suspect that the civilization that was destroyed, although technologically advanced, was much more spiritually advanced than we are today."

Such knowledge, he believes, is part of the legacy of the ancients that we must strive to recover. "What comes across again and again," he says, "particularly from documents like the ancient Egyptian pyramid texts, which I see as containing the legacy of knowledge and ideas from this lost civilization, is a kind of science of immortality—a quest for the immortality of the soul, a feeling that immortality may not be guaranteed to all and everybody simply by being born. It may be something that has to be worked for, something that results from the focused power of the mind." The real purpose of the pyramids, he suggests, may be to teach us how to achieve immortality. But before we can understand, we must recover from the ancient amnesia.

Hancock believes we are a species with amnesia. "I think we show all the signs that there's a traumatic episode in our past that is so horrible that we cannot somehow bring ourselves to recognize it. Just as the victim suffering from amnesia as a result of some terrible episode fears awakening memory of that trauma and tries to avoid it, so we have done collectively." The amnesia victim is, of course, forced to return to the source of his pain and "if you wish to move forward and continue to develop as an individual, you have to overcome it. You have to confront it, deal with it, see it face-to-face, realize what it means, get over it, and get on with your life," he says. "That is what society needs to be doing."

In the institutional resistance to considering ancient achievement, Hancock sees a subconscious pattern based on fear: "There's a huge impulse to deny all of this, because suddenly all the foundations get knocked out from under you and you find yourself swimming loosely in space without any points of reference anymore." The process needn't be so threatening, though. "If we can go through that difficult experience and come out on the other side," he says. "I think we'll all emerge better from it. I'm more and more convinced that the reason we are so messed up and confused and totally disturbed as a species at the end of the twentieth century is because of this—because we've forgotten our past."

If it is true that those who cannot learn from history are doomed to repeat it, then there are lessons in our past that can be ignored only at our peril. Clearly written into the mythology of many societies are stories of cataclysmic destruction. Hancock cites the work of Giorgio de Santillana, of M.I.T., an authority on the history of science who is the coauthor, along with Hertha von Dechend, of the book *Hamlet's Mill: An Essay Investigating the Origins of Human Knowledge and Its Transmission through Myth,* in which the authors hypothesize that an advanced scientific knowledge was encoded into ancient myth.

Hancock points out, "Once you accept that mythology may have originated with highly advanced people, then you have to start listening to what the myths are saying." What the myths are saying, he believes, is that a great cataclysm struck the world and destroyed an advanced civilization and a golden age of mankind. And cataclysm is a recurrent feature in the life of the earth and will return.

The messages from many ancient sources, including the Bible, point to a recurrence of such a cataclysm in our lifetime. Notwithstanding such views, Hancock insists he is not a prophet of doom. His point is, he says, "We've received a legacy of extraordinary knowledge from the past, and the time has come for us to stop dismissing it. Rather, we must recapture that heritage and learn what we can from it, because there is vitally important information in it."

The stakes couldn't be higher. "I'm convinced that we're locked today in a battle of ideas," he says. "I think it's desperately important that the ideas that will lead to a recovery of our memory as a species triumph. And therefore we have to be strong, we have to be eloquent and argue clearly and coherently. We have to see what our opponents are going to do, how they are going to try to get at us, and the dirty tricks that they are going to try and play. We have to fight them on their own ground."

15 The Central American Mystery

What Could Explain the Failure of Mainstream Science to Unravel the Origins of Mesoamerica's Advanced Ancient Cultures?

Will Hart

It has been twenty-three years, yet I remember the morning like it was yesterday. A mist shrouded the jungle above the Temple of the Inscriptions. A series of roaring sounds suddenly split the silence as a band of howler monkeys made their way through the trees. It startled me. I thought the sounds might be those of a jaguar, but the cacophony added to the sense of mystery.

My head was exploding. By the time I had reached Palenque, we had already visited dozens of archeological sites, from the northernmost part of Mexico down to the Yucatán Peninsula and Quintana Roo. I was steeped in questions and mysteries. Several things had become clear to me: The cultures that built the pyramids and other buildings had been advanced in the arts and sciences. I had seen many beautiful things, as well as mind-tugging enigmas.

The Olmec civilization surprised me the most. I had read about the Maya and knew of the Aztecs, but I was unprepared for what I found in Villahermosa: large stone heads with Negroid features and stone stelae carved with depictions of curious ambassadors. The figures clearly were not from any Mexican culture.

Giant Olmec face
(ART BY TOM MILLER)

These artifacts were more than just a fascinating puzzle; they represented a headache for science. They were an anomaly. Who had carved the heads? Who had created the stelae? Where did they get the models for these heads and figures? These were questions that arose because of the way scientists have reconstructed the human history of Mesoamerica. Africans don't fit, nor do the cloaked Caucasian figures carved on the stelae. They shouldn't be there; however, they are surely there.

Scientists do not claim to have solved this enigma. Anthropologists and archeologists admit they do not know much of anything about Olmec culture. Thus, we don't know the ethnic group or the language and we know nothing of the Olmecs' social organization, beliefs, or traditions. No one has any idea why they carved the helmeted heads and then buried them. It doesn't make a lot of sense. We don't usually bury monuments (if that is what they are).

The only records we have are the monuments they left behind, which are impressive. But how do we understand them? Where do they fit into the mosaic of human history? There are no direct clues in Mexico. The Olmecs didn't leave us any written records. However, we do have a clue.

The Bible is an extremely important document. It doesn't matter whether or not you are a believer. It contains a very ancient accounting of human history compiled from a variety of early sources. At least, this is true of the Book of Genesis. But it is not always easy to decode. Do we find any reference in the Bible that might help us solve the Olmec enigma?

Turning to Genesis, chapter 11, we read: "Now the whole Earth used the same language and the same words." This indicates that there was a period in man's history when a global human civilization existed. We learn that during that epoch, men wanted to build a tower: "Come, let us build for ourselves a city, and a tower whose top will reach into heaven; and let us make for ourselves a name; lest we be scattered abroad over the face of the whole Earth."

The fact that the Olmec civilization presents science with an anomaly indicates something quite profound: The data does not fit the current model. Scientists can't change the observable data; it is as hard as data can get. But they could change the *model* to conform to the data. There is the rub. Anthropologists and archeologists have a huge investment in that model, an intellectual edifice that has been built up over generations.

Scientists would rather ignore the tough questions and leave the Olmecs alone in the dim mists of forgotten antiquity. That is not a very scientific approach. Where is the pursuit of truth? What happened to the scientific method? It is just not acceptable. Why?

Some ancient society built the huge mound, dragged the basalt heads about sixty miles from the quarry to the burial site (those heads weighed from five to twenty-five tons), and carved the figures into the stelae. They wouldn't have gone to all that trouble unless the people the monuments represented were important to them. This is a logical assumption to make and we can only hope that scientists in the distant future will reach the same conclusion when they study Mount Rushmore.

Since we have the artifacts, we know that there has to be an *explanation* for who the builders were. As with any other mystery, you search for clues. You begin in the most likely places and work your way down the list: Mexico. The problem is that the Olmecs disappeared from the scene long before Cortez arrived. None of the cultures contemporary with the Aztecs made any references to the Olmecs; they seemed to know nothing about them. And no other Negroid heads have been found in Mesoamerica. Another curious fact is that the developmental period that must have preceded the mound building and head carving is nowhere in evidence.

The Olmecs just suddenly appeared, then disappeared!

It took me years of investigation to finally realize that the most probable answer was in the Bible, and ironically, the Bible was just about the last place I had thought to look. Did the Olmecs come from outer space, as some researchers have proposed? Not necessarily. For one thing, there is no evidence to support this theory. Second, the Negroid heads and the people depicted on the stelae are obviously human.

The idea that there was a global civilization in ancient times does not conform to the current model of science. However, it is corroborated by the reference in the Bible. The problem with the scientific model is that it can't explain the available data, and that is a *serious* issue that has many consequences. If the problem was limited to the Olmec civilization, we might just let it go. But there are artifacts in Egypt, South America, and other parts of Mexico that also don't fit the orthodox scheme.

Scientists have often shown a willful blindness regarding artifacts and developments that they can't explain using their belief system. Worse, they have either ignored key questions or discredited the facts. Many other hard facts, the remains of lost civilizations, and the cultural records of numerous peoples corroborate the Olmec enigma and the Bible.

References to a cataclysmic flood occur in 230 different cultures. Mayan history includes the story of how the Maya came from a land to the east that had been destroyed. Herodotus's *History* recounted of the tale of lost Atlantis. Accounts such as these may sound like romantic myths spun out of early imaginations; however, when you stand at an ancient site surrounded by strange ruins . . . you begin to wonder if they just might contain more than a grain of truth.

I climbed the steps of the Temple of Inscriptions and visited the tomb of Pacal. Then I decided to take a long trip down to the Rio Usamacinta, to Bonampak and Yaxchilan. It was one hundred miles of bad dirt road, heavily rutted in places. It finally became so muddy that we mired the van up to the axles. We had nearly reached the destination; Bonampak was a short walk. I visited Bonampak.

My next destination was Yaxchilan, a ruin secreted in the jungle about eight miles from Bonampak. I decided to try and hack my way there with a machete, against the advice of the natives, who had warned me: "La selva está cerrado!" They were right. I gave up after a grueling four-hour stint in which I traveled less than a quarter of a mile, spent mostly on my belly trying to avoid razor-sharp thorn shrubs. The insects were ravaging my body.

Yaxchilan is situated on the river and is alleged to have been the center of the flourishing Mayan civilization in this region. In February 1989, James O'Kon did manage to make it to this site, one that archeologists had been studying for a century. A particular mound of rocks caught O'Kon's trained eye. Scientists had dismissed it as a minor mystery but the amateur archeologist was also a forensic engineer, and he immediately knew what this mound really was: part of a bridge.

He turned to modern technology to help prove a bridge had once existed at the site. O'Kon, a former chairman of the forensic council of the American Society of Civil Engineers, had used similar techniques during routine investigations. He compiled field information at the Mayan site and used computers to integrate archeological studies, aerial photos, and maps; to develop a three-dimensional model of the site; and to determine the exact positioning and dimensions of the bridge.

Archeologist James O'Kon holds up a drawing of a Mayan bridge.
(PHOTOGRAPH BY WILL HART)

O'Kon ended up making a startling discovery: The Maya had constructed the longest bridge span in the ancient world. When he finished his calculations and computer models, the bridge turned out to be a six-hundred-foot span, a hemp-rope suspension structure with two piers and three spans. It connected Yaxchilan, in Mexico, with its agricultural domain in the Peten (now Guatemala), where Tikal is situated.

What archeologists had assumed was an insignificant rock pile turned out to be part of a crucial finding: a pier twelve feet high and thirty-five feet in diameter. Aerial photos located a second support pier on the opposite side of the river. Both piers were constructed of cast-in-place concrete with an exterior of stone masonry, which is exactly how the Mayan pyramids were made.

In interviews O'Kon, who has been studying the ancient Maya for thirty years, said, "The Maya were very sophisticated mathematically and scientifically." He claimed that the design requirements of the Mayan bridge paralleled twentieth-century bridge-design criteria.

Today we marvel at the ruins and speculate on how and why the Maya built the ceremonial sites. We shouldn't forget that they were an advanced race. They understood astronomy. They had an accurate calendar. They understood the concept of "zero" at least seven hundred years before the Europeans did. The Maya built paved roads and, as we have now learned, the longest suspension bridge in the ancient world.

What occurred to me while standing atop another pyramid, at Coba in Quintana Roo, surveying a trackless jungle was the fact that the Maya had achieved all this *in a jungle*. No other advanced civilization I could think of had emerged from a jungle environment. It deepens the mystery of this lost race.

The *sacbe* are a system of roads that interconnect the sites. This is another feature that has long puzzled scientists and independent investigators alike. The roads were built up with rocks, leveled, and paved over with limestone cement. They vary in width from eight feet to thirty feet. The mystery is simple: Why would a "Stone Age" people without wheeled vehicles or dray animals need such an elaborate and sophisticated road network?

O'Kon turned his attention to the sacbe after finishing his work on the bridge and discussed the fact that he had found the sixty-mile road that extended from Coba to Yaxuna to be as straight as an arrow with a negligible deviation. His studies have revealed the Maya were not Stone Age (he refers to them as "technolithic"). They didn't use iron, because the nearest mines were 1,500 miles away. O'Kon claims, "They used jade tools and they were harder than steel."

You almost have to stand at a site and imagine the scene as it was during the peak of Mayan civilization to really grasp the magnitude and appreciate what this culture achieved. Today we see ruins and jungle and pyramids that are little more than bare stone, crumbling buildings surrounded by wilderness. However, in that day, the pyramids were coated with stucco. They were smooth and they gleamed in the sun. The walls of the structures were painted in various designs of bright colors. The courtyards were paved. The flat white roads radiated out in all directions, connecting the centers.

Yet despite the Maya's advanced knowledge of astronomy and mathematics and their achievements in art and architecture, scientists still consider them a Stone Age culture.

Time is the essence of life. Human beings have always been immersed in it, and have kept track of it in one way or another: measuring it as minutes, hours, days, weeks, months, years, centuries, and millennia. We know of many of its dimensions and we have used them to our advantage. We know, supposedly, how long ago dinosaurs roamed the earth, how long it takes for various radioactive isotopes to decay, when our early hominid ancestors branched off from apes, the layout of the human genome, the exact dates of lunar and solar eclipses long into the future.

Time causes all living things to grow old and die. It seems so obvious and ubiquitous, we are like fish and time is water. We never ask the basic questions: What is time? Do we understand it? Is it more than a system of measurement, whether of the present moment or of the age of the universe?

All cultures certainly have a focus on time; however, the Maya had an *obsession* with it. They tracked and measured the synodic period of Venus, which is 584 Earth days. The 365-day Mayan calendar year was more precise than the Gregorian calendar. They devised three different calendrical systems: the *tzolkin* (sacred calendar), the *haab* (civil calendar), and the long count.

The tzolkin is a cycle of 260 days (thirteen months of twenty days each) and the haab is the solar cycle. These two calendars were combined in an interlocking fashion to produce a cycle of 18,980 days, which was known as a calendar round, about fifty-two years.

Each day had a particular glyph and meaning ascribed to it, and at the end of the fifty-two-year cycle a renewal ceremony would be performed. The long count period lasted for about five thousand years. This was equivalent to an age. According to the Maya, humanity is in the fifth "Sun" or "Age." That will end about five thousand years from the beginning of their calendar, which started in 3011 B.C.E. and expires in 2012.

The longest cycle in Mayan cosmology is 26,000 years, which corresponds to the precession of the equinox. Why did the Maya have such a fascination with astronomy? Why did they create such an intricate calendrical system? Would a Stone Age agrarian society need all this advanced astronomical and mathematical knowledge? How did they acquire it in such a short time? How would they have had any awareness of such a complex phenomenon as the synodic length of Venus or the precession of the equinoxes?

The Maya are either more ancient than science allows or they had more sophisticated technology than we know of. Perhaps someone passed down this knowledge to them? Is it coincidental that the beginning of the fifth Age was 3000 B.C.E., which corresponds to the birth of the Jewish and Chinese calendars? The assertion that the "world" is only five thousand years old may have more truth to it than we know. Is it also a coincidence that so many Christians believe we are now in the end of times?

The Mayan obsession with time may have been based on a deep awareness of how it functions on a cosmic scale and then unfolds on Earth in short- and long-term cycles. That may be the message that the lost civilizations have been trying to deliver to us, and we may just be starting to get it.

16 Destination Galactic Center

John Major Jenkins Thinks Today's World Has
Much to Learn from the Ancient Maya

Moira Timms

Ancient Mayan trumpets erupt in a wash of primal, shamanic sound. The huge dome of the planetarium, like some fish-eye lens, glows with myriad pre-dawn stars. As the sun rises and breaks through the artificial horizon to everyone's left, the ancient music fades, and the crack between the worlds is open once more. In his calm, focused way, the researcher and author John Major Jenkins begins his presentation and delivers the goods: According to ancient Mayan cosmology, we live today in a time of rare galactic alignment, when our solar system aligns with the heart of our galaxy, the galactic center. Our age is a time of transformation fixed by the Mayan calendar's end date on December 21, 2012.

John Major Jenkins

Jenkins, an internationally recognized expert on ancient astronomy and the Mayan calendar, recently spoke of his work and life. "I am devoted to reconstructing lost cosmologies," he says, "to unraveling the knotted threads of a vast, global paradigm now forgotten." He emphasizes that his work is both an explication and a celebration of the Primordial Tradition, or *perennial philosophy*—terms that refer to the universal truths at the core of the world's major religions and philosophies that have endured down the ages.

"I believe the human race can grow spiritually by reviving the ancient Primordial Tradition that has become buried beneath the materialism of the modern world," he says. And it is Jenkins's discerning and painstaking retro-sleuthing into that tradition that has penetrated the rich substrata beneath the materialism of our time and discovered ancient hidden "treasure"—namely, the galactic alignment not only at the core of the Mayan calendar, but also at the center of Vedic cosmology and various Old World traditions, including Mithraism, sacred architecture, and Greek sacred geography. He lays out the details of his progressive reconstruction in two groundbreaking books: *Maya Cosmogenesis 2012: The True Meaning of the Maya Calendar End Date* and *Galactic Alignment: The Transformation of Consciousness According to Mayan, Egyptian, and Vedic Traditions.*

In the mid-1990s, while researching the 2012 end date of the Mayan calendar, Jenkins decoded what he calls the "galactic cosmology" of the Maya. He realized that the ancient Maya understood the 26,000-year cycle known as the precession of the equinoxes and the earth's changing orientation to the galactic center. For the ancient Maya, tuning in to this stellar shifting inevitably led to the realization that at some point in the far future, the December solstice sun would align with the Milky Way's center, which can be seen as a "nuclear bulge" between the constellations of Sagittarius and Scorpio. The Maya thought of the Galactic Center as the ever-renewing womb of the Great Mother, and targeted the alignment with the end date of their calendar.

Jenkins's approach is to skillfully cross-pollinate the discoveries of archaeoastronomy, iconography, and ethnography, blending them into a profoundly coherent synthesis. This has enabled him to revive a fragmented worldview that he calls "multidimensional." He is interested not in inventing a new system, but in reviving the old one, one that because of its galactic focus is advanced in ways that modern science can barely appreciate. By accessing the myths, symbols, texts, and voices of the Primordial Tradition, Jenkins says that "it is clear that the Primordial Tradition is galactic in nature—the Galactic Center is its orientational locus and is the transcendental source of the wisdom it encodes, which now appears ready to make a dramatic appearance on the stage of human history . . . like a lost Atlantean dimension of the human soul."

Because the astronomical mapping laid out in Jenkins's recent books plugs so meaningfully into the sockets of the alignments and geodetics of so many sacred sites, the esoteric Hermetic dictum of "As above, so below" is now revealed fact. This is particularly true at Izapa in Chiapas, Mexico. "This is the site that gives us the 2012 calendar," says Jenkins. "Here, the Mayan wisdom about what the 2012 alignment means for us is encoded into the monumental sculpture!"

Three ceremonial monument groups at Izapa contain the "legacy" to our time in terms of understanding the galactic cosmology of the ancient Maya. Jenkins decodes the ball court group at Izapa as "ground zero of this knowledge, and there is plenty there to help us understand what we, today, are fated to live through. The encoded message of the ball court is a testimony to the brilliance of the ancient Izapan skywatchers."

A VISION QUEST

Jenkins recalls that as a child he was fascinated by gadgets and science. "I would take things apart and—sometimes—put them back together. Thomas Edison was my hero." By high school, Jenkins says, he had exhausted science as an avenue of self-knowledge and began reading philosophy. "And that," he says, "led to Eastern mysticism. This opened up a Gnostic path for me, a path of inner knowing, and I began to practice Yoga and meditation. I studied Tibetan mysticism, practiced celibacy, and wrote devotional poetry. I was trying to grow spiritually and free myself from the suburban nightmare of materialism that surrounded me."

By the time Jenkins reached twenty, that which was building within him was difficult to contain. "An inner spiritual crisis was welling up inside me, and I embarked on a pilgrimage that took me around the southeast United States. My mobile hermitage was a 1969 Dodge van that I lived in for seven months. As my pilgrimage reached a crescendo, I meditated, chanted, and fasted, in locations along the Gulf Coast or in Forest Service campgrounds in the Florida panhandle." Jenkins wrote of this period in his 1991 book, *Mirror in the Sky*. "This is the first time I have publicly shared this aspect of my past," he says.

"The pilgrimage spontaneously culminated in a three-day vigil, crying for a vision, chanting, and praying. It was a crisis of connection with a higher guiding force that I yearned to serve. In the early predawn hours on the cusp of Pisces, I had a mystical vision of the boon-bestowing goddess Govinda, who I also call the Earth Guardian." Jenkins says that the experience was attended by what is called, in Yoga, a kundalini rising. "It wasn't 'just' a dream or vision, as it was attended by an actual physical process called 'a turnabout in the deepest seat of the being' or 'the backward flowing method' described in the Taoist book *The Secret of the Golden Flower*."

Jenkins believes this experience with the goddess was the "boon" that bestowed upon him his mission, that led him to the Maya, a path that he now pursues in service to the Great Mother and the perennial wisdom. "It opened up a path of knowledge for me," he says. "Less than a week after that vision, I met the person who encouraged me to travel to Mexico and visit the Maya." Around that time Jenkins also read (the now classic) *Mexico Mystique,* by Frank Waters.

Today, almost twenty years later, Jenkins says that the connection with that original guiding force "continues to actively work within me, so I can continue to be a mouthpiece for the perennial philosophy. But balancing that call with the demands of making a living and paying the bills has, at times, been daunting."

THINKING AND KNOWING

Jenkins's mystical leanings are not that apparent in his recent books, which are academically rigorous and well documented without denying the deeper spiritual truths. In his view, "The intellect is not inconsistent with spirituality. Early on in my research, when my writings shifted from poetry and song writing to nonfiction research, I felt it would be critical to be clear and concise with my findings, mainly because spiritual materialism in New Age publishing seemed to be diluting the pristine purity of the universal truths with which it was coming into contact.

"Metaphors drawn from the profane modern culture and new terms were being coined for eternal truths . . . distortion of the ancient wisdom was happening. So I decided to place my rational intellect in service to the higher intellect, which is to say the heart. The heart is really higher than the brain." With this approach, Jenkins's work exemplifies the ability to go beyond the astronomy and venture more deeply into the metaphysics of spiritual transformation that awaits us on our approach to the galactic gateway.

The galactic gateway, and its meaning for our time, is the focus of *Galactic Alignment.* As we approach the 2012 end date of the Mayan calendar, it is clear that the knowledge expounded in many of the world's wisdom texts regarding the end of the present world age comes together and is solidly interpreted in Jenkins's latest book. According to his findings, the last of the four Hindu cycles of time, called *Yugas,* completes in synchrony with the Mayan end date, as does the Age of Pisces.

Christian millenarianism, via the year 2000, is also surprisingly close to the galactic alignment. The 2012 date itself is the astronomically defined time when the winter solstice Sun aligns with the center of the Milky Way. Jenkins surveys the work of the galactic philosopher Oliver Reiser to offer a scientific interpretation of how our solar system and the galactic plane become aligned, and what possible effects might result for life and consciousness on Earth.

An inevitable question is, "Does our changing relationship to the greater universe mean anything?" Jenkins's anticipation of this question is fully developed in *Galactic Alignment,* but the basis for a response to the question, he insists, is that "what is happening now was the centerpiece of many, many ancient systems and ancient philosophies, in virtually all of the world's traditions. If our own civilization—including our scientific and religious leaders—fails to see any meaning in this factual event, then we stand alone, divorced from the world's traditions that did."

Professor Jocelyn Godwin, of Colgate University, himself an author on esoteric subjects, sees value in exploring the 26,000-year processional cycle (of which the galactic alignment is the "completion" event) in terms of what it *means*. He says, "John Major Jenkins is the most global and erudite voice of a swelling chorus of 'Galactic Center' theorists. By framing the subject in the context of the Primordial Tradition, he raises it to a new level of seriousness, and of reassurance."

Jenkins emphasizes that his work does not promote a new "system" or "model," but rather offers a reconstruction of lost knowledge. And he notes that, in retrospect, his pursuits seem to have been guided by the initial inspiration of his original contact with the Earth goddess of his vision. He senses that "strings have been pulled behind the scenes" to help manifest his work, which is ultimately about the rebirth of the world. He says he finds the amount of misunderstanding and misinformation that is circulating "incredibly sad" and that, most of all, he wants his work to be an inspiration, to help people understand more deeply ancient teachings about human transformation.

THE BEGINNING IS NEAR, THE BEGINNING IS NEAR!

In many of the world's major cultures of antiquity, the center of the Milky Way galaxy was conceived of as the womb of the Great Mother goddess, the source and center of manifest worlds, and the ultimate means of our renewal at the end of a historical "chapter." The Galactic Center region was, to the Maya, a source point, or birthplace.

Because of this, Jenkins's early "rebirth" experience with the boon-bestowing goddess is especially meaningful, because it led him so directly into the work that has been the revelation of the whole mythic structure surrounding the 2012 astronomical time, when the Sun will be "re-birthed" in the "womb" of the Great Mother at the center of the Milky Way. Jenkins believes it is especially important to understand that 2012 indicates an alignment *process* and that any expectations should not focus on one precise day.

Nevertheless, 2012 has entered popular consciousness and can be considered the end of a Great Year of precession, a death of the old and the birth of the new—just as with the turning of the day or the lunar month or the solar year. Our precessional journey around the great wheel of the zodiac is humanity's 26,000-year gestation period, and the birth time is era-2012. As in all beginnings, new life is the purpose, but there is always a possibility of mishap or disaster if all is not in harmony with the force and magnitude of the "rite of passage" known as birth. Resistance versus acceptance can lead to different results.

Questions naturally arise concerning what Jenkins sees on the horizon between now and 2012. Jenkins eases his way into his response. "It may be unpopular to say it, but it's true," he says. "What 2012 was intended to target is not about 2012; it is about a process-oriented shift. It's about an open door, a once-in-a-precessional-cycle zone of opportunity to align ourselves with the galactic source of life." He points out that there are forces already set in motion "propelling us through a crucible of transformation unlike anything experienced in millennia . . . The sobering and humbling fact is that we are being called to create, nurture, and help unfold something that will not flower until long after we, as individuals, have died. The larger life wave of humanity is at stake." And he reminds us of the Native American teaching to look ahead seven generations in order to make wise decisions, and suggests this should be our guiding maxim as well.

As to the 2012 date itself, *Galactic Alignment* points the compass of time not to a cause-and-effect event, but rather to a higher process of spiritual transformation (which can be intense and challenging). If the 2012 date means anything *specific*, it is more likely to be a rally date for the traditional Maya, whose calendrics designated the 2012 date as the end of a World Age, a truth deeply embedded in their creation mythology.

The Mesoamerican masterminds who wove together mythology, political organization, religion, and astronomy into one seamless whole must surely have wanted the modern Maya to understand and reclaim the greatness of their people's past achievements.

In *Galactic Alignment* Jenkins explores how the galactic alignment is a central doctrine in global traditions. He finds it in Mithraism, Vedic astronomy, the doctrine of the Yugas, Islamic astrology, European sacred geography, Christian religious architecture of the Middle Ages, and various Hermetic traditions. "For me, this means that the galactic alignment wisdom of the Maya 2012 end date is even at the core of Western spirituality, and can unify traditions that on the surface seem so very different."

One wonders how Jenkins sees the core of his work, and what is next for him. "The core? My ongoing relationship with Sophia, the higher wisdom. It was that vision in 1985 and my work with the Tree of Life symbology that have led me into these areas of exploration. The archetype of the Great Mother of renewal and wisdom is a recurring motif that emerges in almost all of my books—even if I wasn't intending it at the outset. Overall, the core of the work is about healing, renewal, and opening up a little door at the end of time that leads into a new world, a new cycle in the drama of human unfolding."

PART FOUR

SEARCHING FOR
THE FOUNTAINHEAD

17 Megalithic England: The Atlantean Dimensions

A Conversation with John Michell

J. Douglas Kenyon

Among those who have argued in their writings that there was once a great and shining, albeit forgotten-to-history, fountainhead of civilization whose ghosts even now continue to haunt us, few have been more eloquent than John Michell.

The author of more than a score of works on ancient mysteries, sacred geometry, UFOs, unexplained phenomena, and the like, Michell is familiar to American readers primarily through his visionary classic *The View Over Atlantis* (a revised and rewritten version of this book, published in 1995, is entitled *The New View Over Atlantis*). *The Earth Spirit* comprises Michell's profusely illustrated essays on the ways, shrines, and mysteries of the subtle animating forces of the planet and their near universal celebration since the dawn of time.

Michell argues that across much of the earth are ancient earthworks and stone monuments built for an unknown purpose, and that their shared features suggest they might be part of a worldwide system that he believes served the elemental science of the archaic civilization that Plato called Atlantis. Michell suggests, in this connection, that the most significant modern discovery is that of leys, a mysterious network of straight lines that link the ancient places of Britain and have their counterparts in China, Australia, South America, and elsewhere.

In *The New View Over Atlantis,* the Cambridge-educated scholar's vision of a high megalithic civilization with a mastery of principles far beyond present-day understanding is so thoroughly and beautifully worked out that it becomes difficult, if not impossible, to credit orthodox notions that the sources of our megalithic heritage were but Stone Age hunter-gatherer societies with little on their primitive minds but survival and procreation. In detailed descriptions of phenomena such as the precise terrestrial and celestial alignments of ancient monuments along long ley lines, advanced ancient sciences of numbers and sacred geometry, and sophisticated prehistoric engineering, Michell paints a picture of a vast and coherent worldwide order beyond anything imaginable today.

"We live within the ruins of an ancient structure," he wrote in the first edition of *The New View Over Atlantis,* "whose vast size has hitherto rendered it invisible." Emerging from current research is the awesome

John Michell at Avebury
(PHOTOGRAPH BY TOM MILLER)

image of an ancient structure so great that its outlines have heretofore escaped understanding, one patiently awaiting our ascent to a sufficient height whence its masterful design, stretched out beneath us, can at last be appreciated.

Colin Wilson described *The View Over Atlantis* as "one of the great seminal books of our generation—a book which will be argued about for generations to come." In an interview with *Atlantis Rising,* Michell was asked if he had been keeping up with the new research by Graham Hancock, Robert Bauval, and others into celestial alignments of the monument of Egypt's Giza plane with the constellation Orion and other stars. He has, and hears an echo of evidence he has found in British sites in "much older stone," where alignments with significant stars also indicate the route of the soul after death.

"Everywhere in the ancient world you see this terrific obsession with death, reflected in the orientation of monuments," he observes. To him it seems plain that the ancients possessed a kind of science of immortality along the lines that Graham Hancock has suggested.

Unlike Colin Wilson, who theorizes that the ancients possessed advanced psychic faculties but had no technology as we understand the term, Michell believes it is very clear that they did. He sees it in their elaborate work of siting and constructing monuments well before the pyramids, and he sees it in their highly developed sciences of numbers and geometry.

"It's truly just extraordinary that so many numerical harmonies are put into basically very simple structures," he marvels, "and how they designed others to concentrate on the long term. In this very beautiful pattern is implied the kind of philosophy that says we can construct, here on Earth, the path to the heavens." He cites the frequent use of the number 12, as in the twelve tribes of Israel and a connection with the twelve signs of the zodiac, hinting at an attempt to order life on Earth according to the pattern of things in the heavens.

The question of technology becomes more pressing, but even more difficult to answer, when one considers how the giant stones of ancient sites were actually cut, tooled, and moved. "It is a mystery, actually," he concedes, "this incredible precision. And again in megalithic times, the extraordinary weights involved—raising blocks of one hundred tons or more, transporting them, and setting them up. They used terrific labor ingenuity and, no doubt, principles that aren't recognized today."

Could such principles have included some kind of levitation? "There are very persistent references from the Classical writers to the power of sound," he says, "of the use of song and music and tone to make things lighter, work songs where there's a rhythm got up, where you can move things without a lot of effort."

Whatever lost secrets the ancients may have possessed, Michell believes that we can recover them and, in fact, will, when the time is right. "Human ingenuity is such that we can do anything we want. If [the ancient knowledge] was actually needed, then it would return again. There's no doubt about that," he says. As to the suggestion that we may have been left hidden caches of records such as the legendary Hall of Records in Egypt, he thinks it very likely that such treasure troves exist, but is not certain we will recognize them when we see them.

"Plato went on about a certain canon of law possessed by the ancient Egyptians by which numerical proportions and musical harmonies, which dominate a society, enable it to continue on the same level for literally thousands of years," he explains. "Ancient civilization lasted far longer than we can conceive of today, so it seems to me that the whole society was based upon an understanding of the harmonies by which the universe is laid. And acting upon these by corresponding rituals, and that sort of thing, could hold the society together through crises." However, he concedes, being sufficiently developed to appreciate the wisdom of such laws may be another matter.

The possibility that we may have begun, at least in some quarters, to resonate in harmony with the ancient chords of wisdom could open the door to a *return* of ancient wisdom. In religious stories such as the Revelation of Saint John, Michell sees the description of a "New Jerusalem" coming down ready-made through a parting of the heavens as the manifestation of an awakening and a wholesale change from the patterns of a previous age.

Such a revelation comes, he believes, from nature, and "it is invoked," he says. "When we need it, we ask for it and it comes. Today, when people are so uncertain, I think we are looking for a truth and understanding that is beyond this world of chaos—of secular theories, and of all the scientific theories that follow one after the other but never establish anything—we're looking for the higher truth that is always there. When we ask for *that,* we'll get *that.*"

In a chaotic world where dissonance and dissonant music apparently reign supreme, there seems little hope that such a force can be overcome, but Michell remains optimistic. "It will overcome itself," he says. "Certainly it has always been recognized that music is the most powerful of the arts. As Plato said, forms of government eventually follow the forms of music. That's why the ancients were very careful in controlling music—no cacophony was allowed. The same music was heard at festivals every year and people were held under a kind of enchantment [whereby] the mind was held under one influence.

"Music is by far the most powerful means for therapy. Certainly the music—and the other art forms too—that we see now threatens chaos in society. It's a vessel that not only reflects what happens but also actually determines what *will* happen. As to what will come about, I have no idea. I think more and more it's in the hands of God and that there is now working out an alchemical process and that changes come about through nature—through the natural process of cause and effect. Things are chaotic and we have a reaction and a yearning for a source of order—there's a quest for *that* and an invocation of *that,* and then there follows a *revelation.*"

Can the hoped-for change come without cataclysm? "Every man-made thing, every created thing comes to an end sooner or later," Michell says. "It's as inevitable as tomorrow's sunrise that all these fruits shall have lain down. That which is artificial does not last long. Look at the fall of Communism. It seemed so assured, so completely in control, and it vanished practically overnght, destroyed by its own inherent contradictions. People just couldn't stand it anymore. It's so like the description of the fall of Babylon [in Saint John's Revelation]. One day it's going with all its wealth, parading its splendor, and the next day it's as if it never had been. There is no doubt that all the institutions we know will collapse. As to how orderly this process will be? The further we go into megalomania and dependence on artificial systems, the more drastic will be the reaction."

Michell sees a clear parallel between the destruction of Babylon described in the Book of Revelation and Plato's description of the fall of Atlantis, and he believes the story is a warning about the danger in certain ordering: "Plato made it very clear he's describing a geometrical pattern, the ground plan of

Atlantis, which is actually not adequate—like a man-made thing—based on the number 10, where his ideal city was based on the number 12. He saw in Atlantis the mortal element prevailed and it collapsed . . .

"It is about an error in the foundation law," Michell says, "which became more and more exaggerated and eventually led to the downfall of the whole thing. Life is bringing us through this process of revelation what was not even conceivable one hundred years ago or less—the idea of there being a cosmological pattern expressible numerically, geometrically, beautifully, which is the best possible reflection of the cosmos. That process establishes perfect patterns in one's own mind and then later on becomes the pattern for society.

"Then, of course, again over many generations, what began as a revelation becomes the iron law and becomes unjust and leads to that process whereby the ideal turns into Babylon and is fit for destruction. The best possible cosmological pattern that is kept up in the institutes of society will enable the society to last for a very long time, but no material thing lasts forever. Eventually it turns into dust."

But the good news, says Michell, is that human nature will always outlive any system of tyranny imposed upon it and, like the phoenix, will rise again. Today, he believes, we are living like bats in the ruins of a haunted house among the relics and ruins of the past, not just physically but also mentally, caught in outmoded forms of thought. If one is going to free oneself from the age-old spells, Michell says, one must challenge the dominant myths as he once did, with the most dominant theory of biology, evolution.

"It's not exactly that they are wrong," he explains. "It's that they are partial and arbitrary. That's the way they teach in school and college. You have to challenge them to get anywhere near adjusting your mind to the reality of things. If you take to heart anyone's scientific explanation, you will have an uneasy life: for, as you know, the theories that are portrayed as certainties are always changing. If you believe what they tell you in school now, by the time you get to be my age you'll be very old-fashioned indeed."

18 Plato, the Truth

How Does the Credibility of the Best-Known
Chronicler of Atlantis Stand Up?

Frank Joseph

*The Egyptian legend of Atlantis also current in folk-tale
along the Atlantic seaboard from Gibraltar to the Hebrides
and among the Yorubas in West Africa is not to be dismissed as pure fancy.*

ROBERT GRAVES, *THE GREEK MYTHS*

As the only surviving report from antiquity describing Atlantis, Plato's
account is the single most important source of its kind at the disposal
of investigators pursuing the lost civilization. His version continues to attract
the attention of both skeptics seeking to debunk Atlantis, and true believers
who contend that every word is quite literally factual. However, an impartial
reading of Plato's account as it is matter-of-factly presented in his dialogues,
the *Timaeus* and the *Critias*, leaves most readers impressed that the events
described so plainly might just as well be found in the more easily verified
writings of Herodotus or Thucydides.

To be sure, gods, goddesses, and Titans are employed, as one may expect,
to stand for the powers of nature, fate, and the remote past, just as they were
called upon to do in virtually every other Greek history. As such, the myths
were metaphors more than actual religious personages. But this is largely the
story of men and events well within the realm of Mediterranean experience,
and does not overly tax our imagination.

The story as it stands seems far less fabulous than factual, if only for its
straightforward, unadorned rendering. As William Blackett wrote in his book
Lost History of the World in 1881, "The case is put very differently by Plato.
Divested of the simplicity of story-telling, and free from the concealment of
mysticism and fancy, his account of the occurrence takes the form of a great
historical event."

The most common argument against the validity of the existence of
Atlantis as presented in the *Timaeus* and the *Critias* is that Plato meant them

to be understood merely as fictional recapitulations of his ideal state. While he obviously admires its high culture, Atlantis was *not* a mirror image of the society described in *The Republic*. There are very significant, nay, fundamental, differences between the two. His authoritarian ideal of a regime ruled by philosopher-kings was a single, race-conscious state, not a far-flung confederation of various peoples under the old system of monarchs constrained from wielding absolute power by a counsel of royal equals.

Even if Atlantis had been tailored after his work *The Republic* (which it was not), the addition of unnecessary, unphilosophic material (lengthy descriptions of architecture, racetracks, etc.) could not have illustrated any ideas that were not already thoroughly covered in *The Republic,* and would have therefore been so much superfluous repetition, something unparalleled in any of the man's writings.

Moreover, Atlantis grows corrupt, the reason for its punishment by the gods, hardly the fate of a society Plato hoped to immortalize as his ideal. His story achieves a more proper perspective when we understand that it was not intended to stand alone as some kind of an anomaly among his other philosophic works, but was rather the first part of an unfinished anthology concerning the major events that most shaped the history of the world until his time. It would have been, by its very nature, an interpretive history, another work on philosophy.

The *Timaeus* deals with the creation of the world, the nature of man, and the first civilized societies. The *Critias,* which survives only in draft form, was to be a full account of the Atlanto-Athenian war and its aftermath; its final section was to describe the critical events of the recent past, up to the fourth century B.C.E. So, the Atlantis story was intended as part of a far greater project, but essentially no different in character from the rest of Plato's writings. More significant, if his account was pure invention, it would not correspond as well as it does with accessible history, nor go on to logically fill so many gaps in our knowledge of pre-Classical antiquity by bridging such a great deal of otherwise disconnected, isolated information.

But Plato's accuracy as historian could not be verified until our own century. His description of a holy spring that ran through the Acropolis was deemed entirely mythical until the discovery of Mycenaean potsherds from the thirteenth century B.C.E. showing a fountain in the midst of the Acropolis led some researchers to reconsider his account. Then, in 1938, renewed excavations revealed that earthquake activity had closed an underground spring beneath the Acropolis precisely where Plato said it had been. During the 1950s, joint teams of Greek, German, and American archeologists found their reconstruction of fifth-century-B.C.E. Athens matched Plato's description of the city with unexpected exactitude. We have, therefore, every reason to assume his description of Atlantis is just as accurate. Both his identification of the fountain at the Acropolis and his precise knowledge of Athens reflect favorably on his historical reliability.

There is also some evidence that Plato's account was not altogether unknown to the Greeks in Classical times before he set it to paper. At the Panathenaea Festival, held every year in Athens, women wore a peplum, a kind of skirt, embroidered with symbolic designs commemorating the goddess of their city. Some of the peplum depictions represented Athena's victory over the forces of Atlantis, not a particularly remarkable fact in itself, except that the Panathenaea was founded 125 years before Plato's birth.

The *Voyage to Atlantis,* rediscovered and tragically lost in modern times, was another earlier source, composed 150 years before Plato's time by Dionysus of Miletus. A few other tantalizing fragments still exist, singed scraps from the incinerated Great Library of Alexandria, such as a fleeting reference to the second-century Roman writer Elianus, whose *Historia Naturalis* described how the rulers of Atlantis dressed to demonstrate their descent from Poseidon. The story was given special credence by another philosopher, Proklos, who told how Krantor, an early follower of Plato, seeking to validate the legend of Atlantis, in 260 B.C.E. personally journeyed to the Egyptian temple at Sais. There he discovered the original tablets, which confirmed the account. Translated, they paralleled Plato's narrative detail for detail.

Krantor was a prominent scholar at the Great Library of Alexandria, the center of Classical learning, where the story of Atlantis was generally regarded as a credible episode in history by the leading minds of the age, including the chief chronicler of the Roman Empire, Strabo. Long before its destruction, the Great Library apparently contained a good deal of supportive materials that almost universally convinced its researchers that Plato had described an actual city in the "outer ocean."

It was only after the success of the Christian revolution that the facts concerning Atlantis, like most of "pagan" civilization, were lost. The story was condemned as heresy because it was not found in the Bible and because it supposedly predated God's creation of the world in 5508 B.C.E., a date arrived at by the curious chronology of Christian theologians.

The subject remained closed until the discovery of America, when so many mysterious parallels between the New World and the Old reminded scholars of Plato's Atlantic empire. Among the first was a sixteenth-century explorer and cartographer, Francisco Lopez de Gomara, who was struck by descriptions of an "opposite continent" (America) in the *Timaeus*. But the Alexandria of Classical antiquity was, after all, only seventy-five miles from Sais, and any investigator who wished to verify the details of Plato's account did not have to travel far to read the tablets at the Temple of Neith.

According to the Roman historian Marcelinus (330–395 C.E.), scholars at the Great Library knew of a geologic convulsion that "suddenly, by a violent motion, opened up huge mouths and so swallowed up portions of the Earth, as in the Atlantic sea, on the coast of Europe, a large island was swallowed up." The historiographer Theopompus believed Plato's story, as did the famous naturalist Pliny the Elder. The original source materials they once possessed, lost since the collapse of Classical civilization, and the fragmentary evidence remaining to us argue consistently on behalf of Plato's credibility.

As Zadenk Kukal, a modern critic of the dialogues, has written, "It is probable that even if Plato had not written a single line about Atlantis, all the archeological, ethnographic, and linguistic mysteries that could not be explained would lead to some primeval civilization located somewhere between the cultures of the Old and New Worlds."

R. Catesby Taliaferro writes in the foreword to the Thomas Taylor translation of the *Timaeus* and the *Critias*, "It appears to me to be at least as well attested as any other narration in any ancient historian. Indeed, he [Plato], who proclaims that 'truth is the source of every good both to gods and men,' and the whole of whose works consist in detecting error and exploring certainty, can never be supposed to have willfully deceived mankind by publishing an extravagant romance as matter of fact, with all the precision of historical detail." Plutarch, the great Greek biographer of the first century C.E., wrote in his *Life of Solon* that the Greek legislator cited in Plato's story "had undertaken to put into verse this great history of Atlantis, which had been told to him by the wise men of Sais."

The city itself played an important role in the Atlantis epic. It was one of the oldest major settlements in Egypt and served as the first capital of the Lower Nile after the unification, which was around 3100 B.C.E.—in other words, at very start of dynastic, historic Egypt. As an indication of its and the Atlantean tablets' antiquity, the Temple of Neith—where they were enshrined, was established by Pharaoh Hor-aha, the first dynastic king of a united Egypt.

Even Sonchis, the obscure character who told the story to Solon, was a historical figure whose very name contributes to the authenticity of the legend. Sonchis is a Greek derivation of the Egyptian god Suchos, known in his Nile homeland as Sebek. Sebek was a water deity who, appropriately enough, worshiped at Sais—where the Atlantis report was recorded—with his mother, Neith. It was in her temple, Plato wrote, that the tablets were preserved.

Neith was one of the very oldest of predynastic figures, the personification of the Waters of Chaos from which the Primal Mound, the First Land, arose. She was known as the keeper of the most ancient histories of both gods and men. The Minoan Mother Earth goddess and the Greek Athena are later manifestations of Neith. She fell into almost complete neglect after the passing of the Old Kingdom. But the First Birth-Giver experienced a popular revival during the Saite Period of the twenty-sixth dynasty, when her temple and its oldest records were restored—precisely the time Plato said Solon visited Egypt. Herodotus wrote that Pharaoh Ahmose had just finished refurbishing the Temple of Neith when Solon arrived in Sais.

It is difficult to believe that Plato went to such lengths of mythic and historic detail to create a mere fable. It is no less unlikely that he suspected any connections among the priest Sonchis; the god Sebek; his mother, the goddess Neith; and their intimate relation to the story of Atlantis recorded so appropriately and unearthed in so timely a fashion at Sais.

Another point worth noting: Krantor said the story was inscribed on tablets mounted on a pillar in the Temple of Neith, while the *Critias* tells that the royal proclamations in Atlantis were inscribed on tablets posted to a column in the Temple of Poseidon: The one seems to reflect and memorialize the other.

There are many unquestionably authentic touches throughout the narrative. For example, the *Critias* tells us that each of the wealthy leaders in Atlantean society was required to provide for the national armaments, including "four sailors to make up a compliment of twelve ships." Although it fell out of use in Plato's more "democratic" times, in Periclean days and for some centuries before, wealthy men known as Trierarchoi each had to undertake the funding of a warship, complete with crew and weapons.

Of course, many more of those fragments still existed, even in Classical times, when the story was generally accepted as a historical event. One of those believers was the geographer Poseidonous of Rhodes (130 to 50 B.C.E.), who conducted his studies at Cadiz—the Gades in the *Critias*—in the Atlantean kingdom of Gadeiros. Strabo wrote of him, "[H]e did well in citing the opinion of Plato that the tradition concerning the island of Atlantis might be received as something more than fiction." Modern critics are less generous. They continue to demean the story as nothing more than a fabulous allegory intended to dramatize principles already laid out in *The Republic,* with no basis in actual history except perhaps for a sketchy reference to Minoan Crete.

In 1956, however, Albert Rivand, professor of classical history at the Sorbonne, declared that both the *Timaeus* and the *Critias* embodied ancient, historic traditions, and contained results of the latest contemporary research carried out in Plato's day. As Ivan Lissner wrote, "That a distinguished French scholar who had spent decades studying the Platonic texts should reach this conclusion is most significant, because it invests the geographical and onto-logical allusions in the two books with greater weight."

Standing alone, Plato's account is simple enough. But background infor-mation on the principles in the narrative should raise it above the level of a dry report and lend the reader a feeling of living history.

More famous in his day than the author of the *Timaeus* and the *Critias* was their chief character, Solon, one of the Seven Sages, who "grew old ever learning new things" and whose name became synonymous for a wise law-giver. Timaeus, born in Locris, in southern Italy, was an explorer and Pythagorean astronomer. Critias the Younger was an orator, statesman, poet, philosopher, and one of the leaders of the Thirty Tyrants. He was also a first cousin of Plato's mother. A vigorous man, he died on the battlefield at Aegospotamis, in the Piraeus, in 403 B.C.E. as he approached his ninetieth birthday.

Solon's unfinished manuscript was passed on to his brother Dropides, the great-grandfather of Critias, and through succeeding generations it became something of a family heirloom. Though these leading characters were real enough flesh-and-blood figures who related the tale with great accuracy (as mentioned above, Krantor verified Plato's version by comparing it with the original Egyptian tablets), the *Timaeus* and the *Critias* are not stenographic records of word-for-word conversations, but rather speeches organized to illus-trate ideas by ordering arguments into the most logically convincing presenta-tion, a standard exercise in the Classical schools of high rhetoric. So when Critias says he hopes he has not forgotten all the details of the Atlantis story, the integrity of the whole narrative does not hang by the memory of an old man. Instead, Plato uses a standard rhetorical device to present his description.

More likely than not, he had Solon's unfinished manuscript in front of him as he wrote out the speeches. He hints as much when he has Critias say, "My great-grandfather, Dropides, had the original writing, which is still in my possession." It is even possible Plato saw the original tablets at the Temple of Neith, as many scholars are sure he traveled to Egypt himself on at least one occasion. His narrative gains additional credence in the high standing of the men involved. No fictional improvisations, their lives were linked to the preservation of the account.

The *Critias* also differs from the rest of Plato's work, not only because of its incompleteness, but also, unlike in the other dialogues, Socrates does not interrupt the narrative with questions, a sign, judging from his behavior in *The Republic,* of agreement. Of course, he may have been saving his questions for later, but that would not have been like him. We, however, should continue to question the story for more answers.

19 The Aegean Atlantis Deception

Was Plato's Grand Tale Nothing More Than the
Saga of an Insignificant Greek Island?

Frank Joseph

Although Atlantis has been generally associated by most investigators with the Atlantic Ocean, as a preponderance of the evidence suggests, fringe theorists have occasionally assigned the island to sometimes bizarre locations, almost always for ulterior reasons. The latest of these eccentric interpretations gained some acceptance among professional archeologists and historians, probably because it did not disturb their modern bias against transoceanic voyages in pre-Classical times.

The theory originally belonged to a pre–World War I writer for the *Journal of Hellenic Studies*, K. T. Frost, who moved Atlantis from the Atlantic Ocean to the Mediterranean island of Crete. Since then, his hypothesis has been expanded by (perhaps not surprisingly) mostly Greek scholars (Galanopoulas, Marinatos, et al.) to include the Aegean island of Santorini, anciently known as Thera. Their advocation of a Greek identity for Atlantis was the latest in an unfortunate chauvinist tendency on the part of some Atlantologists to associate their own national backgrounds with the lost civilization.

Such extra-scientific motivations for conveniently finding Plato's island in the investigator's own homeland have not done the search much credit. But the ulterior motives currently driving professional scholars of all nationalities (mostly Americans these days) to insist that Crete or its neighboring island and Atlantis are one and the same are more harmful. It is important, therefore, to understand why they want to explain away Atlantis in what has come to be known as the Minoan Hypothesis.

Thera was part of the Minoan commercial empire, and excavation on Santorini (its modern name) uncovered a high level of early civilization that once flourished there. The small island was actually a volcanic mountain that exploded in much the same way as the eruption at Krakatoa, and quite literally plunged into the sea. The resulting two-hundred-foot-high wall of water

144

that swept over Crete wrecked havoc among its coastal ports, while accompanying earthquakes badly damaged the inland capital, Knossos. The Minoans were knocked so off balance by this natural disaster that they could not organize an effective resistance to Mycenaean aggression, and their civilization disappeared, absorbed in part by invaders from Greece. Seizing upon these events more than a thousand years before his time, Plato, it is suggested, modeled Atlantis directly after Crete and/or Thera as an analogy for his ideal state.

Although Thera is only a fraction of the size of his Atlantis and lies in the Aegean Sea instead of the Atlantic Ocean, which he specified, and was destroyed 7,800 years after the destruction described in the dialogues, these apparent discrepancies are handily dismissed by the assumption that Plato simply inflated his account by a factor of 10. He did so, it is claimed, deliberately—to make for a grander tale, his figures were mistranslated from the original Egyptian.

Both Atlanteans and Minoans, it is argued, built great palaces and powerful cities, operated thalassocracies (seaborne empires), practiced a pillar cult, traded in precious metals, and had elephants roaming about. This interpretation is not without supporting details. Eumelos, cited by Plato in the *Critias* as the first Atlantean king after Atlas, is echoed in the Minoan island of Melos and, in fact, is mentioned on an inscription of archaic Greek at Thera itself bearing his name.

The Minoan theorists go on to argue against the Atlantic Ocean as the correct site for Plato's island because only in the Aegean Sea have relatively small tracts of land ever suddenly disappeared beneath the surface, such as the city of Helice, in the Gulf of Corinth. The Azores, too, are ruled out as a possible location; supposedly no islands in the area are known to have sunk over the past 72,000 years. The numerous early-flood legends, particularly the Babylonian Epic of Gilgamesh, are cited as literary evidence for Thera's destruction. Even the concentric arrangement of the Atlantean capital, as described by Plato, may to this day be seen in the waters of Santorini Bay.

It is true that, like Atlantis, Thera was a volcanic island and part of an advanced thalassocracy, which vanished after its chief mountain exploded and sank into the sea. But move beyond this general comparison and the Minoan Hypothesis begins to unravel. Thera was a minor colony of Minoan civilization, a small outpost, not its capital, as the dialogues have Atlantis. Mycenaean influences from the Greek mainland *did* supplant Minoan culture on Crete, but the transition appears to have been largely, if not entirely, nonviolent, certainly nothing resembling the scope of Plato's Atlanto-Athenian war that raged across the Mediterranean World.

The Minoans never made a move to occupy Italy or Libya, nor did they threaten to invade Egypt, as the Atlanteans were supposed to have done. From everything scholars have been able to learn about them, the Minoans were an extremely unwarlike people more interested in commercial than military conquests, while the Atlanteans are portrayed as aggressively bellicose. As Kenneth Caroli, a leading writer on the subject, concludes, "Thera's candidacy as Atlantis rests largely on its cataclysmic destruction alone, while Plato's story had far more to do with a war between two antagonistic peoples than with the disaster that later overwhelmed them both."

A CASE OF MISTAKEN IDENTITY

The Minoans operated a dynamic navy to combat piracy and keep open the sea routes of international trade, but their Cretan cities were not ringed by

The volcano at Santorini

*Modern Thera, with its popular association with Atlantis,
has developed a thriving tourist industry.*

high walls or battlements of any kind; compare Knossos or Phaistos with the armed towers and defense-in-depth of the walls surrounding Atlantis. Moreover, these leading cities of Minoan Crete were laid out in the architectural canon of the square grid, unlike the concentric circles upon which Atlantis was built. Some theorists claimed to have actually seen such a concentric arrangement underwater, within the bay created when Thera's volcanic mountain collapsed into the sea.

But Dorothy B. Vitaliano, a prominent geologist specializing in volcanology with the U.S. Geological Survey, reports that the subsurface topography at Santorini "was not in existence before the Bronze Age eruption of the volcano; it has been created by subsequent activity which built up the Kameni Islands in the middle of the bay, to which a substantial amount of land was added as recently as 1926. Any traces of the pre-collapse topography would long since have been buried beneath the pile of lava whose highest portions emerge to form these islands."

Clearly, a recent geological feature has been mistaken for an ancient city. Structures designed in concentric circles prevailed, not in the Mediterranean World, but in the Atlantic, such as the circular temples of the Canary Islands and Britain's Stonehenge.

Caroli points out that "the Atlantean capital lay on a substantial plain surrounded by high mountains on a large island." Thera does not fit this description.

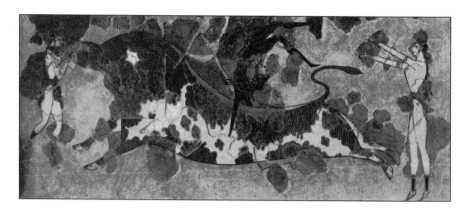

Minoan bull ceremony

The Cretans and Therans did not plate floors, walls, and columns with metal, as Plato says the Atlanteans did. Plato's description of Poseidon's temple implies a structure with metal-covered walls, decorative pinnacles, and at least two pillars that were metal-plated. All this sounds like a Bronze Age Phoenician temple.

Atlantis featured interconnecting canals and lay close to the sea; Phaistos and Knossos are inland and have no canals. Nothing of the kind existed at Knossos or any other Minoan city. Neither of these Aegean locations had a harbor, because their lightweight ships could be hauled up on the beach, unlike the oceangoing Atlantean ships, which required the deep-water ports mentioned in the *Critias*.

In any case, the harbor arrangement described by Plato was impossible in the eastern Mediterranean Sea, because its main channel would have been fouled by stagnation without the ebb and flow of tides that do occur "beyond the Pillars of Heracles." This point alone is sufficient to prove that he was describing a real place in the Atlantic Ocean, not in the Aegean.

Melos, the Minoan island associated with the king Eumelos of Plato's dialogues, is so tiny that it could never have supported the capital of an allied kingdom. Actually, we learn in the *Critias* that Eumelos ruled over that region closest to the Pillars of Heracles called Gades, today's Cadiz, on the Atlantic coast of Spain. That much in Plato is certain. It takes quite a stretch of the imagination, to say nothing of the facts, to relocate Eumelos in the Aegean. Although it is the only name mentioned in the dialogues that does indeed appear in the eastern Mediterranean, no other Atlantean king finds a correspondence in that part of the world.

The island of Atlantis was supposed to have been rich in precious metals;

Crete and Thera have few. Then there is the self-evident fact that Crete did not sink into the sea, as Atlantis was alleged to have done. Thera's volcanic mountain *did* collapse beneath the Aegean, but its island survives to this day; in the *Critias,* both city and island were utterly destroyed.

That rituals involving bulls were practiced by both Atlantean and Minoan civilizations proves nothing, because the animal was similarly venerated in mainland Greece, Egypt, Assyria, the Hittite empire, and Iberia, as far back as Neolithic and even Paleolithic times.

AN OCEAN OF SUNKEN ISLANDS

Contrary to the Minoan theorists, who assert that no sizable territories have sunk into the Atlantic Ocean, as recently as 1931 the Fernando Noronha Islands were points of contention between Great Britain and Portugal, until they sank after one week of seismic activity. Nor was Atlantis the only island-city to have gone under the Atlantic. The Janonius Map of 1649 identified Usedom, formerly a famous mart, which was swallowed up by the waves of the sea. The same island was mentioned five centuries earlier by the Arab cartographer Edrisi. Actually, the town in question was Vineta on the northwest corner of the island of Usedom, near Rugen Island in the North Sea. The North Frisian island of Rungholt, although not as large as Usedom, was likewise once inhabited before it sank at about the same time.

Of course, none of these islands may be identified with Atlantis, but each *does* demonstrate that an Atlantean event was by no means beyond the geologic purview of the Atlantic Ocean.

A LABYRINTH OF MISINFORMATION

As for the flood legend common to the Epic of Gilgamesh, the Old Testament, and early myth, it cannot have resulted from the destruction of Thera, because the deluge myth prominent in Middle Eastern civilization traces back to Sumerian origins, predating the downfall of Minoan Crete by more than a thousand years. The Greek tradition of Theras, the mythic founder of Thera, has no elements in common with Plato's story, nor does it hint of anything remotely Atlantean.

The Minoan Hypothesis was so much in vogue among archeologists during the 1970s that the famed oceanographer Jacques Cousteau spent the better part of his time, energies, and nearly two million dollars provided by the government of Monaco searching the depths around Santorini. Lured to the

Aegean by a fashionable theory designed to dismiss Plato, not explain him, Cousteau turned up nothing resembling Atlantis.

A CONFUSION OF DATES

While at first glance and from a distance the Minoan Hypothesis may appear tenable, it begins to disintegrate the closer one approaches it. Practically point for point, an Aegean Atlantis does not match Plato's straightforward account and is uniformly contradicted by the evidence of geology, history, and comparative mythology. As a last-ditch effort to save something of their excuse for a Cretan interpretation, its advocates claim that Plato merely used the general outline of events at Thera as a vague, historical framework on which to present his notion of a consummate culture in the fictionalized guise of Atlantis.

But here too they err because the dialogues define Atlantis as the enemy of Plato's idealized state. So often has it been repeated that he invented Atlantis to exemplify his "ideal society." In any case, the ideal city Plato does describe, Megaera, is square, not circular.

But only one piece of evidence is required to invalidate the Minoan Hypothesis in a single stroke. The cornerstone its supporters depended upon was the date for the collapse of Thera's volcano into the sea, because it was *this* disaster, they argued, that brought down Minoan civilization in 1485 B.C.E. The attendant tsunamis that crashed along the shores of ancient Crete, and the earthquakes that toppled her cities, were compounded by Greek armies who took advantage of the natural catastrophe to wage war on the disorganized Minoans, plunging them into a dark age from which they never reemerged.

The pivotal date was arrived at by a process of ice-core drilling. Caroli explains: "Ice cores reveal 'acidity peaks' at the times of major eruptions, because ash falls on the ice caps and affects their chemistry. Long cores by hollow pipes used as drills (some hundreds of feet in length) taken from both Greenland and Antarctica have been examined to determine the past climate of the Earth.

"By analyzing the chemistry of these cores, 'acidity peaks' can be found," he says, "many of them visible to the naked eye as dark streaks in the ice made by the ash that fell long ago. Some of these cores, mainly those from Greenland, have annual layers, like tree rings, or sedimentary glacial deposits at lake bottoms. These can and have been counted back for thousands of years. The oldest of these 'long cores' was drilled in 1963 at Camp Century in north-central Greenland. For years, it was the only core that went back far enough and had been studied in sufficient detail to potentially reveal the timing of Thera's eruption."

It is now understood that Thera erupted between 1623 and 1628 B.C.E., almost 150 earlier than the Minoan theorists believed. The significance of this discrepancy renders their entire interpretation invalid, because Minoan civilization did not disappear in the wake of a natural disaster. "By all indications," Caroli points out, "the Minoans not only survived the eruption, but reached their peak *after* it."

Proponents of an Aegean Atlantis call upon Egyptian history for corroboration, but here too they find contradiction to their assertion that Minoan civilization was shattered by Thera's eruption. Pharaoh Amenhotep III dispatched an embassy to the cities of Crete and found them still occupied nearly a century after their supposed destruction. The Egyptian records were confirmed in the late 1970s when excavators around Knossos discovered evidence for the final occupation by the Minoans in 1380 B.C.E. This was one hundred years later than even the original, incorrect date for the eruption of Thera and its assumed destruction of Aegean civilization, the alleged source for Plato's story of Atlantis.

Caroli's assessment seems conclusive: "And so the Minoan hypothesis is left with no war, no maritime civilization destroyed by catastrophe, the wrong kind of disaster, the wrong date, and no comparable dark age as a result. What does that leave us? To my mind, not much."

20 Atlantology: Psychotic or Inspired?

Media Stereotypes Aside, What Kind of Person Pursues Knowledge of a Forgotten Civilization?

Frank Joseph

A mainstream archeologist interviewed about Atlantis on a recent special for The Discovery Channel declared that the only people who believe in such garbage are cranks, fools, and charlatans. His assessment is shared by conventional scientists who insist that no one of any intellectual worth would demean him- or herself by seriously considering any sunken civilization. True, virtually no university-trained researchers today are willing to risk the wrath of conservative academics not above sabotaging the careers of independent-minded colleagues.

Solon

But contrary to the establishment's defaming characterization of those interested in the historical possibility of Atlantis, the subject has for centuries attracted some of the best brains in the world. Solon, one of the Seven Wise Men of Greece, introduced social reforms and a legal code that formed the political basis of Classical civilization. He was also the first great poet of Athens. In the late sixth century B.C.E., the great law-giver traveled to Sais, the Nile Delta capital of the twenty-sixth dynasty, where the Temple of Neith was located.

Here a history of Etelenty was preserved in hieroglyphs inscribed or painted on dedicated columns, which were translated for him by the high priest Sonchis. Returning to Greece, Solon worked all the details of the account into an epic poem, *Atlantikos,* but was distracted by political problems from completing the project before his death in 560 B.C.E.. About 150 years later, the unfinished manuscript was given to Plato, who formed two dialogues, the *Timaeus* and the *Critias,* from it.

As one of the very greatest historical figures in Classical Greek history, Solon's early connection with the story of Atlantis lends it formidable credibility. But neither he nor Plato was the only towering figure of Classical antiquity to embrace the reality of Atlantis. Statius Sebosus was a Greek geographer and contemporary of Plato mentioned by the Roman scientist Pliny the Elder for his detailed description of Atlantis.

All the works of Statius Sebosus were lost with the fall of Classical civilization. Dionysus of Miletus, also known as Skytobrachion, for his prosthetic leather arm, wrote *A Voyage to Atlantis* around 550 B.C.E., predating not only Plato, but also Solon. A copy of Dionysus's manuscript was found among the personal papers of the historical writer Pierre Benoit. Tragically, it was lost between the restorers and borrowers who made use of this valuable piece of source material after Benoit's death.

Another Greek historian, Dionysus of Mitylene (430 to 367 B.C.E.), relying on pre-Classical sources, reported that "from its deep-rooted base, the Phlegyan isle which stern Poseidon shook and plunged beneath the waves with its impious inhabitants."

The volcanic island of Atlantis is suggested in the fiery (Phlegyan)

Poseidon

isle destroyed by the sea god. Tragically, this is all that survives from a lengthy discussion of Atlantis in the lost Argonautica, mentioned four hundred years later by the Greek geographer Diodorus Siculus as one of his major sources for information about the ancient history of North Africa. Interestingly, Dionysus was a contemporary of Plato.

A utopian novel written by Francis Bacon in 1629, *The New Atlantis,* was the first written discussion of Atlantis since the fall of Classical civilization and probably sparked Athanasius Kircher's interest in the subject; he published his own scientific study of Atlantis in *The Subterranean World* thirty-six years later. Although a work of fiction, *The New Atlantis* came about through excited discussions in contemporary scholarly circles of reports from travelers to America. They said that the indigenous peoples had oral accounts of a land comprising numerous points in common with Plato's sunken civilization; they even called it Aztlan, which paralleled a native version of the Greek Atlantis. *The New Atlantis* actually incorporates some Atlanto-American myths Bacon heard repeated in London.

A German polymath of the seventeenth century, the Jesuit priest, Athanasius Kircher was a pioneering mathematician, physicist, chemist, linguist, and archeologist. He was the first to study phosphorescence and he was the inventor of numerous futuristic innovations including the slide projector and a prototype of the microscope. The founding father of scientific Egyptology, he led the first serious investigation of temple hieroglyphs. Kircher was also the first scholar to seriously investigate the Atlantis legend. Initially skeptical, he cautiously began reconsidering its credibility while assembling mythic traditions about a great flood from numerous cultures in various parts of the world.

"I confess for a long time I had regarded all this," he said of various European traditions of Atlantis, "as pure fables, to the day when, better instructed in Oriental languages, I judged that all these legends must be, after all, only the development of a great truth." His research led him to the immense collection of source materials at the Vatican Library, where, as Europe's foremost scholar, he had at his disposal all its formidable resources. It was here that he discovered a single piece of evidence that proved to him that the legend was actually fact.

Among the relatively few surviving documents from Imperial Rome, Kircher found a well-preserved, treated-leather map purporting to show the configuration and location of Atlantis. The map was not Roman, but had been brought in the first century C.E. to Italy from Egypt, where it had been executed. It survived the demise of Classical times and found its way into the Vatican Library. Kircher copied it precisely (adding only a visual reference to the New World) and published it in *The Subterranean World*. His caption describes it as a map of the island of Atlantis, originally made in Egypt after Plato's description, which suggests it was created sometime following the fourth century C.E., perhaps by a Greek mapmaker attached to the Ptolemys. More probably, the map's first home was the Great Library of Alexandria, from which numerous books and references to Atlantis were lost, along with another million-plus volumes, when the institution was burned by religious fanatics. By relocating to Rome, the map escaped that destruction.

Similar to modern conclusions forced by current understanding of geology in the Mid-Atlantic Ridge, Kircher's map depicts Atlantis not as a continent but as a large island about the size of Spain and France combined. It shows a tall, centrally located volcano, most likely meant to represent Mount Atlas, together with six major rivers, something Plato does not mention (the *Critias* speaks of large rivers on the island of Atlantis, but we are not told how many). Although the map vanished after Kircher's death in 1680, it was the only known representation of Atlantis to have survived the Ancient World. Thanks to his research and book, it survives today in what is considered to be a close copy of the original.

Kircher was the first to publish such a map, probably the most accurate of its kind to date. Curiously, it is depicted upside down, contrary to maps in both his day and ours. Yet this apparent anomaly is proof of the map's authenticity, because Egyptian mapmakers, even as late as Ptolemaic times, designed their maps with the Upper Nile Valley (located in the south; "Upper" refers to its higher elevation) at the top, because the river's headwaters are located in the Sudan.

Olof Rudbeck (1630–1702) was Sweden's premiere scientific genius: professor of medicine (Uppsala), discoverer of the lymph glands, inventor of the anatomical theater dome, leading pioneer of modern botany, designer of the first university gardens; initiator of Latin as the *lingua franca* of the scientific world community; historian of early Sweden. A brilliant scholar fluent in Latin, Greek, and Hebrew, Rudbeck possessed a grasp of Classical literature that was nothing less than encyclopedic. Combining his vast knowledge of the ancient world with personal archeological research in his own country, he concluded during a long, intense period of investigation (1651 to 1698) that Atlantis was fact, not fiction, and the greatest civilization in prehistory.

He believed that Norse myths and some physical evidence among his country's megalithic ruins showed how a relatively few Atlantean survivors may have had an impact on Sweden, contributing to its cultural development, and laid the foundation (particularly in ship construction) for what would much later be remembered as the Viking Age (the ninth to twelfth centuries C.E.).

Critics have since misrepresented Rudbeck's work by claiming he identified Sweden with Atlantis itself, but he never made such an assertion. In their sloppy research they have confused him with another eighteenth-century scholar, the French astronomer Jean Bailey, who concluded (before being executed during the French Revolution) that Spitzbergen, in the Arctic Ocean, was all that remained of Atlantis.

Born in Kraljevic, Austria, on February 27, 1861, Rudolf Steiner was a university-trained scientist, artist, and editor who founded a Gnostic movement based on comprehension of the spiritual world through pure thought and the highest faculties of mental knowledge. This was the guiding principle of anthroposophy, knowledge produced by the higher self in man, as he defined it, a spiritual perception independent of the senses. Such instinctual awareness of the divine energies that interpenetrate the entire universe is not new; on the contrary, it was exercised by our ancestors during the deep past, when they more freely and fully participated in the spiritual processes of life. A gradual attraction to vulgar materialism through development of the high cultures in the ancient world increasingly diminished their innate sensitivities, which eventually atrophied but did not die out.

To awaken these faculties dormant in all men and women required, Steiner believed, training their consciousness to look beyond mere matter. These concepts were developed in his 1904 book, *Cosmic Memory: Prehistory of Earth and Man*. He maintained that before Atlantis gradually sank, in 7227 B.C.E., its earliest inhabitants formed one of mankind's root races, a people who did not require

Rudolf Steiner

speech but instead communicated telepathically in images, not words, as part of their immediate experience with God.

According to Steiner, the story of Atlantis was dramatically revealed in Germanic myth, wherein fiery Musplheim corresponded to the southern, volcanic area of the Atlantic land, while frosty Niflheim was located in the north. Steiner wrote that the Atlanteans developed the first concept of good versus evil and laid the groundwork for all ethical and legal systems. Their leaders were spiritual initiates able to manipulate the forces of nature through control of the life force and development of etheric technology.

Seven epochs comprise the "post-Atlantis period," of which ours, the Euro-American epoch, will end in C.E. 3573. *Cosmic Memory* goes on to describe the earlier and contemporary Pacific civilization of Lemuria, with stress on the highly evolved clairvoyant powers of its people. Steiner defined Atlantis as the turning point in an ongoing struggle between the human search for community and our experience of individuality.

The former, with its growing emphasis on materialism, dragged down the spiritual needs of the latter, culminating eventually in the Atlantean cataclysm. In this interpretation of the past, Steiner opposed Marxism. To him, spirit, not economics, drives history. Steiner's views of Atlantis and Lemuria are important if only because of the educational Waldorf movement he founded, which still operates about one hundred schools attended by tens of thousands of students in Europe and the United States. He died on March 30, 1925, in Dornach, Switzerland, where he had founded his school of spiritual science twelve years earlier.

James Lewis Thomas Chalmers Spence, born on November 25, 1874, in Forfarshire, Scotland, was a prominent mythologist who inherited Ignatius Donnelly's position as the world's leading Atlantologist of the early twentieth century. An alumnus of Edinburgh University, Spence was made a fellow of the Royal Anthropology Institute of Great Britain and Ireland, and elected vice president of the Scottish Anthropology and Folklore Society. Awarded a Royal Pension for services to culture, he published more than forty books. Many of them, such as the *Dictionary of Non-Classical Mythology* coauthored with Marian Edwards, are still in print and widely regarded as the best source materials of their kind.

Lewis Spence

His interpretation of the Maya's *Popol Vuh* (Book of Consul) won international acclaim, but he is best remembered for *The Problem of Atlantis* (1924), *Atlantis in America* (1925), *The History of Atlantis* (1926), *Will Europe Follow Atlantis?* (1942), and *The Occult Sciences in Atlantis* (1943). During the early 1930s, he edited a prestigious journal, *The Atlantis Quarterly*. *The Problem of Lemuria* (1932) is still probably the best book on its subject.

Lewis Spence died on March 3, 1955, and was succeeded by the British scholar Edgerton Sykes. Trained as an engineer, Sykes was a foreign correspondent for the British press, invaluable because of his quadrilingual fluency. During his long life in the diplomatic service and as a fellow of the Royal Geographical Society, he published an estimated three million words in numerous books and magazine articles, many of them devoted to a rational understanding of the Atlantis controversy.

Sykes's erudite journals and encyclopedias of comparative myth went a long way in sustaining and expanding interest in Atlantis throughout the mid-twentieth century. He died in 1983, just before his ninetieth birthday, but a legacy in the form of his large library of Atlantis-related material is preserved in its own room at Edgar Cayce's Association for Research and Enlightenment in Virginia Beach, Virginia.

Contrary to mean-spirited characterizations by conservative archeologists, it says something for the credibility of Atlantis that many of the greatest thinkers in the history of Western civilization have been among its most prominent advocates.

Artist Rob Rath's conception of Atlantean ruins

21 | Atlantis in Antarctica

Forget about the North Atlantic
and the Aegean, Says Author Rand Flem-Ath

J. Douglas Kenyon

In the not-too-distant future, Atlantis-seeking archeologists may have to trade in their sun hats and scuba gear for snow goggles and parkas.

If a rapidly growing body of opinion proves correct, instead of the bottom of the ocean, the next great arena of exploration for the fabled lost continent could be the frozen wastelands at the bottom of the earth. And before scoffing too vigorously, proponents of probable locations for Atlantis—such as the North Atlantic Ocean and the Aegean Sea, as well as other candidates—would be well advised to give the new arguments for Atlantis in Antarctica a fair hearing.

Already enlisted in the ranks of those who take the notion very seriously are such luminaries as John Anthony West and Graham Hancock. Founded on a scientific theory developed by the late Dr. Charles Hapgood in close interaction with no less a personage than Albert Einstein, the idea appears robust enough to withstand the most virulent attacks expected from the guardians of scientific orthodoxy. At any rate, it will not take a wholesale melting of the ice cap to settle the question. A few properly directed satellite pictures and the appropriate seismic surveys could quickly determine whether or not an advanced civilization has ever flourished on the lands beneath the ice.

Leading the charge of those betting that such evidence will soon be forthcoming are Canadian researchers Rand and Rose Flem-Ath, the authors of *When the Sky Fell: In Search of Atlantis*, a book that contains the couple's painstaking synthesis of Hapgood's theory of Earth's crust displacement and their own groundbreaking discoveries. The result has already won many converts.

Graham Hancock believes the Flem-Aths have provided the first truly satisfactory answer to the question of precisely what happened to Plato's giant lost continent. Since devoting a chapter in his best-selling *Fingerprints of the Gods: The Evidence of Earth's Lost Civilization* to the work of the Flem-Aths, Hancock continues to discuss in media appearances the importance of their Antarctic theories. Flem-Ath himself talked about his ideas on the February 1996 NBC Special "The Mysterious Origins of Man."

To get to the bottom of all the excitement, if not the planet, *Atlantis Rising* interviewed Rand Flem-Ath at his home on Vancouver Island in British Columbia.

The author has not forgotten how his own interest in Atlantis began. In the summer of 1966, while waiting for an interview for a librarian's position in Victoria, British Columbia, he was working on a screenplay involving marooned aliens hibernating in ice on Earth for 10,000 years. Suddenly, on the radio, came pop singer Donovan's hit "Hail Atlantis." "Hey, that's a good idea," Flem-Ath thought. "I wanted ice, so I thought, 'Now where can I have ice and an island continent?' and I thought of Antarctica."

Later, researching the idea, he read everything he could find on Atlantis, including Plato's famous account in the *Timaeus* and the *Critias,* where Egyptian priests described Atlantis—its features, location, history and demise—to the Greek lawgiver Solon. At first the story didn't work for Flem-Ath, but that changed when he made a startling discovery—unmistakable similarities between two obscure but remarkable maps.

A 1665 map by the Jesuit scholar Athenasius Kircher, copied from much older sources, seemed to have placed Atlantis in the North Atlantic but,

Kircher map of Atlantis

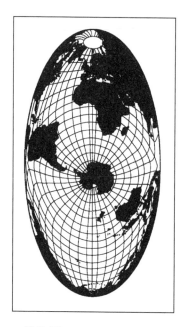

*U.S. Navy map projection
from the South Pole*

strangely, had put north at the bottom of the page, apparently forcing study upside down. The 1513 Piri Ri'is map, also copied from much more ancient sources, demonstrated that an ice age civilization had sufficient geographic knowledge to accurately map Antarctica's coast as it existed beneath an ice cap many millennia old (as pointed out by Charles Hapgood in *Maps of the Ancient Sea Kings: Evidence of Advanced Civilization in the Ice Age*). What seemed obvious to Flem-Ath was that both maps depicted the *same landmass*.

Suddenly Antarctic Atlantis "stopped being a science-fiction story," Flem-Ath says. The revelation had dawned that it might be "something that could have been real." Further study of Plato yielded even more clues. "I noticed that the description is *from* Atlantis," he recalls. Soon, armed with a U.S. Navy map of the world as seen from the South Pole, he discovered a new way of understanding Plato's story and a new way of looking at Kircher's map. Viewed from this southern perspective, all of the world's oceans appear as parts of one great ocean, or as what is described in Plato as "the real ocean," and the lands beyond as a "whole opposite continent." Sitting in the middle of that great ocean, at the very navel of the world, is Antarctica. Suddenly, it was possible to understand Kircher's map as drawn, with north at the top, Africa and Madagascar to the left, and the tip of South America on the right.

The term "Atlantic Ocean," Flem-Ath soon realized, had meant something quite different in Plato's time. To the ancients, it included *all* of the world's oceans. The idea becomes clearer when one remembers from Greek mythology that Atlas (a name closely related to Atlantis and Atlantic) held the entire world on his shoulders.

Rand Flem-Ath

The "whole opposite continent," which surrounded the "real ocean" in Plato's account, consisted of South America, North America, Africa, Europe, and Asia, all fused together in the Atlantean worldview as though they were one continuous landmass. And, in fact, these five continents were at that time (9600 B.C.E.) one landmass in the geographic sense.

Flem-Ath would render Plato's account to read: "Long ago the World Ocean was navigated beyond the Straits of Gibralter by sailors from an island larger than North Africa and the Middle East combined. After leaving Antarctica you would encounter the Antarctic archipelago (islands currently under ice) and from them you would reach the World Continent which encircles the World Ocean. The Mediterranean Sea is very small compared to the World Ocean and could even be called a bay. But beyond the Mediterranean Sea is a World Ocean which is encircled by one continuous landmass."

A common mistake in most readings of Plato, Flem-Ath believes, is the inappropriate attempt to interpret the ancient account in the light of modern concepts. Another example is the familiar reference to the Pillars of Hercules, beyond which Atlantis was said to reside. Though it is true that the term sometimes referred to the Straits of Gibralter, an equally valid interpretation is that it meant "the limits of the known world."

For Flem-Ath, the world as seen from Antarctica matched perfectly the ancient Egyptians' account of the world as seen from Atlantis. The ancient geography was, in fact, far more advanced than our own, which made sense if Atlantis was, as Plato argued, an advanced civilization.

Platonic theories notwithstanding, the most difficult challenge—explaining how Atlantis might have become Antarctica—remained. How could land currently covered with thousands of feet of ice have once supported *any* kind of human habitation, much less a great civilization on the scale described by Plato? For the Flem-Aths, the answer, it turned out, had already been worked out—thoroughly, convincingly, and published in the *Yale Scientific Journal* in the mid-1950s.

In his theory of Earth crust displacement, Professor Charles Hapgood had—citing vast climatalogical, paleontological, and anthropological evidence—argued that the entire outer shell of the earth periodically shifts over its inner layers, bringing about major climatic changes. The climatic zones (polar, temperate, and tropical) remain the same because the Sun still shines from the same angle in the sky, but as the outer shell shifts, it moves through those zones. From the perspective of earth's population, it seems as though the sky is falling. In reality, the Earth's crust is shifting to another location.

Some lands move toward the tropics. Others shift, with the same movement, toward the poles; yet others escape great changes in latitude. The consequences of such movements are, of course, catastrophes, as throughout the world massive earthquakes shake the land and enormous tidal waves batter the continental shelves. As old ice caps forsake the polar zones, they melt, raising sea levels higher and higher. Everywhere, and by whatever means possible, people seek higher ground to avoid an ocean in upheaval.

Charles Hapgood

The Flem-Aths corresponded with Hapgood from 1977 until his death in the early eighties, and though he differed with them about the location of Atlantis (his candidate was the Rocks of Saint Peter and Saint Paul), he praised their scientific efforts to buttress his theory. In the summer of 1995, Flem-Ath was allowed to read Hapgood's voluminous, 170-page correspondence with Albert Einstein, wherein he discovered a much more direct collaboration between the two men than had been previously supposed.

Upon first hearing of the research (in correspondence from Hapgood), Einstein responded: "very impressive . . . have the impression that your hypothesis is correct." Subsequently, Einstein raised numerous questions that Hapgood answered with such thoroughness that Einstein was eventually persuaded to write a glowing foreword for Hapgood's book *Earth's Shifting Crust: A Key to Some Basic Problems of Earth Science.* Earth crust displacement is not mutually exclusive with the now widely accepted theory of continental drift. According to Flem-Ath, "they share one assumption, that the outer crust is mobile in relation to the interior, but in plate tectonics the movement is extremely slow." Earth crust displacement suggests that over long periods of time, approximately 41,000 years, certain forces build toward a breaking point. Among the factors at work: a massive buildup of ice at the poles, which distorts the weight of the crust; the tilt of the earth's axis, which changes by more than three degrees every 41,000 years (not to be confused with the wobble that causes the precession of the equinoxes); and the proximity of the earth to the Sun, which also varies over thousands of years.

"One of the common mistakes," says Flem-Ath, "is to think of the continents and the oceans as being separate, but really the fact that there's water on certain parts of the plates is irrelevant. What we have in plate tectonics are a series of plates that are moving very gradually in relationship to each other. But what we have in Earth crust displacement is that all of the plates are considered as one single unit, as part of the outer shell of the earth, which changes place relative to the interior of the earth."

The theory, says Flem-Ath, offers elegant explanations for such phenomena as the rapid extinction of the mammoths in Siberia, the near universal presence of cataclysmic myths among primitive peoples, and many geographic and geological anomalies left unexplained by any other theory. Most of the evidence usually cited to support the idea of an ice age serves the theory of Earth crust displacement even better. Under the latter, some parts of the planet are always in an ice age; others are not. As lands change latitude, they move either into or out of an ice age. The same change that put western Antarctica in the ice box also quick-froze Siberia but thawed out much of North America.

Although many establishment geologists insist that the Antarctic ice cap is much older that the 11,600 years indicated by Plato, Flem-Ath points out that the core sampling on which most of the dating is based is taken from Greater Antarctica, which was indeed under ice, even during the time of Atlantis. The suggestion here is that a movement of about 30 degrees or about two thousand miles occurred within a relatively short span of time.

Artist Tom Miller's conjectural vision of Atlantis in Antarctica

Before such a movement, the Palmer peninsula of Lesser Antarctica (the part closest to South America and whose sovereignty is presently disputed by Chile, Argentina, and Great Britain) would have projected an area the size of western Europe beyond the Antarctic circle into temperate latitudes reaching as far as Mediterranean-like climes. In the meantime, Greater Antarctica would have remained under ice in the Antarctic circle.

"An area such as that described by Plato," says Flem-Ath, "would be the size of Pennsylvania, with a city comparable to modern-day London"—not a bad target for satellite photography. Concentric circles or other large geometric features should be easily discernible through the ice.

Flem-Ath believes that in most areas, Plato should be taken at his word, though he does suspect that there may have been some fabrications in the story. The war between the Atlanteans and the Greeks, for example, he believes may have been cooked up to please the local audience. In regard to the scale of Atlantean achievement, however, he takes Plato quite seriously and is very impressed. "The engineering feats described," says Flem-Ath, "would have required incredible skill, more so than even what we have today."

As for the notion that Plato's numbers should be scaled down by a factor of ten—a frequent argument used to support claims that Atlantis was really the Minoan civilization in the Aegean—he doesn't buy it. "A factor of ten error might be understandable when you are using Arabic numbers, with a difference between one hundred and one thousand of one decimal place, but in Egyptian numbering the difference between the two numbers is unmistakable." For him the argument is similar to the one for a North Atlantic location, in which a modern concept has been inappropriately superimposed upon an ancient one.

So far Flem-Ath's ideas have been largely ignored by the scientific establishment, but he believes that at least Hapgood's arguments may be getting close to some kind of acceptance. "Quite often new ideas take about fifty years to be absorbed," he says, "and we're getting close to the time."

If, in fact, satellite photography and seismic surveys produce the indications that Flem-Ath expects, what next? "The ice in the region that we are talking about is relatively shallow," he says, "less than half a kilometer, and once we've pinpointed the area, it should be relatively easy to sink a shaft and find something."

That "something" could be among the finest and most dramatic artifacts ever discovered—quick-frozen and stored undisturbed for almost 12,000 years. Is this a prospect hot enough to melt the hearts of even the most hardened skeptics? We shall see.

22 Blueprint from Atlantis

Do Alignments of Ancient Monuments
Have Something to Tell Us about the
History of Earth's Shifting Crust?

Rand Flem-Ath

In November 1993 I received a fax from John Anthony West that started me on a four-year quest. The article that slipped through the fax machine that day had been written by an Egyptian-born construction engineer by the name of Robert Bauval. Little did I suspect that Bauval would soon become known for his revolutionary theory that the pyramids of Egypt were a mirror image of the constellation of Orion. Bauval discusses this in his book, coauthored by Adrian Gilbert, *The Orion Mystery: Unlocking the Secrets of the Pyramids.* However, in the article I read that day, Robert Bauval had taken his idea even further. He revealed that not only the pyramids but also that most famous of all sculptures, the Sphinx, were oriented to the constellation of Orion as it appeared in 10,500 B.C.E. This he discusses in another book, co-written with Graham Hancock, entitled *The Message of the Sphinx: A Quest for the Hidden Legacy of Mankind.*

John followed up his fax with a telephone call; this was to be one of our earliest conversations. He had read the original manuscript of our book *When the Sky Fell: In Search of Atlantis* and had volunteered to write an afterword. Our theory that Antarctica could hold the remains of Atlantis was framed by the concept of a geological phenomenon known as Earth crust displacement, about which I had spent years corresponding with Charles Hapgood.

I had concluded, based on extensive research into the origins of agriculture and the late Pleistocene extinctions, that 9600 B.C.E. was the most probable date of the last displacement. After discussing details about the afterword for *When the Sky Fell,* John, in his usual direct manner, asked me: "If Bauval is right that the Sphinx points to a date of 10,500 B.C.E., how do you reconcile that date with your time period of 9600 B.C.E., for the last displacement of the earth's crust?"

John had put his finger on a very important point. If the Sphinx had been built before the crustal displacement, as Bauval's data indicated, then the monument's orientation would have been changed as the earth's crust shifted, resulting in a misalignment. But the fact remains that the Sphinx and, indeed, the whole Giza complex are precisely aligned with the earth's cardinal points. "Either Bauval's calculations of the astroarcheology are incorrect or your date of 9600 B.C.E. is wrong," John said. "How sure are you of that date? Could you be wrong by nine hundred years?"

"John," I replied, "a host of archeological and geological radiocarbon dates indicate unequivocally that the last catastrophe occurred in 9600 B.C.E. I'm sticking with that. Perhaps the ancient Egyptians were memorializing an earlier date that was tremendously significant to them, not necessarily the date that the Sphinx was carved."

In October 1996, Robert Bauval and I continued the friendly debate at a conference in Boulder, Colorado. I was convinced that the Sphinx was constructed immediately after 9600 B.C.E. and I explained why. Imagine, I began, that an asteroid or giant comet hit the United States today, utterly destroying the continent and throwing the whole culture back to the most primitive of living conditions.

Then imagine that a team of scientists, perhaps safely under the ocean in a submarine, survived the cataclysm and decided to commemorate their nation and leave a message for the future by constructing a monument aligned to the heavens. What date would they choose to mark the memory of the United States of America? Would it be 1996, the year that their world ended? I don't think so. I believe that they would orient their monument to 1776: the date that the nation was born. And in the same way, I think that although the Sphinx was created around 9600 B.C.E., it is oriented to 10,500 B.C.E. because that date was significant to their culture.

Now, it happens that inconsistencies and puzzles in science are like oxygen to my blood! My entire philosophy of science is predicated on the motto that anomalies are gateways to discovery. I usually conduct my research in a methodical and painstaking (some might say obsessive) manner. However, over the past twenty years of investigating the problem of Atlantis and the earth's shifting crust, I have discovered again and again that chance plays a critical role in discovery.

Between writing novels, my wife, Rose, works part time at the local university library, and her serendipitous approach to research ideally balances my own meticulous methods. I can't begin to count the number of times that she has brought home a book that turned out to be exactly what I needed. So when she presented me with *Archaeoastronomy in Pre-Columbian America,* I eagerly flipped it open.

Written in 1975 by Dr. Anthony F. Aveni, one of the leading astroarche-ologists in the world, the book dropped right into my lap a critical piece of the puzzle that I was trying to solve. It appears that almost all of the major megalithic monuments of Mesoamerica are oriented east of true north. Aveni wrote that the people of Mesoamerica did tend to lay out many of their cities oriented slightly east of true north. Fifty of the fifty-six sites examined align east of north.

However, I found Aveni's explanation for this alignment wanting. He believes that the Street of the Dead, the famous avenue at Teotihuacan (near Mexico City), is the key to the whole mystery of why the monuments are strangely misaligned. This street, which runs directly toward the Pyramid of the Moon, is misaligned fifteen and a half degrees east of north. Because it points within one degree to the Pleiades constellation (a set of stars important to Mesoamerican mythology), Aveni views this skewed alignment as a kind of template, a master plan, for the rest of the megaliths throughout Mesoamerica. While this is true for Teotihuacan's Street of the Dead, it is not true for the other sites that Aveni lists in his book. His argument that the other forty-nine sites are merely inadequate copies of the holy alignment of Teotihuacan rang hollow.

I had a different idea, a theory based on the science of geodesy, which is the study of the measurement of the shape and the size of the earth. In addi-tion to astronomical observatories, what if these Mesoamerican sites were part of a vast geographical survey? My study of ancient maps had convinced me that the Atlanteans had mapped the world. What if the orientations of the most ancient cities of Mexico were remnants of a lost science, the science of geography? What if the alignment of the ancient cities was a stone stencil, a precise blueprint of a prediluvian Earth?

Teotihuacan lies upon the longitude of 98:53 west. If we subtract the 15:28 degrees that it is misaligned, we get a location of 83:25 west, less than half a degree off Charles Hapgood's location of the North Pole prior to 9600 B.C.E. In other words, the Street of the Dead was fifteen and a half degrees west of the longitude that Hapgood had calibrated for the old pole.

When I made this discovery, I was naturally very excited. Could it be that the ancient monuments of Mexico were oriented to the pole before the last Earth crust displacement? The implications were profound. Such an orienta-tion would point to the existence of a civilization that must have held scien-tific knowledge of the earth's geography. They also must have possessed sophisticated surveying methods that they put to use in America before the earth's crust shifted.

I soon discovered that several important Mesoamerican sites (Tula, Tenayucan, Copan, and Xochicalco, for instance) matched my geodetic theory. Each of their misalignments, when subtracted from their current longitude, yielded the longitude of the North Pole before the last Earth crust displacement (83 degree west). What if, I wondered, there were other sites in the Old World that were orientated to the old pole?

I began to research sites in Iraq, cradle of the most ancient civilizations. Unlike in Mesoamerica, these sites had not been studied in relation to their misalignment to the earth's cardinal points. I had to piece together the evidence from site to site, from author to author. But the tedious task was worth the startling result obtained. I soon discovered that many of the oldest sites in the Middle East are west of today's North Pole. Like the ancient sites of Mesoamerica, they were oriented to the old pole.

In the ancient city of Ur, its ziggurat (a stepped pyramid symbolizing a sacred mountain) and its shrine to the Moon god, Nanna, are oriented west of north (toward the old pole in the Hudson Bay).

Without control of the holy city of Nippur, no ruler could rightfully claim to be the king of Sumeria. The remains of the city lie south of Baghdad, where some of the most famous tablets in archeology were unearthed at the turn of the twentieth century. The tablets disclosed the Sumerian belief in the existence of a long-lost island paradise called Dilmun. The myth of Dilmun, which we show in *When the Sky Fell*, is remarkably similar to the mythology of the Haida people of British Columbia, and relates how the island paradise was destroyed by the god Enlil in a Great Flood. Enlil's incredible power is honored at Nippur with a temple and a ziggurat that is skewed west of north. The ziggurat and White Temple of the Sumerian city of Uruk also point to Hudson Bay rather than true north.

The more I looked, the more ancient sites I found in the Middle East that pointed to the North Pole before the last Earth crust displacement. Perhaps the most poignant is Jerusalem's Wailing Wall, the only remains of Herod's Temple, built upon the site of Solomon's Temple.

I now knew that I was looking at a unique geodesic phenomenon that demanded exploration. My next step was to calculate the former latitudes of the key megalithic and sacred sites of the world. If the latitudes were located at significant numbers, I could be sure that I was really on to something.

The first site I measured was, of course, the eternally compelling Great Pyramid at Giza. I calculated its coordinates against 60 degrees N 83 degrees W (Hudson Bay pole). Giza had been 4,524 nautical miles from the Hudson Bay pole, which meant its latitude was at 15 degrees north prior to 9600 B.C.E.

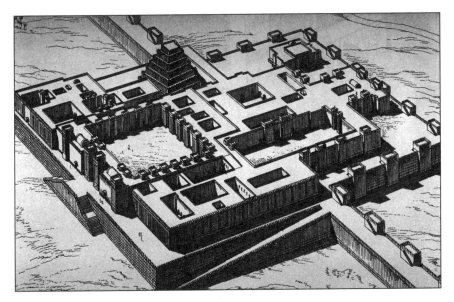

Sumerian ziggurat

I found it odd that Giza, which today lies at 30 degrees north (one third of the distance from the equator to the pole), should have been so neatly at 15 degrees north (one sixth the distance) before the last Earth crust displacement. So I decided to study Lhasa, the religious center of Tibet, because I knew that this city, like Giza, lies at 30 degrees north today.

Lhasa's coordinates are 29:41N 91:10E, which calculated at 5,427 nautical miles from the Hudson Bay pole. The distance from the equator to the pole is 5,400 nautical miles (90 degrees times 60 seconds = 5,400), so Lhasa had rested just twenty-seven nautical miles (less than half a degree) off the equator during the reign of Atlantis. This was getting spooky. The Earth crust displacement had shoved Giza from 15 degrees to 30 degrees while moving Lhasa from 0 degree to 30 degrees. Was this coincidence?

The coincidence started to become extreme when I compared the location of Giza and Lhasa (and a host of other ancient sites) with the position of the crust over three Earth crust displacements. I was amazed to discover that latitudes like 0 degree, 12 degrees, 15 degrees, 30 degrees, and 45 degrees came up again and again. Each of these numbers divides the earth's geography by whole numbers.

This seemed way beyond chance, so I christened them "sacred latitudes." Most of these sites will be familiar to anyone who takes an interest in archeology or the sacred sites of the world's major religions. All of these places are within thirty nautical miles (a day's walk) from sacred latitudes, and are thus more accurately aligned geodesically than Aveni's astronomical calculations.

The careful reader will note that several of these sites show up in more than one table. They are actually situated at the crossing points of two (even three) sacred latitudes. For example, Giza lies at the intersection of 15 degrees (Hudson Bay pole) and 45 degrees north (Greenland Sea pole) and today is at 30 degrees north. Lhasa, which today is near 30 degrees north, was at the equator during the Hudson Bay pole and only thirty-two nautical miles from 30 degrees north during the Greenland Sea pole.

So what was going here?

I believe that sometime before the devastating Earth crust displacement, scientists in Atlantis recognized that the increasing earthquakes and rising ocean level that they were experiencing were a warning of a coming geological catastrophe. Trying to preserve their civilization from this unavoidable disaster, they became obsessed with discovering exactly what had overtaken the globe in the remote past.

Teams of geologists fanned across the planet with a mission to gauge the former positions of the earth's crust. If they could determine exactly how far the crust had shifted in the past, they might have some idea of what they could expect to face in the future. In the process of their investigations, they left geodesic markers at the points they considered critical to their calculations.

After the earth crust displacement that destroyed Atlantis, the old calibrations were rediscovered by survivors who knew nothing of that forgotten and desperate geographic survey. They naturally believed that these marvelous geodesic markers, from those who had gone before, were messages from the gods. The sites became sacred and cities were built around them (it's no accident that Teotihuacan is an Aztec term meaning "Place of the Gods"), and their very practical purpose was lost.

Further generations continued to worship at these huge shrines, but eventually the winds of time began to erode the original structures. New altars were built on top of the remnants of the artifacts left by the surveyors from Atlantis. But during each reconstruction, whispers from the past compelled the new architects to preserve the original orientations that pointed to the Hudson Bay pole at the time when Atlantis thrived.

The secrets buried beneath the slowly crumbling cities remained hidden for thousands of years. Eventually, some intrepid souls in Egypt, Mesopotamia, India, China, and America had the courage to begin excavations. The story of the remarkable discoveries uncovered by those who dared to dig under holy sites is only now emerging. The secret mission of the Knights

Templar in Jerusalem and the sophisticated devices that Moses took from Egypt are but two of these fascinating accounts.

I believe we can explain the enigmatic location of the ancient megaliths in a way that finally makes sense of their puzzling misalignments. These sacred sites, which we sense contain clues to our true history, continue to draw visitors who marvel over their awesome construction feats and wonder at the intelligence and vision of our anonymous ancestors. But my explanation covers only the tip of a very deep iceberg. There are many more sites that can be discovered using simple calculations derived from latitude changes after crustal displacements, not the least of which are sites on Atlantis itself, the island continent of Antarctica.

I never thought to find another adventure to compare with my eighteen-year search for Atlantis. But the unique placement of the earth's most sacred sites has emerged as a mystery that compels me with the same kind of fascination as that journey did.

23 Japan's Underwater Ruins

Have Remains of Ancient Lemuria Been Found?

Frank Joseph

In March 1995, a sport diver unintentionally strayed beyond the standard safety perimeter near the south shore of Okinawa. A battleground for the last land campaign of World War II, the island was about to become the scene of another kind of drama. As the diver glided through unvisited depths some forty feet beneath the clear blue Pacific, he was suddenly confronted by what appeared to be a great stone building heavily encrusted with coral.

Approaching it, he could see that the colossal structure was black and gaunt, a sunken arrangement of monolithic blocks, their original configuration obscured by the organic accretion of time. After encircling the anonymous monument several times and taking several photographs of it, he rose to the surface, reoriented himself, and kicked for shore. The next day, photographs of his find appeared in Japan's largest newspapers.

The structure sparked instant controversy and attracted crowds of diving archeologists, newsmedia people, and curious nonprofessionals, none of whom was able to ascertain its identity. They could not even agree on whether or not it was man-made, let alone ancient or modern. Was it the remnant of some forgotten military coastal

Yonaguni formations
(Photographs courtesy of Fuji Television)

172

defense from the war? Or could it possibly date back to something entirely different and profoundly older?

Already there were whispers of the lost culture of Mu, preserved in legend as "the Motherland of Civilization," which perished in the sea long before the beginning of recorded time. But Okinawa's drowned enigma was hermetically locked within too thick an encrustation. The structure looked anciently man-made.

Nature, however, sometimes made her own forms appear artificial. The popular and scientific debate concerning its origins went back and forth. Then, in late summer of the following year, another diver in Okinawan, waters was shocked to see a massive arch, or gateway, of huge stone blocks, beautifully fitted together in the manner of prehistoric masonry found among the Incan cities on the other side of the Pacific Ocean, in the Andes Mountains of South America.

This time there was no doubt. Thanks to swift currents in the area, coral had been unable to gain any foothold on the structure, leaving it unobscured in the hundred-foot visibility of the crystal-clear waters. It was certainly man-made and very old. It seemed nothing short of miraculous, an unbelievable vision standing in apparently unruined condition on the ocean floor.

But its discovery was only the first of that summer's undersea revelations. Fired by the possibility of more sunken structures in the area, teams of expert divers fanned out from the south coast of Okinawa using standard grid-search patterns. Their professional efforts were soon rewarded. Before the onset of autumn, they found five subsurface archeological sites near three offshore islands.

The locations varied from depths of one hundred to twenty feet, but are all stylistically linked, despite the great variety of their architectural details. They comprise paved streets and crossroads, huge altarlike formations, grand staircases leading to broad plazas, and processional ways surmounted by pairs of towering features resembling pylons.

The sunken buildings apparently cover the ocean bottom (although not continuously) from the small island of Yonaguni in the southwest to Okinawa and its neighboring islands—Kerama and Aguni—311 miles away.

If ongoing exploration reveals more structures linking Yonaguni with Okinawa, the individual sites may be separate components of a huge city lying at the bottom of the Pacific.

The single largest structure so far discovered lies near the eastern shore of Yonaguni at one hundred feet down. It is approximately 240 feet long, 90 feet across, and 45 feet high. All the monuments appear to have been built from granitic sandstone, although no internal passages or chambers have been found. To a degree, the underwater structures resemble ancient buildings on Okinawa itself, such as Nakagusuku Castle.

More of a ceremonial edifice than a military installation, Nakagusuku dates back to the early centuries of the first millennium B.C.E., although its identity as a religious habitation site is older still. Its builders and the culture it originally expressed are unknown, although the precinct is still regarded with superstitious awe by local Okinawans. Other parallels with Okinawa's oldest sacred buildings are found near Noro, where burial vaults designed in the same rectilinear style are still venerated as repositories for the islanders' ancestral dead. Very remarkably, the Okinawan term for these vaults is *moai*, the same word Polynesians of Easter Island, more than six thousand miles away, used to describe the famous large-headed, long-eared statues dedicated to their ancestors!

Possible connections far across the Pacific may be more than philological. Some of the sunken features bear even closer comparison to the *heiau* found in the distant Hawaiian Islands. Heiau are linear temples of long stone ramparts leading to great staircases surmounted by broad plazas, where wooden shrines and carved idols were placed. Many heiau still exist and continue to be venerated by native Hawaiians. In terms of construction, the Okinawan examples comprise enormous single blocks; the heiau are made up many more, smaller stones.

They were first built, according to Hawaiian tradition, by the Menehune, a red-haired race of master masons who occupied the islands long before the arrival of the Polynesians. The original inhabitants left, unwilling to intermarry with the newcomers.

Okinawa's drowned structures find possible counterparts at the eastern limits of the Pacific Ocean, along Peruvian coasts. The most striking similarities occur at ancient Pachacamac, a sprawling religious city a few miles south of the modern capital of Lima. Although functioning into Incan times (as late as the sixteenth century), it predated the Incas by at least 1,500 years and was the seat of South America's foremost oracle. Pilgrims visited Pachacamac from all over the Tiawantisuyu (the Incan empire) until it was sacked and desecrated by the Spaniards under Francisco Pizarro's high-spirited brother, Hernando, with twenty-two heavily armed conquistadors. Enough of the sun-dried, mud-brick city remains, with its sweeping staircases and broad plazas, to suggest parallels with the sunken buildings around Okinawa.

Two other pre-Incan sites in the north, just outside Trujillo, likewise have some leading elements in common with the overseas, undersea structures. The so-called Temple of the Sun is a terraced pyramid built two thousand years ago by a people known as the Moche. More than 100 feet high and 684 feet long, the irregularly stepped platform of unfired adobe bricks was formerly the colossal centerpiece of a city sheltering 30,000 inhabitants. Its resemblance to the structure found at Yonaguni is remarkable.

On the other side of the Pacific, the first emperor of Japan was remembered as Jimmu, whose immediate descendant was Kamu, among the "legendary" founders of Japanese society. Another ancestral emperor was Temmu, who was said to have committed to memory the *Kojiki* ("Records of Ancient Matters") and the *Nihongi* ("Chronicles of Japan"). In northern Japan runs a river deemed sacred because it carried the first semi-divine beings into the country; it is called the Mu River. In Japanese, the word *mu* means "that which does not exist or no longer exists," just as it does in Korean. Does it harken back to a land that "no longer exists"?

In ancient Rome, the Lemuria was a ritual conducted by the head of each household to appease the spirits of the deceased who returned annually. Lemuria was also the Roman name for a huge island kingdom that the Romans believed once lay in "the Far Eastern Sea," sometimes imagined to have been the Indian Ocean. It vanished to become "the abode of troubled souls."

The Lemurian ceremony was instituted by Romulus in expiation for the murder of Remus. Here, too, we encounter Mu in relation to the founding of a civilization, as the brothers were accepted as the progenitors of Rome. In Latin, their names are pronounced with the accent on the second syllable: RoMUlus and ReMUS.

In the early nineteenth century, when English biologists were in the process of mammal classification, they applied the ancient term *lemur* to describe primitive tree primates first found in Madagascar, because the creatures possessed large, glaring eyes, just like the ghostly lemures described in Roman myth. When lemurs were discovered outside Africa, in such widely separated locations as southern India and Malaya, scientists theorized that a continent in the Indian Ocean may have connected all these lands before it sank beneath the waves. Oceanographers have since established that no such continent ever existed.

But collectors of oral traditions throughout the island peoples of the Pacific were perplexed by recurring themes of a vanished motherland from which ancestral culture bearers arrived to replant society's seeds. On Kaua'i, the Hawaiians told of the Mu (also known as the Menehune mentioned earlier) who arrived in the dim past from a "floating island."

The most important ancestral chant known to the Hawaiians was the "Kumulipo," which recounts a terrific flood that destroyed the world long ago. Its concluding lines evoke some natural catastrophe in the deep past: "Born the roaring, advancing and receding of waves, the rumbling sound, the earthquake. The sea rages, rises over the beach, rises to the inhabited places, rises gradually up over the land. Ended is the line of the first chief of the dim past dwelling in cold uplands. Dead is the current sweeping in from the navel of the Earth. That was a warrior wave. Many who came vanished, lost in the passing night." The survivor who escaped the "warrior wave" was Kuamu.

Despite an abundance of folk traditions spanning the Pacific, all describing a sunken homeland, the first accurate, sonar-generated maps of the ocean bottom revealed nothing resembling a lost continent. But archeological enigmas supporting the myths still exist at such remote locations as tiny Malden Island, where a road of paved stones leads directly into and under the sea. The uninhabited island is also home to forty platform pyramids.

A provocative architectural theme, linking South America to Japan through Polynesia and suggesting a lost intermediary culture, is the sacred gate. The aesthetic focus of Tiahuanaco, a great ceremonial city high in Bolivia's Andes near Lake Titicaca, is two ritual gates. One is above the sunken court at the entrance and dramatically frames the twelve-foot-tall statue of a god or man; the other, at the far end of the complex, is the famous Gateway of the Sun, oriented to various solar phenomena.

Out across the Pacific in the Polynesian island of Tonga stands the Haamonga-a-Maui, "the Burden of Maui," a fifteen-foot-high stone gate weighing 109 tons and aligned with sunrise of the summer solstice. Japan is covered by many thousands of such gates, most of them wooden but all used to define a sacred space. Known as torii, the same word appears in ancient Indo-European languages and survives in the German word for gate: "Tor." An outstanding feature of the sunken structures in the vicinity of Okinawa is an unconnected gate of massive stonework. The Romans, who celebrated a Lemuria festival every May, ornamented their empire with free-standing ceremonial gates.

These intriguing parallels, combined with a wealth of archeological evidence and descriptive native traditions, convinced investigators that some powerful, centrally located "X-culture" indeed existed in the Pacific, from which civilizing influences spread in both directions. Their conclusion seemed borne out with recent discoveries among the Ryukyu Islands, where architectural features of the sunken structures bear tell-tale affinities to pre-Incan structures in Peru and ancestral burial vaults on Okinawa. But the sunken buildings provoke more questions than they answer. How old are they? Why are they under water? Who built them? For what purposes?

The evidence that has been collected thus far suggests that the site did not succumb to a sudden geologic catastrophe. Aside from one or two monuments leaning at irregular angles, none of them displays any structural damage, no cracks or fallen stones. Instead they appear in unruined, virtually pristine condition. They were either overwhelmed by rising sea levels or sank with a slowly collapsing landmass, or some combination of both.

Most researchers opt for the last scenario, as oceanographers tell us that sea levels rose from one hundred feet 1.7 million years ago. Even so, the Japanese sites must be very old. They are constantly being swept clean by strong currents, so radiocarbon-dating material is not available.

The purposes for which they were made appear less difficult to understand, because their strongest resemblance to Hawaiian heiau implies that they were mostly ceremonial in nature. Their expansive staircases lead up to presently barren platforms, where wooden shrines and carved idols were probably set up for religious dramas.

Just who their worshippers and builders were suggests a word most professional American archeologists are unable to pronounce. But in view of the numerous accounts from hundreds of cultures around the Pacific of a flood that destroyed some former civilization, if Okinawa's sunken city is not the lost Lemuria, then what is it?

24 West, Schoch, and Hancock Dive into Lemurian Waters

J. Douglas Kenyon

The issue of underwater ruins in the Pacific remains controversial, even within the alternative science community. Atlantis Rising has not taken a stance one way or the other on the issue, desiring instead to present both sides of the argument in a fair and even-handed manner. I will say, however, that those individuals who believe that these underwater ruins are man-made are supported by the argument presented by Frank Joseph in the foregoing chapter, while those who question this supposition may find themselves agreeing with the positions of Robert M. Schoch, Ph.D., et al., in the following essay.

—EDITOR

In September 1997, the maverick Egyptologist John Anthony West, accompanied by the geologist Robert M. Schoch, Ph.D., and the writer Graham Hancock, visited the island of Yonaguni in Japan, where a mysterious 160-foot pyramidal platform had been found under the waters of the ocean at a depth of eighty feet. In several dives, the three investigated part of what could be one of the most significant discoveries of the century. Subsequent to the trip, West shared with *Atlantis Rising* his opinion regarding the site's archeological authenticity.

John Anthony West
(PHOTOGRAPH BY TOM MILLER)

He and Schoch, it was pointed out, had made the trip predisposed to believe that here could be the great breakthrough most of us have been waiting for—the discovery of undeniable proof of the existence of prediluvian civilization (the area has been under water for at least 11,500 years). The photos they had been shown certainly appeared unambiguous. And, after all, it was their research that had, a few years earlier, shaken the academic establishment by demonstrating that it was water and not windblown sand that had weathered the Great Sphinx of Egypt, thus establishing that it was thousands of years older than previously supposed.

After examining the Yonaguni site, however, both West and Schoch are of the opinion that it is probably natural in origin, though perhaps worked over by human hands in some way—maybe to create a terra-form. Nevertheless, the two continue to believe that even if the Yunaguni site is of strictly natural origin, the spot remains one

Dr. Robert M. Schoch at Yonaguni

of the most—if not *the* most—unusual to be found anywhere. The one thing that West, Schoch, and Hancock agree on unanimously is the need for much more research and a complete examination of the site, as they all feel it is far too early to draw any final conclusions.

In response to West's comments, *Atlantis Rising* contributor Frank Joseph pointed out that West, Schoch, and Hancock visited only one of eight locations that are spread over a 311-mile area, and added that the onus is now on Schoch to demonstrate just how geomorphologic forces could have created the formations, which, if indeed natural, are unique in the world.

After attending a conference of avant-garde researchers held in England by *Quest Magazine* (also attended by West), Joseph reports that while there is still much controversy and complexity surrounding the issue, the consensus at the conference, he felt, was that the formations were of man-made origin. Joseph also added that laboratory analysis by Japanese researchers of some of the stone from the site is consistent with artificial tooling.

25 India 30,000 B.C.E.

Do the Roots of Indian Culture Lie Drowned beneath the Indian Ocean?

David Lewis

The world is full of mysteries. And given its mystical traditions, no place in the world remains more mysterious than India, a country and culture said to be rooted in primordial timelessness.

Westerners have frequently tried to fathom the mysteries of Mother India. Western scholars, relative newcomers on the world stage, have consistently tried to date Indian civilization according to Western time lines, assuming an intellectual superiority that routinely dismisses the accumulated wisdom of millennia, including cultural traditions that speak of humanity's origin, lost continents, and advanced prehistoric civilizations.

But that wasn't always the case. In the mid- to late nineteenth century, when scientific ideas about human origins had only begun to take shape in Europe, many early geologists and archeologists accepted the idea of the biblical flood and lost continents for which they found much hard evidence, even a landmass in the Indian Ocean—the great Southern Continent of the British naturalist Alfred Russell Wallace. Today, mainstream science still theorizes that landmasses such as Gondwanaland and Pangaea must have existed, although they are relegated to extremely ancient epochs: 180 to 200 million years ago.

Temple deity, Sri Lanka

180

Could the Valles Marineris on Mars be the lightning scar of the mythical god of war?

Venus as seen by the Hubble Space Telescope (NASA) is thought to have been a major player in a series of global catastrophes recorded all over the world.

The Crab Nebula as seen from the Hubble Space Telescope. The lower of the two large stars seen in the box is the Crab Pulsar, which emits optical, as well as electro-magnetic, pulses.

Above, two views of the Great
Sphinx of Egypt.

Bottom right, eroded stone in
the Sphinx enclosure provides
clear evidence of the kind of
water weathering that could
result only from long-term
precipitation. The inescapable
inference is that the Sphinx is
at least 2,500 years older than
previously believed by
orthodox Egyptologists.

(Photographs by J. Douglas Kenyon)

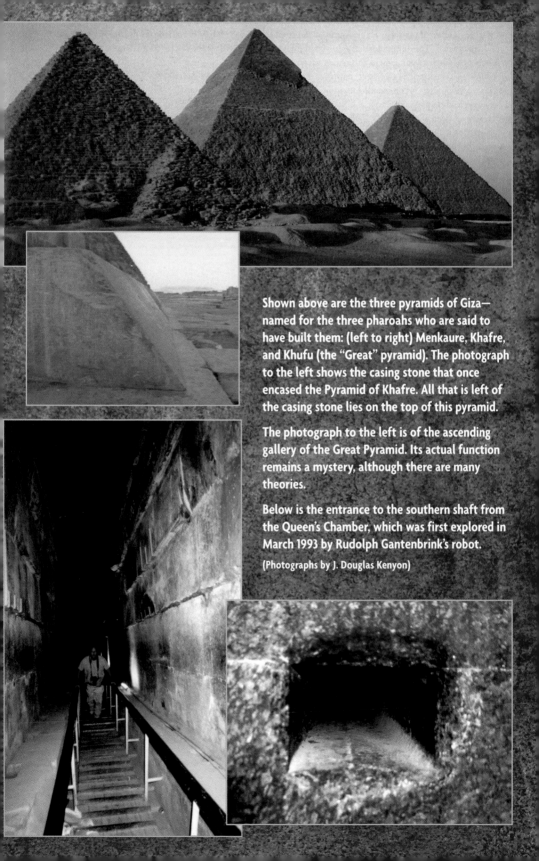

Shown above are the three pyramids of Giza—named for the three pharoahs who are said to have built them: (left to right) Menkaure, Khafre, and Khufu (the "Great" pyramid). The photograph to the left shows the casing stone that once encased the Pyramid of Khafre. All that is left of the casing stone lies on the top of this pyramid.

The photograph to the left is of the ascending gallery of the Great Pyramid. Its actual function remains a mystery, although there are many theories.

Below is the entrance to the southern shaft from the Queen's Chamber, which was first explored in March 1993 by Rudolph Gantenbrink's robot.

(Photographs by J. Douglas Kenyon)

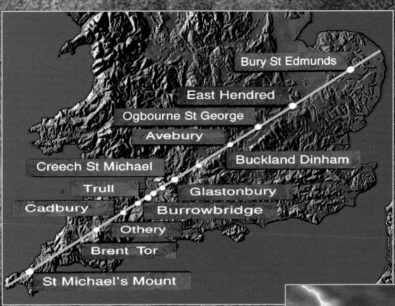

Depicted above is the main axis of Britain's archaic
system of ley lines. Leys are ancient and very precise
alignments of megalithic structures along perfectly
straight lines. They often are many miles in length
and their course, in many cases, remains visible today.
This one, following the path of the sun at summer
solstice from Land's End in the west of England to
Bury St. Edmunds in the east, is hundreds of miles
long and connects dozens of ancient shrines along
the longest continuous stretch of terrain in Britain.
At right is a conjecture of how the gigantic pieces
of Stonehenge—many weighing over 40 tons—might
have been moved into place using a lost science
of levitation. Like many ancient temples, Stonehenge
is thought to have served as, among other things,
an observatory—precisely aligning the movements
in the sky above to the earth below.

Above is Tom Miller's illustration of Plato and Atlantis as suggested by Plato's writings.

Above is the island of Thera. Some researchers believe this may have been the original island of Atlantis, although its dates don't correspond to the dates that Plato attributed to Atlantis.

Drawn in 1513 by Piri Ri'is, a celebrated Turkish admiral, the map above is believed to have been based on much older maps, perhaps from the lost library of Alexandria. It accurately reveals the actual coastline of Antarctica, which has been buried under thousands of feet of ice for thousands of years.

The illustration at right is Tom Miller's depiction of what the destruction of Atlantis might have looked like.

The highly complex relief carving on the tomb of Pacal in Palenque, Mexico, is believed by some to depict an ancient astronaut and by others to depict a soul in transition to the afterlife.

The Street of the Dead (below) in Teotihuacan, Mexico. Some who argue that Earth's poles shifted in remote antiquity say this site was once oriented to the old North Pole before a cataclysmic displacement of Earth's crust.

The ancient Izapa stone shown here is said to foretell what can be expected from Earth's approach to the galactic center in the next few years.

(Photograph by John Major Jenkins)

The Temple of Luxor seen at night. R. A. Schwaller de Lubicz demonstrated that the Golden Section, conventionally credited to the Greeks, was used in the construction of this temple, with great sophistication and centuries earlier.

The obelisk at Luxor. This massive stone weighs more than four hundred tons. Scientists have long argued over how it was possible to quarry and move such a massive object.

MOTHER OF ALL MOTHERLANDS

Lemuria, the term for a lost continent in the Pacific or Indian Ocean, came to life in the 1860s when geologists found a striking similarity between fossils and sedimentary strata in India, South Africa, Australia, and South America. These geologists surmised that a great continent or at least a land bridge or series of islands must have existed in the Indian Ocean, and this landmass was named Lemuria by the English biologist Philip L. Scalter after the lemurs of Madagascar.

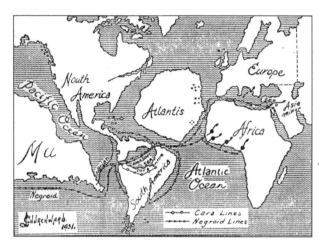

James Churchward's map of Mu

Madame Helene Blavatsky, founder of the Theosophical Society, wrote extensively in the late nineteenth century of Lemuria and, in the 1920s, Colonel James Churchward claimed to have discovered certain ancient tablets in India describing long-lost Mu (Lemuria), a golden civilization said to have existed in the Pacific. Churchward devoted his life and study to bringing the lost Lemurian culture to life in a series of books.

Continental drift theory, which proposes the extremely slow drifting of continents, and then the concept of plate tectonics, did away with Lemuria in the minds of many, while satisfying one of the essential tenets of modern scientific thinking about origins. This essential tenet is called uniformitarianism, which holds that all natural developments on Earth come about extremely slowly, incrementally, and in a more or less uniform fashion. Great floods, global cataclysms, and the submergence of continents in recent prehistory smack of the biblical, and so the anti-biblical Darwinists of bygone days imposed the doctrine of uniformitarianism upon the early geologists and archeologists. The idea that grand-scale cataclysms had anything to do with prehistory, once considered heretical, only recently came into fashion on the heels of evidence that a large-impact asteroid struck the Yucatán area, causing the extinction of the dinosaurs many millions of years ago.

But consider the ancient south Asian traditions that mimic the findings of early geologists, those that say an inhabited continent once existed in what is now the Indian Ocean. This is a belief that thrives, to this day, among peoples of southern India, in Sri Lanka, and in the islands of the Andaman Sea off Malaysia.

One tradition emerges from the writings of ancient Ceylon that refers to a lost civilization in the area now occupied by the Indian Ocean and a landmass that connected the Indian subcontinent with the island of Sri Lanka—the kind of tradition dismissed as fable by the modern-day intelligentsia.

"In a former age," an ancient Ceylonese text states, "the citadel of Rawana (Lord of Lanka), 25 palaces and 400,000 streets were swallowed by the sea." The submerged landmass, according to one ancient account, rested between Tuticorin on the southwest Indian coast and Manaar in Ceylon, not a landmass of the size once envisioned by the early geologists, but—if it actually existed—a submerged portion of the Indian subcontinent just the same.

Another cultural tradition, cited in Allan and Delair's *Cataclysm! Compelling Evidence of a Cosmic Catastrophe in 9500 B.C.E.,* that of the Selungs of the Mergui archipelago off southern Burma, also speaks of a sunken landmass: "Formerly [the] country was of continental dimensions, but the daughter of an evil spirit threw many rocks into the sea . . . the waters rose and swallowed up the land . . . . Everything alive perished, except what was able to save itself on one island that remained above the waters."

One of the Tamil epics of southern India, the *Silappadhikaram,* frequently mentions a vast tract of land called Kumari Nadu, otherwise known as Kumari Kandam (and later identified as Lemuria by European scholars), stretching far beyond India's present-day coasts into the Indian Ocean. Ancient south Indian commentators wrote in detail of a prehistoric Tamil Sangham, a spiritual academy, situated in that ancient land. They also wrote of the submersion of two rivers, the Kumari and the Pahroli, in the middle of the continent, and of a country dotted with mountains, animals, and vegetation.

The *Silappadhikaram* tells of a country with forty-nine provinces, and mountain ranges that yielded precious gems (Sri Lanka and other parts of India are sources of precious gems to this day). This Pandyan kingdom, according to tradition, reigned from 30,000 B.C.E. to 16,500 B.C.E. At least one lineage of modern-day south Indian mystics claims direct descent from those extraordinarily ancient times, when their spiritual progenitors achieved extremely long lives through yogic mastery, walking as virtual gods. This was a phenomenon said to have been duplicated successively to the present, carried on in remote regions of the Himalayas.

In addition, India's epic poem the *Mahabarata,* dated by some nonanglicized Indian scholars to the fifth millennium before Christ, contains references that place its hero, Rama, gazing from India's present-day west coast into a vast landmass now occupied by the Indian Ocean. These Indian epics also allude to advanced technology in the form of *vimana,* aircraft that were used to transport the society's elite and to wage war. Less celebrated ancient Indian writings describe these aircraft in detail and at great length, puzzling both scholars and historians. What's more, the great Indian epics vividly describe militaristic devastation that can be equated only to nuclear war.

The Sanskrit scholar and the renowned physicist J. Robert Oppenheimer, father of the hydrogen bomb, apparently interpreted the ancient epic as having described a prehistoric nuclear conflagration. After the first atomic test in Alamagordo, New Mexico, Oppenheimer chillingly quoted the *Mahabharata,* saying, "I have become death, the destroyer of worlds." In a later interview, when asked if the Alamagordo test was the first time an atomic bomb had been detonated, Oppenheimer replied that it was the first time *in modern history.*

Oppenheimer notwithstanding, are tales of flying machines, lost continents, and prehistoric nuclear war merely mythical or do these ancient references provide us with a historical record, long forgotten and then dismissed by modern science, with its modern prejudices, as fantasy?

THE KNOWLEDGE FILTER

To begin to answer that question, we must first look at the history of scholarship as it pertains to India.

Since the nineteenth century, Western scholars have routinely dismissed the historical significance of the cultural traditions of ancient peoples, those of southern Asia included. With a decidedly ethnocentric bias—the intellectual stepchild of Western colonialism—the experts reinterpreted Eastern history, casting whole systems of ancient philosophy and science, in the experts' minds, into the historical dustbin. This historical dustbin is the repository of all things conflicting with European models, such as biblical Christianity and scientific materialism. Here we find the very inception of the "knowledge filter," now well known to students of alternative archeology, geology, and other disciplines involved with the search for lost origins.

India, with her treatment by the West and her acquiescence to that

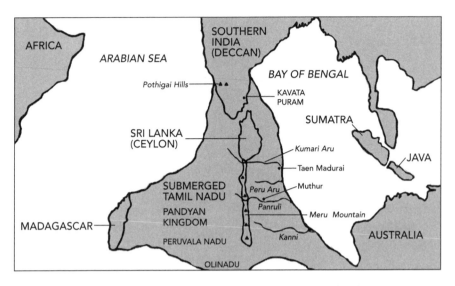

Speculative map showing submerged Tamil Nadu landmass

treatment, typifies the way in which Western intellectualism conquered the world. Call it the "West is best" model: a strict adherence to European doctrines that deny traditions and attempt to offer decidedly more ancient theories regarding the origins of civilization than those of the Western scholars. On top of this, add a scientific materialism that denies all nonmaterial theories regarding the origins of man, life, and reality.

Having found, for example, that root words of India's ancient Sanskrit turned up almost universally in the world's major languages, Western scholars devised an ethnocentric scheme to explain the phenomenon—one that India's first prime minister, Jawaharlal Nehru, and many other modern Indian intellectuals came to accept. A previous European people must have once existed, the scholars told us, an Indo-European race upon which the world, and India, drew for its linguistic roots and genetic stock.

The scholars also expropriated the now mythic Aryans of ancient India to flesh out this scenario. This mythic race, we were told, derived from Europe and then invaded the Indus Valley, in the north of India—making Sanskrit and Vedic culture a product, rather than a progenitor, of Western civilization—and rather young at that.

But the Aryan invasion theory has since fallen into disrepute, after being downgraded to a *migration* theory. James Schaffer, of Case Western University, a noted archeologist specializing in ancient India, had this to say on the matter: "The archeological record and ancient oral and literate traditions of south

Asia are now converging," Schaffer recently wrote. "A few scholars have proposed that there is nothing in the 'literature' firmly placing the Indo-Aryans outside of south Asia, and now the archeological record is confirming this. . . . We reject most strongly the simplistic historical interpretations, which date back to the eighteenth century [the time of the British invasion of India]. . . . These still-prevailing interpretations are significantly diminished by European ethnocentrism, colonialism, racism, and anti-Semitism."

None of this, of course, speaks well of Western scholarship.

Southern India, a land whose cultural roots are said by some to stretch into an even more profound antiquity than that of the north, suffered a similar fate. Speakers of a proto-Dravidian language, the forerunner of a family of languages spoken in the south—and some say of Sanskrit itself—entered India from the northwest, we were told. Both theories were necessitated by Western beliefs, at first about the supremacy of the Garden of Eden theory of origins and then, with the arrival of the Darwinists, the widely held "out-of-Africa" theory—the doctrine that man evolved from a more primitive form in southern Africa and slowly made his way across Asia, then to the New World, just 12,000 years ago.

But the Aryan invasion theory has been debunked. No skeletal evidence shows any difference between the supposed invaders and the indigenous peoples of India. And satellite imagery now shows that the ancient Harappan civilization of the Indus Valley and Mohenjo-Daro probably declined and disappeared due to climatic changes—that is, the drying up of the *mythical* Saraswati River—rather than the descent of imaginary Aryan hordes. Burying the Aryan invasion theory, however, opens a Pandora's box for orthodox scholars regarding the prehistory not just of India, but of the world. If Sanskrit predates the world's other languages, along with India's genetic stock, how to explain prehistory in conventional terms?

David Hatcher Childress attributes the demise of Harappa and Mohenjo-Daro to something far more controversial than climate change: *a prehistoric nuclear conflagration* involving aircraft and missiles (Rama's highly destructive "flaming arrows"). This is a picture that may seem bizarre on the face of it, but it is represented convincingly in the ancient writings—as Oppenheimer observed—and with some geological evidence, according to Childress.

Meanwhile, even orthodox thinking dates Indian village culture, thought to be the forerunner of Mohenjo-Daro and the Harappan civilization, to an extremely ancient age. Excavations at Mehgarh, in modern-day Pakistan, have pushed back that date in India to 6000 B.C.E., before the so-called advent of civilization in the Middle East. Some orthodox scholars credit India not only with the first alphabet, but also as the cradle of

Ancient Tamil Nadu statue

civilization whence sprang Mesopotamia, Sumeria, and Egypt. Linguistic evidence, moreover, offers intriguing clues: The indigenous languages of places as distant as Kamchatka and New Zealand bear a similarity to Tamil, the language of southern India. Tamil words turn up, furthermore, in the world's great Classical languages: Sanskrit, Hebrew, and Greek.

But how far does the knowledge filter go? How much of the actual history of India still lies in the dustbin created by Western ethnocentrism, colonialism, and scientific materialism?

The demise of the Aryan invasion theory may represent only the tip of the iceberg of misconceptions about the age and nature of the ancient Indian subcontinent, its culture, its people, and its accomplishments. It has long been claimed that Mother India holds a history that stretches into the dim and forgotten mists of the past, to a time before all myth began, when great *rishis*, men of profound wisdom and phenomenal spiritual attainment, walked the earth.

This ancient India, said to be a product of the gods, dates to the times out of which grew the epic poems the *Ramayana* and the *Mahabarata* and the ancient traditions of Tamil Nadu in southern India. This ancient India was a land whose culture was said by some to predate that of the north, having once existed as part of Kumari Kandam, a great southern continent thought to have stretched from present-day Madagascar to Australia and dating to a staggering 30,000 B.C.E.

Obscure texts of the Siddhanta tradition of Tamil Nadu reportedly say that a great deluge inundated Kumari Kandam. This is a notion that is echoed in the writings of Colonel James Churchward and of W. S. Cervé, both of whom claim knowledge of texts, Indian and Tibetan, respectively, that speak of a long-lost continent situated in the East.

WHERE HAVE ALL THE MAMMALS GONE?

While continental drift theory presupposes extremely slow and regular movement of landmasses over many hundreds of millions of years, a great deal of evidence exists that Earth's surface did indeed change with extreme rapidity and violence in recent prehistory. A great, sudden extinction took place on the planet, perhaps as recently as 11,500 years ago (usually attributed to the end of that last ice age), in which hundreds of mammal and plant species disappeared from the face of the earth, driven into deep caverns and charred muck piles the world over. Modern science, with all its powers and prejudices, has been unable to adequately explain this event.

Instead, one might reasonably say, it has tried to *explain away* the evidence with ever more cumbersome ice age theories meant to account for everything and anything of a cataclysmic nature that happened in recent prehistory. Gradual glacial movements caused all the death and destruction, we are told, though such assertions do not account for much of the worldwide evidence indicating that, on review, a global cataclysm must have taken place. Indeed, scientists can't explain why massive glaciers would slide in the first place.

Allan and Delair, in *Cataclysm!*—a stunning and exhaustive work of scholarship—amass a formidable quantity of *known* evidence corroborating the flood/conflagration legends stored in the world's mythological record. If we suspend belief in the textbook accounts of recent prehistory, Allan and Delair fill the void in a most convincing way. And much evidence centers on southern Asia that would explain how a continent would have been lost to the sea in recent prehistory.

Records gathered in 1947 by the Swedish survey ship *Albatross* reveal a vast plateau of hardened lava for at least several hundred miles southeast of Sri Lanka. The lava, evidence of a severe rupture in the earth's crust, fills most of the now submerged valleys that once existed there. The immense eruption that gave off the lava may have coincided with the downfall of Wallace's Southern Continent (aka Kumari Kandam) for which much zoological and botanical evidence exists that would give such a landmass a recent date, according to Allan and Delair.

Amid the troves of evidence compiled by early geologists and resurrected by Allan and Delair are Asian caves filled with the bones of numerous and diverse species of recent prehistoric animals *from around the world* that could have been driven to their final resting place only by vast amounts of water, propelled by some spectacular, cataclysmic force of nature.

In light of Allan and Delair's work, other geographic anomalies, such as India's Deccan trap, a vast triangular plain of lava several thousand feet thick covering 250,000 square miles, and the Indo-Gangetic trough, a gigantic crack in the earth's surface stretching from Sumatra through India to the Persian Gulf, can be interpreted as evidence of a fantastic cataclysm that sank Kumari Kandam at the time of the great extinction. And this Deccan area is geologically distinct from the Indo-Gangetic plain and the Himalayas of the north. The rocks of the Deccan are among the oldest in the world, with no trace of ever having been under water, and frequently overlaid with sheets of trap rock or basalt that once flowed over them as molten lava.

DISTANT LEGACIES?

Other titillating fragments of anomalous evidence suggest a pervasive if not advanced seafaring or even airborne culture having once existed in Kumari Kandam: for example, the identical nature of the Indus Valley script to that found at Easter Island on the other side of the Pacific Ocean. According to certain south Indian researchers, the thought-to-be-indecipherable scripts are written in a proto-Tamil language, one that would link the culture of distant Easter Island and its famous megalithic statues with ancient southern India, or Kumari Kandam—an idea echoed in the lore of Easter Islanders about a great Pacific continent from which their people originated.

And continuing eastward to North America, new dating methods have placed the Spirit Cave mummy—the remains of a forty-year-old man discovered in 1940 in a cave east of Carson City, Nevada—in the seventh millennium B.C.E. Although the remains have been claimed by modern American Indians, the mummy's facial features appear to be that of a Southeast Asian man. With a dispute raging over the dating of the mummified man's lifetime and the uncertainties and biases regarding the dating of artifacts and fossils in general, the Spirit Cave mummy may be the remains of an ancient inhabitant of Kumari Kandam, or perhaps at least an ancestor.

Whether or not the Spirit Cave mummy hails from Kumari Kandam, actually or genetically, a new look at old research in the field of human origins and the probability of ancient advanced civilization having once existed has begun to seriously upset the applecart of the Western scientific paradigm. The trouble for "West-is-besters," and with them dyed-in-the-wool scientific materialists, is that most cultures of the world offer traditions and a mythological record that contradict the aggressive assumptions of Western science, its assertions about prehistory and about the nature of man. More and more frequently, incremental revelations in a variety of fields, from archeology, to the new physics, to near-death studies, support the ancient traditions.

And even as "West-is-best" assumptions continue to proliferate in textbooks and universities around the globe, records written in the earth and in ancient texts quietly reappear like ghosts from the forgotten past. The records of Mother India, where those ghosts are gods, are no exception.

PART FIVE

ANCIENT HIGH TECH

26 A Conversation with Peter Tompkins

Secrets of Forgotten Worlds

J. Douglas Kenyon

For the many who date their personal discovery of the wisdom of the ancients and the power of unseen forces with the late 1960s and early '70s, two books enjoyed nearly unequaled influence. *The Secret Life of Plants* and *Secrets of the Great Pyramid* were both runaway best sellers, which, if nothing else, put the orthodox establishment to considerable trouble defending itself.

While today notions such as the preference of plants for good music and the miraculous measurements of the Great Pyramid may have become somewhat passé, twenty-five years ago they caused quite a stir and in the process earned not a little notoriety for the author Peter Tompkins. For one who had dared to challenge so flagrantly the titans of the scientific establishment, Tompkins achieved not only celebrity but also, for a time, an unprecedented measure of credibility.

Both books remain in print but Tompkins, though scrupulous in his research, came to be dismissed by the conventional as something of a crank. Two of his other books, *Mysteries of the Mexican Pyramids* and *Secrets of the Soil,* have done little to change his undeserved reputation; nevertheless, he remains busy and unrepentant. He is a seminal, fascinating figure, and *Atlantis Rising* was lucky enough to interview him in order to discuss his views on a number of interests that he shares with the magazine.

Originally from Georgia, Tompkins grew up in Europe, but returned to the United States to study at Harvard. College, though, was interrupted by World War II. Initially employed by the *New York Herald-Tribune,* Tompkins began the war as a correspondent. Soon he was broadcasting for Mutual and NBC. By the end of the war he was working with Edward R. Murrow and CBS. In 1941, his reporting career was interrupted by a stint in the TOI (a precursor of the OSS, which ultimately became the CIA).

Five months were spent behind enemy lines. "At the Anzio landing," he recalls, "General Donovan and General Park sent me into Rome ahead of the landing, and had they not failed to arrive, we would have had a big victory. But as it was, we got stuck. Then I had to send out radio messages four or five times a day about what the Germans were doing—where they were going to attack and in what strength, and so on."

During the mission, Tompkins recruited numerous agents who were sent north to link up with the partisans and help clear the way for the planned Allied advance. Eventually he went to Berlin. When, at the close of the war, Truman abolished the OSS, Tompkins found he had no desire to join the newly organized CIA and went his own way. The years following the war were spent in Italy learning moviemaking and scriptwriting and developing a healthy distaste for censorship: "I realized the only way I could say what I wanted to say was by writing books. They don't get censored."

Eventhen, he was finding his views made him anathema to many. "I got thrown out of more dinner parties," he chuckles, "for talking about metaphysical—or what were considered crazy—notions at the time, so I learned to be quiet."

Peter Tompkins

Being quiet in print, though, has not been his wont. Nor has censorship of a sort been entirely escaped. Tompkins believes his most recent book, *Secrets of the Soils,* which he describes as "a cry to save the planet from the chemical killers," was virtually "squashed by the publisher," afraid of scaring the public. A follow-up on the *Secret Life of Plants,* the book spelled out alternatives to the use of chemical fertilizers that Tompkins says "are absolutely useless and only lead to killing the soil and the microorganisms, poisoning the plants and, ultimately, animals and humans." Tompkins believes such fertilizers to be primary contributors to the spread of cancer.

The writer has found his plans thwarted not just by publishers. One idea to use a promising technology he had chanced upon to virtually X-ray the Great Pyramid was apparently blocked by Zahi Hawass and the Egyptian Antiquities Authority. "It would have cost about fifty grand to X-ray the whole pyramid and find out what the hell really is in there," he says. "It seemed to me that it would make an interesting television program, but no one was interested. It was very strange."

On the recent highly publicized work of the Belgian astronomer Robert Bauval purporting to show an alignment between the pyramids and the constellation Orion, Tompkins shrugs: "It's a hypothesis, but it's not provable.

I'm only interested in those things about the Great Pyramid that are solid, that are indisputable." Tompkins wants more than "endless theories," of which he claims to have a roomful. But, he concedes, "if you think of the Dogon and the Sirius connection, it's obvious that, on this planet, people knew a great deal more about astronomy, and may have been linked in one way or another with the stars. But I'm only interested when someone comes along with fairly hard proof."

Proof of advanced ancient astronomical knowledge, Tompkins believes, is abundant in much of the ancient architecture. "It's obvious that all the great temples in Egypt were astronomically oriented and geodetically placed," he says. He is especially interested in Tel el-Amarna, which he sees as the subject of a possible future book. The astronomical knowledge incorporated into the city built by Akhenaton Tompkins considers "mind blowing," as he puts it. Unfortunately for his plans, though, Livio Catullo Stecchini, the Italian scholar and authority on ancient measurement upon whom Tompkins relied for much of his work in *Secrets of the Great Pyramid,* is dead.

Interestingly, Tompkins never permitted *Secrets of the Great Pyramid* to be published in Italy because the publisher wanted to omit Stecchini's appendix. The injustice still angers Tompkins: "Here's an unrecognized Italian genius, but the Italians said if you print it, you can't have the book."

Tompkins's subsequent book, on the Mexican pyramids, further reinforced his view that the ancients were possessed of advanced astronomical knowledge. Though not convinced that the similarities between Egypt and Mexico prove the existence of a mother culture like Atlantis, as some have suggested, he does believe "it's obvious that people went back and forth across the Atlantic." And he believes the Mexico builders used the same system of measurements as the Egyptians. "I should write another whole book on the subject of what was known on both sides of the Atlantic," he says.

During his Mexico experience, Tompkins succeeded—at great expense and difficulty—in filming the effect of the rising and setting sun at the equinox on the temple at Chichen Itza. "It's absolutely staggering," he says, "but you can see that snake come alive, just on that one day. It goes up and down the steps. We filmed it and it's just beautiful. How did they orient that pyramid so that would happen only on the equinox?"

Answering that question led Tompkins to New Zealand and Geoffrey Hodgeson, who gained fame in the 1920s by clairvoyantly pinpointing the precise position of the planets at a given time. Convinced by Hodgeson's demonstration, Tompkins concluded that he knew the secret by which the ancients were able to achieve their precise astronomical alignments without

Peter Tompkins at Chichen Itza

access to modern instruments. "They didn't need the instruments," he says, "because the instruments were built into them. Clairvoyantly they could tell exactly where the planets were and understand their motion." Such understanding, while available to the ancients, has been largely forgotten by alienated high-tech Western society. "We've closed ourselves in," he says. "We've pulled down the shades on our second sight."

Fascinated by clairvoyance and the potential it represents, Tompkins has tried to deploy it as a resource for his more scientific investigation. When his own search for concrete proof of the existence of Atlantis took him to the Bahamas, he used every tool at his disposal. When one site appeared to be littered with ancient marble columns and pediments, it was a psychic who told him that the spot was nothing more than the final resting place of a nineteenth-century ship bound for New Orleans with a marble mausoleum on board. On the more scientific side, clandestine core sampling of the celebrated Bimini Road convinced him the pavement was not man-made but only beach rock.

It took a University of Miami geologist to give him what he wanted. Dr. Cesare Emiliani showed Tompkins the result of his own core sampling over the years in the Gulf of Mexico. Here was conclusive proof of a great inundation of water in about 9000 B.C.E. Tompkins remembers: "Emiliani said, 'They say that Atlantis has been found in the Azores and found off the coast of Spain and off the East Coast of the United States. All of these places,' he said, 'could have been part of the Atlantean empire that was submerged at exactly the date when Plato said it was.'"

Several years earlier Tompkins had written the foreword for the English translation of Otto Muck's book *The Secret of Atlantis*. Muck's hypothesis that Atlantis had been sunk by an asteroid Tompkins thought very plausible, and he still thinks so, though it remains to be proved. In Emiliani's work, though, Tompkins believes he has found the only geological proof on the subject.

Of course, proved or not, Atlantis, like many other controversial notions, is not likely to be readily accepted by the intellectual establishment. The reasons for this seem clear to Tompkins: "They would have to rewrite all their archeological schoolbooks if some of this is proved. If John West's theory about the Sphinx is correct (that it's over ten thousand years old), it's going to change a lot of stuff." By way of analogy he describes a man he knows in Canada who has developed a cure for cancer, and points out what a threat such a discovery is to the billion-dollar-a-year cancer industry.

A lifetime of searching the hidden byways has made Tompkins philosophical about his own inevitable physical transition. While acknowledging that he is "getting on," he says, "I'm infinitely more peaceful about the prospect of death. Like time, it's sort of an illusion. I mean, you lose the body, but what's that? You've had many before and you'll probably have more after. Maybe you'll do better without them."

At any rate, his productivity has yet to suffer. His next book promises to prove the existence of elemental creatures. The project was inspired by the recent scientific validation of the work of Annie Besant and C. W. Leadbeater in mapping subatomic structure. Before the turn of the century, the two leaders of the Theosophical Society had decided to use their yogic powers to analyze the elements. Leadbeater saw and Besant drew. When their work was published, no one paid any attention. After all, not only was it "impossible" to do what they were doing, but their results also contradicted conventional science.

Then, in the 1970s, an English physicist discovered their work and realized that they were accurately describing quarks and other features of the atom that had only recently been discovered. With such powerful vindication established, Tompkins now goes into the detailed work that the two produced on elemental spirits, as well as the work of the renowned clairvoyant Rudolf Steiner.

"If you put it all together," he says, "and realize these people could actually many years ahead of the discovery of atoms and isotopes accurately describe and draw them, and then look at their description of the nature spirits, their function on the planet, their connection with human beings, and why it is that we should reconnect with them, you have to listen. I mean, it's black and white. You can't escape it."

27 Ancient Agriculture, in Search of the Missing Links

Is the Inescapable Evidence of a Lost Fountainhead of Civilization to Be Found Growing in Our Fields?

Will Hart

One of the most curious aspects of history's mysteries is that there is anything mysterious to puzzle over. Why *should* our history be full of anomalies and enigmas? We have become conditioned to accept these incongruities, but if we turn the situation around, it really does not seem to make sense. We know the histories of America, Europe, Rome, and Greece with some precision back three thousand years, just as we know our own personal histories. We would consider it very odd and unacceptable if we did not.

However, when we go farther back into prehistory than Babylonia to Sumeria and ancient Egypt, things get very fuzzy. There can be few possible explanations: 1) our ideas and beliefs about the way history happened conflict with the truth; 2) we have collective amnesia for unknown reasons and/or some combination of both.

Imagine that you woke up one morning with complete amnesia, no idea of how you got on this planet and no memories of your own past. We are in an analogous situation regarding the history of civilization, and it is just as disturbing. Or let's say that you are living in an old Victorian-style mansion full of odd, ancient artifacts. That is pretty much our situation as we wander around ancient ruins and through the galleries of museums wondering who made all this stuff, and how, and why.

One hundred and fifty years ago, much of the history in the Old Testament was considered pure fiction, including the existence of Sumeria (the biblical Shinar), Akkad, and Assyria. But those forgotten pieces of our past were discovered in the late nineteenth and early twentieth centuries when Nineveh and Ur were found. Their artifacts have completely changed our view of history.

Until fairly recently, we did not know the roots of our own civilization. We had no idea who might have invented the wheel, agriculture, writing, cities, or any of the rest of it. Additionally, for some curious, inexplicable reason, not that many people cared to know, and even historians were willing to let the ruins of human history lie buried under the desert sands. That attitude seems as strange as the mysteries themselves.

Would you simply accept the situation if you had amnesia, or would you do everything in your power to reconstruct your past and your identity?

It seems that there is something we are hiding from ourselves. Some will say it was a mind-wrenching visit by ancient astronauts; others will argue there was an ancient human civilization destroyed by cataclysm. In either event, we have apparently buried and forgotten those episodes because the memory is too painful. Personally, I have not reached a final conclusion regarding those ideas; however, I am sure the orthodox theories presented by conventional archeologists, historians, and anthropologists do not hold up under intense scrutiny.

It is curious that we have developed the capability to send space probes to Mars and to crack the human genome, and even to clone ourselves, but we are still fumbling around trying to understand the mysteries of the pyramid cultures, of prehistory, and of how we made the quantum leap from the Stone Age to civilization in the first place! It does not add up. Why should we, as a species, not have maintained the threads directly and concretely linking us to our past?

I have this gut feeling that investigative reporters and homicide detectives get when they've been digging into an unsolved case for a long time. We are missing some pieces and/or we are not looking at the situation correctly, and we are probably overlooking the meaning of obvious clues because we have been conditioned to think about the facts in a certain way. Additionally, we have not asked all of the right questions. It never hurts to go back to basics and review everything you think you know and what the real "facts" are.

We have always had the choice of trying to make sense of the world or not. Life has given us an incredible amount of leeway and freedom when it comes to knowledge acquisition. Our ancestors mastered the basic rules of the game of survival during the incredibly long time span of the Stone Age. They did not need to know that Earth revolved around the Sun or the nature of atomic structure to succeed. But after the last ice age, something strange occurred, and the human race went through a sudden transformation that sent our race into unknown territory.

We are still reaping the consequences of those explosive events.

Let us go back and set the stage of early human evolution as science depicts it unfolding. Our ancestors found themselves in a world full of natural wonders, facing the challenges that nature set before them, all having to do with basic survival. To begin with, they had no tools and no choice other than to meet the challenges head-on, just as other animals did. We have to keep the realities of this background in perspective. We know exactly how Stone Age people lived because many tribes around the world were still living in this manner during the past five hundred years, and they have been studied intensively and extensively.

We know that humanity was fairly homogeneous throughout the Stone Age. Even 10,000 years ago, people lived pretty much the same way, whether they were in Africa, Asia, Europe, Australia, or the Americas. They lived very close to nature, hunting wildlife and gathering wild plants, using stone tools and stone, wood, and bone weapons. They had learned the art of making and controlling fire and they had very accurate and detailed knowledge about the habits of animals, the lay of the land, nature's cycles, and how to distinguish between edible and poisonous plants.

This knowledge and their way of life had been painstakingly acquired over millions of years of experience. Stone Age humans have been wrongly portrayed and misunderstood. They were not stupid brutes, and there would be no modern mind and no modern civilization without the long evolution they went through to establish the basis for all that would eventually happen. They were keenly aware, entirely in communion with nature, and unquestionably stronger and more muscularly robust than we are today.

In reality, the natural world we inherited from Stone Age man was entirely intact. Everything was as pristine and virginal as it had been during the millions of years of human evolution. Nature bestowed her bounty upon those early humans and they learned to live within that natural framework. Viewed from a statistical perspective, the human status quo is the hunter-gatherer culture that we lived in for 99.99 percent of our existence as a species, at least according to modern science.

It is very easy to understand how our remote ancestors lived; life changed very little and very slowly. Early man adapted and stuck with what worked. It was a simple but demanding way of life that was passed on from generation to generation by example and oral tradition.

There really does not seem to be much mystery about it. But that all starts to change radically after the last ice age. Suddenly, a few tribes began to embrace a different way of life. Giving up their nomadic existence, they settled down and started raising certain crops and domesticating several animal species. The first steps toward civilization are often described but

Ancient Egyptian farmers

never really examined at a deep level. What compelled them to change abruptly? It is more problematic to explain than we have been led to believe.

The first issue is very basic and straightforward. Stone Age people did not eat grains, and grains are the basis of agriculture and the diet of civilization. Their diet consisted of lean wild meats and fresh wild greens and fruits.

To begin with, we will be looking at the evolutionary discordance from a general standpoint by examining the mismatch between characteristics of foods eaten since the "agricultural revolution" that began 10,000 years ago and our genus's prior two-million-year history as hunter-gatherers. The present-day edible grass seeds simply would have been unavailable to most of mankind until after their domestication because of their limited geographic distribution. Consequently, the human genome is most ideally adapted to those foods that were available to pre-agricultural man.

This presents us with an enigma that is every bit as difficult to penetrate as the building of the Great Pyramid. How and why did our ancestors make this leap? As they had little to no experience with wild grains, how did they know what to do to process them, or even that they were indeed edible?

Beyond that, by the time of the abrupt appearance of the Sumerian and

Egyptian threshing

Egyptian civilizations, grains had already been hybridized, which demands a high degree of knowledge about and experience with plants, as well as time. If you have any experience with wild plants or fruits, or any experience of farming, then you know that wild breeds are very different from hybridized cultivars. It is well established that hunter-gatherers had no experience with plant breeding or animal domestication, and it should have taken much longer to go from zero to an advanced state than historians insist it did.

We must ask, Where did their knowledge originate? How did Stone Age man suddenly acquire the skills to domesticate plants and animals and do it with a high degree of effectiveness? We find purebred dog species like salukis and greyhounds in Egyptian and Sumerian art: How were they bred so quickly from wolves?

The following issues make the conventional explanations difficult to support: 1) mankind's very slow process of evolution in the Stone Age; 2) the sudden creation and implementation of new tools, new foodstuffs, and new social forms that lacked precedence. If early humans had eaten wild grains and experimented with hybridization for some lengthy time period and evolved in obvious developmental stages, then we could comprehend it.

But how can we accept the scenario of the Stone Age to the Great Pyramid of Giza?

Plant breeding is an exacting science and we know it was being done in Sumeria, in Egypt, and by the ancient Israelites. If you doubt that statement, consider that we are growing the same primary grain crops that were developed by the ancients. That is a strange fact and it begs close scrutiny. There are hundreds of other possible wild plants that could be domesticated. Why have we not developed new grains from the other wild species of the past three thousand years? How could they pick the best crops with the extremely meager knowledge that they would have possessed had they just emerged from the Stone Age?

They not only figured out all these complex issues, but they also quickly discovered the principles of making secondary products out of cereals. The Sumerians were making bread and beer five thousand years ago and yet their very close ancestors—at least according to anthropologists—knew nothing of these things and lived by picking plants and killing wild beasts. It is almost as if they were given a set of instructions by someone who had already developed these things. But it could not have been from their ancestors, because they were hunters and plant collectors.

It is very difficult to reconstruct these rapid-fire transitions, especially when they were accompanied by radical changes in every other feature of human life. How and why did humans who had known nothing but a nomadic existence and an egalitarian social structure so quickly and so radically change? What compelled them to build cities and create highly stratified civilizations when they knew nothing about such organizations?

During the Epipaleolithic Era, circa 8000–5500 B.C.E., the tribes in the Nile Valley were living in semi-subterranean oval houses roofed with mud and sticks. They made simple pottery and used stone axes and flint arrowheads. They were still seminomadic and moved seasonally from one camp to another. The vast majority of tribes around the globe were living in a similar state. How do we get from there to quarrying, dressing, and manipulating one- to sixty-ton stones into the world's most massive structure, and in such a short time?

This quick transition is all but impossible to explain rationally. All inventions and cultural developments require time and a sequence of easily identified developmental stages. Where are the precursors? It is very easy to trace this path of development during the Stone Age from very primitive tools to chipped ax heads and flint arrowheads. That is what we should find as civilization develops.

But where are the smaller-scale pyramids—much smaller? Where are the crude stone carvings that precede the sophisticated stelae? The slow evolution of forms, from simple to complex, is all that human beings knew, not mud and thatch-roof huts and then large-scale architecture employing megalithic blocks of stone and complex artwork demanding master craftsmanship.

But the developmental phases are simply not there. Sumerian cuneiform tablets describe fairly complex systems of irrigation and farming, bakeries, and the making of beer. The Bible tells us that the ancient Jews raised grapes and made wine, and both leavened and unleavened bread. We take these things for granted but the assumptions underlying them are never questioned. Where did they learn to hybridize bread wheat and turn it into flour and bake the flour into bread in such a short time span? Ditto for viticulture. These are not simple or obvious products.

We assume that their ancestors developed farming skills over a prolonged period of time, which is a logical expectation. But that is not the case. The very first and very primitive agricultural experiments that have been documented by archeologists occurred in Jarmo and Jericho. These were small, humble villages that raised a few simple crops, but they still hunted game and gathered plants, so they were not strictly agricultural communities.

The problem is that there is no intermediate step between them and Sumeria and Egypt, just as there are no small-scale ziggurats, pyramids, or *any* progression showing that Stone Age artisans could suddenly carve intricate statuary and stelae.

The orthodox theories are starting to rely more on the "official" pronouncements of authorities rather than on well-argued and well-documented facts. We have reached a crisis in the fields of anthropology, history, and archeology because the conventional theses are unable to solve an increasingly large number of anomalies. The explanations are thin and threadbare and becoming more ponderous and unable to support their own weight. The pieces do not lock together and fit into a smooth, coherent whole.

We have mentioned previously in this book a quote by the eminent paleo-anthropologist Louis Leakey. Some years ago, while giving a lecture at a university, Leakey was asked by a student about the evolutionary "missing link." He replied, "There is not *one* missing link, there are *hundreds* of links missing." This is even more true for cultural than biological evolution. Until we find those links, we are like amnesiacs struggling to make sense out of our modern lives and our collective history.

28 Atlantean Technology: How Advanced?

What Does the Evidence Really Show?

Frank Joseph

Edgar Cayce said that the inhabitants of Atlantis operated aircraft and submarines, and were in possession of a fabulous technology superior to that achieved in the twentieth century. The question of so advanced a technology in ancient times is the most difficult argument for many investigators to accept, especially Cayce's descriptions of achievements beyond anything known today. He said the Atlanteans were adept at "photographing from a distance" and "reading inscriptions through walls—even at distances."

The Atlantean "electrical knife was in such a shape, with the use of the metals, as to be used as the means for bloodless surgery, as would be termed today—by the very staying forces used which formed coagulating forces in bodies where larger arteries or veins were to be entered or cut," he said.

Refugees from Atlantis supposedly brought to Egypt "electron music where color, vibration, and activities make for toning same with the emotions of individuals or peoples that may make for their temperments being changed. And same may be applied by the entity in those associations with what may be called the temperments of individuals, where they are possessed—as it were—by the influences from without, and those that are ill from diseases that have become of a nature or vibratory influence within the body as to set themselves as a vibration in the body."

Cayce told of "a death ray that brought from the bowels of the Earth itself—when turned into the sources of supply—those destructions to portions of the land." This "death ray" may be today's laser because, Cayce said in 1933, it "will be found in the next twenty-five years." He spoke of "electrical appliances, when these were used by those peoples to make for beautiful buildings without but temples of sin within." The Atlanteans were skilled in "the application of the electrical forces and influences especially in the association and the activities of same upon metals; not only as to their location but as to the manner of the activity of same as related to the refining of some and the discovery of others, and the use of the various forms or transportation of same—or transformation of same to and through those influences in the experience."

At the time Cayce said that the Atlanteans used electrical current for the working of metals, there was no evidence that the ancients knew anything about electricity, let alone how it might be applied to metallurgy. Then in 1938, Dr. Wilhelm Koenig, a German archeologist, was inventorying artifacts at the Iraq State Museum in Baghdad when he noticed what seemed to be the impossible resemblance of a collection of two-thousand-year-old clay jars to a series of dry cell storage batteries. His curiosity had been aroused by the peculiar internal details of the jars, each of which enclosed a copper cylinder capped at the bottom by a disk (also of copper) and sealed with asphalt.

A few years later, Dr. Koenig's suspicion was put to the test. Willard Gray, a technician at the General Electric High Voltage Laboratory in Pittsfield, Massachusetts, finished an exact reproduction of the Baghdad jars. He found that an iron rod inserted into the copper tube and filled with citric acid generated 1.5 to 2.75 volts of electricity, enough to electroplate an object with gold. Gray's experiment demonstrated that practical electricity could have been applied to metalworking by ancient craftsmen after all.

Doubtless, the "Baghdad battery," as it has since become known, was not the first of its kind—it was a device that represented an unknown technology preceding it by perhaps thousands of years, and might have included far more spectacular feats of electrical engineering long since lost.

According to Cayce, the Atlanteans did not confine their application of electricity to metallurgy. They had "the use of the sound waves, where the manners in which lights were used as a means of communication," he said.

"Elevators and the connecting tubes that were used by compressed air and steam" operated in Atlantean buildings.

Atlantean technology soared into aeronautics. Airships of elephant hides were "made into the containers for the gases that were used as both lifting and for the impelling of the crafts about the various portions of the continent, and even abroad. . . . They could not only pass through that called air, or that heavier, but through that of water."

Manned flight is practically emblematic of our times, and we find such references to ancient aeronautics incredible. Yet serious researchers believe Peruvian balloonists may have surveyed the famous Nazca Lines two thousand or more years ago from aerial perspectives. Despite reluctance to take Cayce at his word, equivocal yet tantalizing evidence does exist to at least suggest that manned flight may indeed have occurred in the ancient world.

The earliest substantiated journeys aloft took place in the fifth century B.C.E., even before Plato was born, when the Greek scientist Archytas of Tarentum invented a leather kite large enough to carry a young boy. It was actually used by Greek armies in the earliest known example of aerial reconnaissance.

More amazing was the discovery made in the Upper Nile Valley near the close of the nineteenth century. The story is best told by the famous author and explorer David Hatcher Childress: "In 1898, a model was found in an Egyptian tomb near Sakkara. It was labeled a 'bird' and cataloged Object 6347 at the Egyptian Museum, in Cairo. Then, in 1969, Dr. Khalil Massiha was startled to see that the 'bird' not only had straight wings, but also an upright tail-fin. To Dr. Massiha, the object appeared to be that of a model airplane. It is made of wood, weighs 39.12 grams and remains in good condition.

The Saqqara bird

"The wingspan is 18 cm, the aircraft's nose is 3.2 cm long, and the overall length is 18 cm. The extremities of the aircraft and the wing-tips are aerodynamically shaped. Apart from a symbolic eye and two short lines under the wings, it has no decorations nor has it any landing legs. Experts have tested the model and found it airworthy."

In all, fourteen similar flying models have been recovered from ancient digs in Egypt. Interestingly, the Saqqara example came from an archeological zone identified with the earliest dynastic periods, at the very beginning of pharaonic civilization, which suggests that the aircraft was not a later development but belonged instead to the first years of civilization in the Nile Valley.

The Egyptians' anomalous artifacts may indeed have been flying "models" of the real thing operated by their Atlantean forefathers. The Cairo Museum's wooden model of a working glider implies the ancient Egyptians at least understood the fundamental principles of heavier-than-air, man-made flight. Perhaps such knowledge was the only legacy left from a former time, when those principles were applied more seriously.

The quote from Childress is excerpted from his book *Vimana Aircraft of Ancient India and Atlantis* (coauthored with Ivan Sanderson), the most complete examination of the subject. In it, he was able to assemble surprising evidence from the earliest Hindu traditions of aircraft supposedly flown in ancient times. Then known as *vimanas,* they appear in the famous *Ramayana* and *Mahabharata* and the less-well-known but earliest of the Indian epics, the *Drona Parva.*

Aircraft were discussed in surprisingly technical detail throughout several manuscripts of ancient India. The *Vimaanika Shastra, Manusa,* and *Samarangana Sutradhara,* all classic sources, additionally describe "aerial cars" that were allegedly operating from deeply prehistoric times.

Each of these epics deals with a former age, hinting at the last, bellicose, cataclysmic years of Atlantis. Childress's collection of impressive source materials dating back to the dawn of Hindu literature heavily underscores Cayce's description of flying devices in Atlantis. It is important to understand, however, that these vimanas had virtually nothing in common with modern aviation, because their motive power was utterly unlike combustion or jet engines. They also had little to do with aeronautics as we have come to understand it.

Apparently, the Atlanteans operated two types of flying vehicles: gas-filled dirigible-like craft and heavier-than-air vimanas directed from a central power source on the ground. While the latter represented an aeronautical technology beyond any known aircraft, the balloons Cayce describes featured a detail that suggests their authenticity.

He said their skin was made of elephant hides. They probably would have been too heavy to serve as envelopes for the containment of any lighter-than-air gas. But lighter, expandable, and non-leaking elephant bladders might have worked. In any case, Cayce says that the Atlanteans used the animals, which were native to their kingdom, for a variety of purposes.

The *Critias* also mentions that elephants abounded on the island of Atlantis. Skeptics long faulted Plato for including this out-of-place pachyderm until the 1960s, when oceanographers dredging the sea bottom of the Atlantic Ocean some two hundred miles west of the Portuguese coast unexpectedly hauled up hundreds of elephant bones at several different locations. The scientists concluded that the animals had anciently wandered across a now submerged land bridge extending from the Atlantic shores of North Africa into formerly dry land long since sunk beneath the sea. Their discovery gave special credence not only to Plato, but to Cayce as well.

No less surprising are the submarines known to the early-fifth-century-B.C.E. Greek historian Herodotus and the first-century-C.E. Roman naturalist Pliny the Elder. Even Aristotle wrote about submarines. His most famous pupil, Alexander the Great, was said to have been on board a glass-covered undersea vessel during an extended shake-down cruise beneath the eastern Mediterranean Sea, around 320 B.C.E.

While these submersibles may have gone back twenty-three centuries or so, Atlantis had already vanished about one thousand years earlier. Even so, if such inventions took place in Classical times, they might just as well have operated during the Bronze Age, which was not much different technologically.

Ancient aeronautics paled in comparison to even greater technological achievements, as Atlantean scientists succeeded "in the breaking up of the atomic forces to produce impelling force to those means and modes of transportation, or of travel, or of lifting large weights or of changing the faces or forces of nature itself," said Edgar Cayce. The same life-reading explains that explosives were invented by the Atlanteans. Seven years earlier, he mentioned what he called "the Atlantean period, when those first of the explosives were made." Ignatius Donnelly, the father of modern Atlantology, wrote even earlier that explosives were developed in Atlantis.

Cayce explained that the Atlanteans were able to create such an advanced society because their civilization developed over a more or less continuous history until the final catastrophe. Their cultural evolution had been graced with many centuries of growth in which to develop and perfect the scientific arts. The basis of this ancient technology was an understanding and application of crystal power. Through it, the motive forces of nature were somehow directed to serve human needs. Transportation on, above, and under the sea became possible, and long-distance communication bound together the world of Atlantis.

We find such a high level of material progress set in prehistoric times incomprehensible and beyond belief. Yet many better-known civilizations achieved technological breakthroughs that were forgotten when their societies fell, only to be rediscovered sometimes thousands of years later. In Middle America, for example, Mayan accomplishments in celestial mechanics were not matched until the last century. Incan agricultural techniques, abandoned with the Spanish Conquest, yielded three times more produce than farming methods employed in Peru today.

At the same time Plato was writing about Atlantis, his fellow Greeks were sailing the *Alexandris*. More than four hundred feet long, she was a colossal ship, the likes of which would not be seen again for another two thousand years. A pregnancy test in use among eighteenth-dynasty Egyptians was not discovered until the 1920s. As for Egypt, our modern world's top engineers lack the know-how capable of reproducing the Great Pyramid in all its details. Certainly, far more was lost with the fall of ancient civilization than has yet been found.

Moreover, our times do not have a monopoly on human beings of great genius and inventiveness. That they were able to create complex technologies in other times and societies long since forgotten should not overtax our credulity. And if one of those lost epochs belonged to a place known as Atlantis, we have it on the authority of Western civilization's most influential philosopher and the foremost psychic our country has yet produced.

However they may disagree in their interpretations of the lost civilization, both metaphysical and worldwide mythological sources are almost unanimous in describing a central role for the sophisticated technology of Atlantis in its ultimate destruction. Cayce said that the Atlanteans grew intoxicated with the material wonders made possible through quartz crystal technology. The riches and luxuries it generated inspired them with an insatiable desire for abundance.

They turned the beams of their power crystals into the very bowels of the planet, excavating for even greater mineral wealth. Prodigious amounts of high-grade copper, which fueled the bronze weapons industries of the pre-Classical world, and gold enough to sheet the walls of their city poured forth from Earth's violated cornucopia.

The copper-mining operations of prehistoric Michigan still bear the scars of Atlantean technology. For example, some unknown device enabled the ancient miners of the Upper Peninsula to sink pits vertically through sixty feet of solid rock. Another piece of lost instrumentation directed them to all the richest veins of copper hidden under the hillsides of Isle Royale and the Kewanee Peninsula.

These and similar achievements of the late fourth millennium B.C.E., which allowed the prehistoric miners to remove a minimum of half a billion pounds of raw copper, are no speculation; they have been known to archeologists for more than a century. Perhaps in overreaching themselves through their mining operations, the Atlanteans excavated too deeply into the already seismically unstable Mid-Atlantic Ridge on which their capital perched. They were blind to the geologic consequences of their ecological selfishness, and regarded our living planet as an inexhaustible fount of mineral wealth. Parallels with our times are uncomfortably close.

The Atlanteans reveled in an orgy of self-indulgent materialism. But at some indefinable point, long-suffering Nature rebelled. The threshold of her forbearance had been crossed, and she chastised her sinful children with a terrible punishment. Her fires of hell opened to engulf opulent Atlantis in a volcanic event so cataclysmic that it destroyed the entire island. The crumbling, incinerated city with its screaming inhabitants was dragged to the bottom of the sea and into myth. The "great, terrible crystal"—the source of the Atlanteans' unexampled prosperity—had become the instrument of their doom.

29 Archeology and the Law of Gravity

Orthodox Theory of Ancient Capability Tends to Cave In under Its Own Weight

Will Hart

The massive earthmover makes the average street pickup look like a Tonka truck. Rated to about 350 tons, it is restricted to mining operations, as the federal highway load limit is forty tons and the truck weighs more than that without a load. I was watching it being put through its paces in the local open-pit copper mine in Bisbee, Arizona. A bone-jarring flash suddenly struck me that snapped into place things that I had long been trying to get a perspective on.

The earthmover is the heaviest truck that we have in modern civilization and it can haul the heaviest loads we find littering the landscapes in Egypt, Bolivia, and Peru. At one point in my life, as I was learning the ropes of the literary world, I worked on a cement construction crew in a logging town, where I came to know about handling heavy loads and what a front-end loader could lift and a double flatbed logging truck could haul.

During the course of my thirty years of investigations into the mysteries of ancient civilizations, I have often been puzzled by the way people react to cyclopean blocks of stone being moved long distances or hoisted up into the air. These reactions were either a blank look or a shrug that said "Okay, what's the big deal?" This response frustrated me and made me feel as if I was not communicating adequately the scope and difficulty of the problem. But I have since realized that the reason most people do not grasp the magnitude of the problem—and what the "real" enigmas of our planet are—has to do with simple, direct experience.

One hundred and fifty years ago most people lived on farms in rural areas and were commonly faced with having to haul loads of hay, logs, or whatever. They knew what it took to bale a ton of hay and lift a three-hundred-pound log or chunk of rock. But today machines handle all of these heavy-lifting and moving jobs and we have lost our perspective. I recently had a conversation with a

Gigantic blocks in the Khafre pyramid weigh more than 70 tons each and are many stories above the ground. (PHOTOGRAPH BY J. DOUGLAS KENYON)

friend about these issues wherein I was trying to explain why the Egyptians could not have built the Great Pyramid with primitive tools and techniques.

He was skeptical, until he recalled an event that quickly shifted his attitude. I was telling him that I would be willing to concede that the builders could handle the millions of 2.5-ton blocks if he would deal with the problem of the seventy-ton megaliths over the King's Chamber. The light went on in his head. He suddenly became animated as he told me how he and a group of friends were faced with moving a heavy pool table. They positioned themselves about it, shoulder to shoulder, and gave the old heave-ho.

It came as a great surprise when the pool table remained rooted to the floor; they had not been able to lift it even one inch. My point sank in. You cannot use manpower to lift a seventy-ton block of granite up and out of a quarry and onto a sledge. The task increases exponentially when we consider how one-hundred-ton blocks were hoisted up and positioned more than twenty feet off the ground in the Sphinx Temple. This is an engineering and

1950s-vintage two-hundred-ton steam locomotive
(PHOTOGRAPH BY J. DOUGLAS KENYON)

physics problem that cannot be overcome by numbers, which is how Egyptologists try to solve it. Granite is very dense, and a twenty-foot-long block can weigh seventy tons. How many men can physically fit around it to attempt a lift? Maybe fifty, which is not even enough manpower to hoist ten tons.

This is an intractable problem. As long as Egyptologists insist that men lifted up the cyclopean blocks of stone with nothing but brute force and ropes, this problem will need to be overcome. The rest of the construction formula of the Egyptologists is moot until this primary obstacle is dealt with. If they cannot or will not prove that it was accomplished as they claim, then it is time to go beyond challenging the rest of their baseless theories. We need to discard the whole orthodox house of cards and walk away from the so-called debate.

Returning to the 350-ton cyclopean monsters, our highest-rated commercial cranes are near their limit with this load. If anyone thinks that men, ropes, and sledges lifted and hauled loads that our heaviest equipment can barely handle, I will argue that this belief is a sign of technological illiteracy. Recently I was watching a documentary about a bridge that collapsed while a train was traveling over it. I went through a mental process similar to the copper mine example.

Locomotives, diesel or steam, weigh about two hundred tons. They are rugged, hardworking, heavy-duty pieces of machinery. There are many cyclopean blocks in Egypt and Peru that weigh as much as a locomotive. A monstrous crane was brought in to fish the locomotive out of the river. Imagine placing a locomotive on bare earth or sand. What would happen? It would immediately sink into the ground. There is a good reason that train tracks are built on a gravel bed that has railroad ties laid down crosswise beneath the steel tracks.

Could several thousand men pull a locomotive across the sand? That is extremely doubtful. Some kind of hard-packed road would have to be constructed to take the weight and lessen the tremendous drag. As we saw above, our modern highways hold up only under loads less than forty tons.

The average eighteen-wheel tractor-trailer hauls about twenty tons, so it is obvious that loads exceeding twenty tons are indeed very heavy. Those kinds of loads were hauled all over Egypt. Where is the evidence that the necessary roads were installed? They would not have disappeared, as they would have been made out of stones and brick masonry.

Assuming a few of the ancient stone-block transport roads have been uncovered, they are perfect to test the orthodox sledge-hauling theory. The problem of how the ancients moved the heaviest loads is quite enough to crush the orthodox building theories and time lines into dust, in my estimation. Academics are not known for being mechanically inclined, nor are they the ones doing the sweat labor during excavations out in the field. It is extraordinarily easy to put pen to paper and make a one-hundred-ton block of stone move from the quarry onto a temple wall. It is impossible to meet that challenge in the real world using manpower unaided by modern equipment.

The fact is that the Egyptologist Mark Lehner discovered this years ago when he put together an expert team to try and raise a thirty-five-ton obelisk using ancient tools and techniques. It was filmed by "NOVA." A master stonemason was brought in to quarry the granite block from the bedrock. Unfortunately, he gave up after trying every trick he knew. They called a bulldozer in, which cut it away from the bedrock and lifted it onto a waiting truck. That was really the end of the experiment, and it proved that it was not possible to quarry and lift a block one-tenth the size of the heaviest obelisk still standing in Egypt.

WHAT MORE PROOF IS NEEDED?

Lehner never again tried to use the ancient tools to prove how the pyramids were constructed. In a later experiment aimed at showing that a twenty-foot-tall scale model of the Great Pyramid could be constructed, he brought in barefoot locals with modern chisels, hammers, and a truck with a steel winch to hoist the blocks out of the quarry.

That compromised the entire test, which was silly anyway, as the blocks were less than half the size of the average ones used to build the pyramid. How could that prove that seventy-ton blocks were hoisted up 150 vertical feet to the King's Chamber? His use of the twenty-foot-tall scale model is analogous to the comparison between the plastic Tonka truck and a real earthmover cited earlier in this article. The whole fiasco proved only that he had become intimidated by the magnitude of the construction problems.

We encounter very similar, intractable problems when we examine the precision engineering that went into building the Great Pyramid. We have another example of just how precise and demanding this massive project was in a demonstration that took place in the late 1970s. At that point in time, Japan was the global economic miracle, and riding high. A Japanese team funded by Nissan set out to prove they had the wherewithal to build a sixty-foot scale model of the Great Pyramid using traditional tools and methods.

The Egyptian government approved the project. Their first embarrassment came at the quarry when they discovered they could not cut the stones from the bedrock. They called in jackhammers. The next embarrassing situation came when they tried to ferry the blocks across the river on a primitive barge. They could not control it and had to call for a modern one.

Then they ran into more grief on the opposite bank when they discovered that the sledges sank into the sand and they could not budge them. They called for a bulldozer and a truck. The *coup de grâce* was delivered when they tried to assemble the pyramid and found they could not position the stones with any accuracy, and had to request the aid of helicopters.

National pride and saving face are very important to the Japanese, and this was a shameful episode. They were utterly humiliated when they ultimately discovered that they were not able to bring the four walls together into an apex and their mini-pyramid experiment was a disaster. They left Giza sadder and wiser. Imagine the inconceivably exact planning that went into building the Great Pyramid in order to bring the 481-foot-high walls to a point!

How long did it take the ancient Egyptians to build it? That is the wrong question. The right one is, Could the ancient Egyptians have built the Great Pyramid? The answer is: not with the tools and techniques that Egyptologists claim they used.

These issues have been raised and debated for decades. It is time to bring them to a head and move on. Alternative historians have pointed to the enigmas and orthodoxy has pooh-poohed them. Quite frankly, this gridlock is unproductive. Orthodox historians have shown a disdain for applying the rules and guidelines of scientific methodology to the matter.

Chris Dunn has addressed this issue and pointed out that Egyptologists apply a double standard when it comes to evaluating their soft "evidence" versus the hard facts as outlined above. They set the bar about one foot off the ground for themselves and about eight feet high for alternative historians.

The repeated live TV and canned video programs that have been churned out quite regularly since the mid-1990s, by Zahi Hawass and Mark Lehner, have been aimed at shoring up the party line. In the Fox-TV special broadcast live from the Giza plateau in September 2002, I watched the robot explore the shaft. While most observers have focused on analyzing the "payoff," the most important parts of the program slipped by virtually unnoticed. These were "the filler" segments that recited and added new support for the traditional version of history. It was very deftly layered into the program; in fact, it was "the programming" part of the show.

There really is no "debate" between the orthodox and the alternative history camps because the former group refuses to engage in any fair, open exchange or to provide solid proof of its theories. Every one of their basic construction tenets can be subjected to scientifically controlled tests. Alternative historians have been under the false impression that the other side could be convinced with compelling fact-based arguments and incontrovertible evidence. But that has proved to be a false assumption.

History's mysteries have long since become a political football.

In my opinion, it is time to leave behind that paradigm and time to stop playing by the other side's rigged rules. The debate is over, if it ever existed, so why go on wasting effort trying to open closed minds? That is an exercise in futility. Some very crucial issues need our full attention: What intelligent culture built the pyramid complexes using cyclopean stones? How did they do it and where is the evidence of the technology that was used? Are we the beneficiaries of an alien, yet human, DNA that has to solve this riddle before it can evolve any further? Or are we the inheritors of a strictly Earth-based legacy handed down by a "lost" civilization?

30 An Engineer in Egypt

Did the Ancient Egyptians Possess Toolmaking Skills Comparable to Those of the Space Age?

Christopher Dunn

Within the past three years, artifacts established as icons of ancient Egyptian study have developed a new aura. There are suggestions of controversy, cover-ups, and conspiracy to squelch or ignore data that promises to shatter conventional academic thinking regarding prehistoric society. A powerful movement is intent on restoring to the world a heritage that has been partly destroyed and undeniably misunderstood. This movement consists of specialists in various fields who, in the face of fierce opposition from Egyptologists, are cooperating with each other to effect changes in our beliefs of prehistory.

The opposition by Egyptologists is like the last gasp of a dying man. In the face of expert analysis, they are striving to protect their cozy tenures by arguing engineering subtleties that make no sense whatsoever. In a recent interview, an Egyptologist ridiculed theorists who present different views of the pyramids, claiming their ideas are the product of overactive imaginations stimulated by the consumption of beer. Hmmm.

Wax reveals machined perfection of curve in Giza stone.
(PHOTOGRAPH BY CHRISTOPHER DUNN)

By way of challenging such conventional theories, for decades there has been an undercurrent of speculation that the pyramid builders were highly advanced in their technology. Attempts to build pyramids using the orthodox methods attributed to the ancient Egyptians have fallen pitifully short. The Great Pyramid is 483 feet high and houses seventy-ton pieces of granite lifted to a level of 175 feet. Theorists have struggled with stones weighing from up to two tons to a height of a few feet.

One wonders if these were attempts to prove that primitive methods are capable of building the Egyptian pyramids—or the opposite? Attempts to execute such conventional theories have not revealed the theories to be correct! Do we need to revise the theory, or will we continue to educate our young with erroneous data?

In August 1984 I published an article in *Analog* magazine entitled "Advanced Machining in Ancient Egypt," based on *Pyramids and Temple of Gizeh*, by Sir William Flinders Petrie (the world's first Egyptologist), published in 1883. Since that article's publication, I have been fortunate enough to visit Egypt twice. On each occasion I left Egypt with more respect for the industry of the ancient pyramid builders—an industry, by the way, whose technology does not exist anywhere in the world today.

In 1986, I visited the Cairo Museum and gave a copy of my article, and a business card, to its director. He thanked me kindly, then threw my offering into a drawer with sundry other stuff and turned away. Another Egyptologist led me to the "tool room" to educate me in the methods of the ancient masons by showing me a few tool cases that housed primitive copper implements.

I asked my host about the cutting of granite, as this was the focus of my article. He explained how a slot was cut in the granite, and wooden wedges—soaked with water—would then be inserted. The wood swelled, creating pressure that split the rock. This still did not explain how copper implements were able to cut granite, but he was so enthusiastic with his dissertation, I chose not to interrupt.

I was musing over a statement made by the Egyptologist Dr. I. E. S. Edwards in *Ancient Egypt*. Edwards said that to cut the granite, "axes and chisels were made of copper hardened by hammering."

This is like saying, "To cut this aluminum saucepan, they fashioned their knives out of butter"!

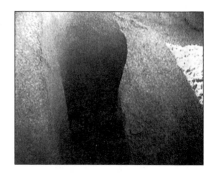

Evidence of the pyramid builders' true quarrying methods: a large hole drilled in the bedrock near the unfinished obelisk at the Aswan quarries.
(PHOTOGRAPH BY CHRISTOPHER DUNN)

My host animatedly walked me over to a nearby travel agent, encouraging me to buy plane tickets to Aswan, "where," he said, "the evidence is clear. You must see the quarry marks there and the unfinished obelisk." Dutifully, I bought the tickets and arrived at Aswan the next day.

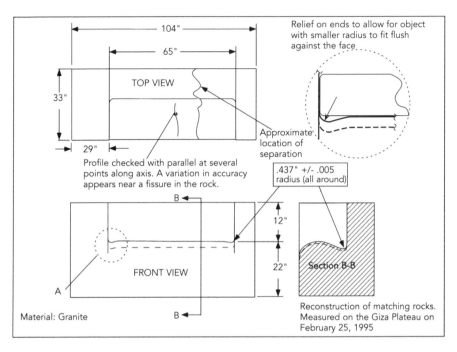

Measuring the curvature of carved stone at Giza
(DRAWING BY CHRISTOPHER DUNN)

The Aswan quarries were educational. The obelisk weighs approximately 440 tons. However, the quarry marks I saw there did not satisfy me as being the only means by which the pyramid builders quarried their rock. Located in a channel that runs the length of the obelisk is a large hole drilled into the bedrock hillside, measuring approximately twelve inches in diameter and three feet deep. The hole was drilled at an angle, with the top intruding into the channel space.

The ancients must have used drills to remove material from the perimeter of the obelisk, knocked out the webs between the holes, and then removed the cusps. While strolling around the Giza plateau later, I started to question the quarry marks at Aswan even more. (I also questioned why the Egyptologist had deemed it necessary that I fly to Aswan to look at them.) I was to the south of the second pyramid when I found an abundance of quarry marks of a similar nature. The granite-casing stones, which had sheathed the second pyramid, were stripped off and lying around the base in various stages of destruction. Typical to all of the granite stones worked on were the same quarry marks that I had seen at Aswan earlier in the week.

This discovery confirmed my suspicion of the validity of Egyptologists' theories on the ancient pyramid builders' quarrying methods. If these quarry marks distinctively identify the people who created the pyramids, why would they engage in such a tremendous amount of extremely difficult work only to destroy their work after having completed it? It seems to me that these kinds of quarry marks were from a later period of time and were created by people who were interested only in obtaining granite, without caring where they got it from.

One can see demonstrations of primitive stonecutting in Egypt if one goes to Saqqara. Being alerted to the presence of tourists, workers will start chipping away at limestone blocks. It doesn't surprise me that they choose limestone for their demonstration, for it is a soft, sedimentary rock and can be easily worked. However, one won't find any workers plowing through granite, an extremely hard igneous rock made up of feldspar and quartz. Any attempt at creating granite, diorite, and basalt artifacts on the same scale as the ancients but using primitive methods would meet with utter and complete failure.

Those Egyptologists who know that work-hardened copper will not cut granite have dreamed up a different method. They propose that the ancients used small round diorite balls (another extremely hard igneous rock) with which they "bashed" the granite.

How could anyone who has been to Egypt and seen the wonderful intricately detailed hieroglyphs cut with amazing precision in granite and diorite statues, which tower fifteen feet above an average man, propose that this work was done by bashing the granite with a round ball? The hieroglyphs are amazingly precise, with grooves that are square and deeper than they are wide. They follow precise contours and some have grooves that run parallel to each other, with only a .030-inch-wide wall between the grooves.

Sir William Flinders Petrie remarked that the grooves could have been cut only with a special tool that was capable of plowing cleanly through the granite without splintering the rock. Bashing with small balls never entered Petrie's mind. But, then, Petrie was a surveyor whose father was an engineer. Failing to come up with a method that would satisfy the evidence, Petrie had to leave the subject open.

We would be hard-pressed to produce many of these artifacts today, even using our advanced methods of manufacturing. The tools displayed as instruments for the creation of these incredible artifacts are physically incapable of coming even close to reproducing many of the artifacts in question. Along with the enormous task of quarrying, cutting, and erecting the Great Pyramid and its neighbors, thousands of tons of hard igneous rock, such as granite and diorite, were carved with extreme proficiency and accuracy. After standing in awe before these engineering marvels and then being shown a paltry collection of copper implements in the tool case at the Cairo Museum, one comes away with a sense of frustration, futility, and wonder.

Sir William Flinders Petrie recognized that these tools were insufficient. He admitted it in his book *Pyramids and Temples of Gizeh* and expressed amazement and stupefaction regarding the methods the ancient Egyptians used to cut hard igneous rocks, crediting them with methods that "we are only now coming to understand." So why do modern Egyptologists identify this work with a few primitive copper instruments and small round balls? It makes no sense whatsoever!

While browsing through the Cairo Museum, I found evidence of lathe turning on a large scale. A sarcophagus lid had distinctive indications. Its radius terminated with a blend radius at shoulders on both ends. The tool marks near these corner radii are the same as those I have witnessed on objects that have an intermittent cut.

Petrie also studied the sawing methods of the pyramid builders. He concluded that their saws must have been at least nine feet long. Again, there are subtle indications of modern sawing methods on the artifacts Petrie was studying. The sarcophagus in the King's Chamber inside the Great Pyramid has saw marks on the north end that are identical to saw marks I've seen on modern granite artifacts.

The artifacts representing tubular drilling, studied by Petrie, are the most clearly astounding and conclusive evidence yet presented to identify, with little doubt, the knowledge and technology in existence in prehistory. The ancient pyramid builders used a technique for drilling holes that is commonly known as trepanning.

This technique leaves a central core and is an efficient means of hole making. For holes that didn't go all the way through the material, the craftsmen would reach a desired depth and then break the core out of the hole. It was not just the holes that Petrie was studying, but also the cores cast aside by the masons who had done some trepanning. Regarding tool marks that left a spiral groove on a core taken out of a hole drilled into a piece of granite, he wrote, "[T]he spiral of the cut sinks .100 inch in the circumference of six inches, or one in sixty, a rate of plowing out of the quartz and feldspar which is astonishing."

For drilling these holes, there is only one method that satisfies the evidence. Without any thought to the time in history when these artifacts were produced, analysis of the evidence clearly points to ultrasonic machining. This is the method that I proposed in my article in 1984, and so far no one has been able to disprove it.

In 1994 I sent a copy of the article to Robert Bauval (author of *The Orion Mystery: Unlocking the Secrets of the Pyramids*), who then passed it on to Graham Hancock (author of *Fingerprints of the Gods: The Evidence of Earth's Lost Civilization*). After a series of conversations with Hancock, I was invited to Egypt to participate in a documentary with him, Bauval, and John Anthony West. On February 22, 1995, at 9:00 A.M., I had my first experience of being "on camera."

This time, with the expressed intent of inspecting features I had identified on my previous trip, in 1986, I took some tools with me: a flat ground piece of steel (commonly known as a parallel in tool shops, it is about six inches long and a quarter-inch thick with edges ground flat within .0002 inch); an Interapid indicator; a wire contour gauge; a device that forms around shapes; and hard-forming wax.

While there, I came across and was able to measure some artifacts produced by the ancient pyramid builders that prove beyond a shadow of a doubt that highly advanced and sophisticated tools and methods had been employed by them. The first object I checked for close precision was the sarcophagus inside the second (Khafra's) pyramid on the Giza plateau.

I climbed inside the box, and with a flashlight and the parallel was astounded to find the surface on the inside of the box perfectly smooth and perfectly flat. Placing the edge of the parallel against the surface, I lit my flashlight behind it. There was no light coming through the interface. No matter where I moved the parallel, vertically, horizontally, sliding it along as one would a gauge on a precision surface plate, I couldn't detect any deviation from a perfectly flat surface. A group of Spanish tourists found it extremely interesting too and gathered around me, as I was becoming quite animated at this point, exclaiming into my tape recorder, "Space-Age precision!"

The tour guides were becoming quite animated, too. I sensed that they probably didn't think it was appropriate for a live foreigner to be where they believed a dead Egyptian should rest, so I respectfully removed myself from the sarcophagus and continued my examination of it from the outside. There were more features of this artifact that I wanted to inspect, of course, but I didn't have the freedom to do so.

My mind was racing as I lowered my frame into the narrow confines of the entrance shaft and climbed outside. As I did so, my mind was reeling: the inside of a huge granite box finished off to a precision that we reserve for precision surface plates? How had they done this? It would be impossible to have done this by hand!

While being extremely impressed with this artifact, I was even more impressed with other artifacts found at another site in the rock tunnels at the temple of Serapeum at Saqqara, the site of the step pyramid and Zoser's tomb. In these dark dusty tunnels are housed twenty-one huge basalt boxes. They weigh an estimated sixty-five tons each and are finished off to the same precision as the sarcophagus in the second pyramid.

The final artifact I inspected was a piece of granite I quite literally stumbled across while strolling around the Giza plateau later that day. I concluded, after doing a preliminary check of this piece, that the ancient pyramid builders had to have used machinery that followed precise contours in three axes to guide the tool that created it. Beyond the incredible precision, normal flat surfaces, being simple geometry, may be explained away by simple methods. This piece, though, drives us beyond the question normally pondered—What tools were used to cut it?—to a more far-reaching question: What *guided* the cutting tool? These discoveries have more implications for understanding the technology used by the ancient pyramid builders than anything heretofore uncovered.

The interpretation of these artifacts depends on engineers and technologists. When presenting this material to a local engineers club, I was gratified by the response of my peers. They saw the significance. They agreed with the conclusions. While my focus was on the methods used to produce them, some engineers, ignoring the Egyptologists' proposed uses for these artifacts, asked, "What were they doing with them?" They were utterly astounded by what they saw.

The interpretation and understanding of a civilization's level of technology cannot and should not hinge on the preservation of a written record for every technique that it had developed. The nuts and bolts of our society do not always make good copy, and a stone mural will more than likely be cut to convey an ideological message rather than the technique used to inscribe it. Records of the technology developed by our modern civilization rest in media that are vulnerable and could conceivably cease to exist in the event of a worldwide catastrophe, such as a nuclear war or another ice age.

Consequently, after several thousand years, an interpretation of an artisan's methods may be more accurate than an interpretation of his language. The language of science and technology doesn't have the same freedom as speech. So even though the tools and machines have not survived the thousands of years since their use, we have to assume, by objective analysis of the evidence, that they obviously *did* exist.

31 The Giza Power Plant, Technologies of Ancient Egypt

A New Book Challenges Conventional Wisdom on the Intended Purpose of the Great Pyramid

Christopher Dunn

In the summer of 1997, Atlantis Rising was contacted by a scientist involved in government research into nonlethal acoustical weapons. He said his team had analyzed the Great Pyramid using the most advanced tools available and concluded that its builders used sophisticated geometries that we have only recently begun to understand—"way beyond Euclidean" or any of the other familiar, ancient systems. Moreover, we were told, the analysis indicated that the only way to understand the configuration of the chambers in the Great Pyramid was in acoustical terms: in other words, by the sophisticated manipulation of sound. For the weapons designer, that meant the Great Pyramid was, in all probability, a weapon—an extremely powerful one at that. Unfortunately, for reasons that remain unclear, we soon found ourselves unable to contact the scientist again, and we were left with a tantalizing bit of information that we could not corroborate. However, as fate would have it, one of the most important investigations of the acoustical potential of the Great Pyramid was being conducted by an old friend of ours, Christopher Dunn.

Chris has written a book entitled The Giza Power Plant: Technologies of Ancient Egypt *in which he produces an overwhelming body of evidence that accounts for many previously unexplained anomalies. In it he tells us that the Giza pyramid was a machine that captured the acoustic energies of the earth to produce awesome power. In this article, Chris excerpts and edits a brief summary of the arguments in his book.*

—Editor

221

T he evidence carved into the granite artifacts in Egypt clearly points to manufacturing methods that involved the use of machinery such as lathes, milling machines, ultrasonic drilling machines, and high-speed saws. They also possess attributes that cannot be produced without a system of measurement that is equal to the system of measurement we use today. Their accuracy was not produced by chance, but rather is repeated over and over again.

After I assimilated the data regarding the ancient Egyptians' manufacturing precision and their possible and in some instances probable methods of machining, I suspected that to account for the level of technology the pyramid builders seem to have achieved, they must have had an equally sophisticated energy system to support it. One of the pressing questions we raise when we discuss ancient, ultrasonic drilling of granite is, "What did they use as a source of power?"

A still more forceful inquiry regarding the use of electricity necessary to power ultrasonic drills or heavy machining equipment that may have been used to cut granite is, "Where are their power plants?" Obviously there are no structures from the ancient world that we can point to and identify as fission reactors or turbine halls. And why should we have to? Isn't it a bit misguided of us to form an assumption that the ancient power plants were even remotely similar to ours?

Christopher Dunn at his home computer
(PHOTOGRAPH BY TOM MILLER)

Nevertheless, there may be some fundamental similarities between ancient and modern power supplies, in that power plants in existence today are quite large and need a supply of water for cooling and steam production. If such an advanced society existed in prehistory and if indeed it had an energy system, we could logically surmise that its power plants, in all probability, would have been the largest construction projects it would have attempted. It also may follow that, as the largest creations of the society, those power plants would stand a good chance of surviving a catastrophe and the erosion of the elements during the centuries that followed.

The pyramids easily meet these requirements. These geometric relics of the past, which have been studied, speculated about, and on which so much debate has centered, are located near a water supply, the Nile River, and, indeed, are the largest building projects that this ancient society completed. In light of all the evidence that suggests the existence of a highly advanced society utilizing electricity in prehistory, I began to consider seriously the possibility that the pyramids were the power plants of the ancient Egyptians.

Like just about every other student of the Egyptian pyramids, my attention was focused on the Great Pyramid, primarily because this is the one that everybody else's attention had been focused on, resulting in more research data being available for study. The reports of each successive researcher's discoveries inside the Great Pyramid are quite detailed. It is as though researchers became obsessed with reporting data, regardless of how insignificant it may have seemed. Much of their data focuses on the dimensional and geometric relationship between the Great Pyramid and Earth.

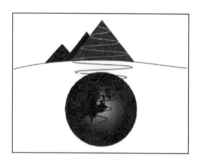

The Great Pyramid and Earth in resonance

To review John Taylor's findings: A pyramid inch is .001 inch larger than a British inch. There are twenty-five pyramid inches in a cubit and there were 365.24 cubits in the square base of the Great Pyramid. There are 365.24 days in a calendar year. One pyramid inch is equal in length to 1/500 millionth of Earth's axis of rotation. This relationship suggests that not only were the builders of the Great Pyramid knowledgeable about the dimensions of the planet, but they also based their measurement system on them.

What else is unique about the Great Pyramid? Although it is a pyramid in shape, its geometry possesses an astounding approximation of the unique properties of a circle, or sphere. The pyramid's height is in relationship to the perimeter of its base as the radius of a circle is in relationship to its circumference. A perfectly constructed pyramid with an exact angle of 51° 51'14.3" has the value pi incorporated into its shape.

Further understanding of this relationship requires the study of not just every detail of the Great Pyramid, but also those of Earth. Earth is a dynamic, energetic body that has supported civilization's demand for fuel for centuries. To date, this demand has been predominantly for energy in the form of fossil fuels. More recently, scientific advances have allowed us to tap into the power of the atom, and further research in this area promises greater advances in the future.

There is, however, another form of abundant energy in the earth that, in its most basic form has, for the most part, been largely ignored as a potential source of usable energy. It usually gets our attention when it builds up to a point of destruction. That energy is seismic, and it is the result of the earth's plates being driven by the constant agitation of the molten rock within the earth. The tides are contained not only within the oceans of the world; the continents, too, are in constant movement, rising and falling as much as a foot as the Moon orbits Earth.

The earth's energy includes mechanical, thermal, electrical, magnetic, nuclear, and chemical action, each a source for sound. It would follow, therefore, that the energy at work in the earth would generate sound waves that would be related to the particular vibration of the energy creating it and the material through which it passes. The audible hum of an electric motor—operating at 3,600 rpm—would fall well below the level of human hearing if it were to slow down to one revolution every twenty-four hours, as in the case of Earth. What goes unnoticed as we go about our daily lives is our planet's inaudible fundamental pulse, or rhythm.

On the other end of the scale, any electrical stimulation within the earth of piezoelectrical materials—such as quartz—would generate sound waves above the range of human hearing. Materials undergoing stress within the earth can emit bursts of ultrasonic radiation. Materials undergoing plastic deformation emit a signal of lower amplitude than when the deformation is such as to produce cracks. Ball lightning has been speculated to be gas ionized by electricity from quartz-bearing rock, such as granite, that is subject to stress.

Because the earth constantly generates a broad spectrum of vibration, we could utilize vibration as a source of energy if we developed suitable technology. Naturally, any device that attracted greater amounts of this energy than is normally being radiated from the earth would greatly improve the efficiency of the equipment. Because energy will inherently follow the path of least resistance, any device offering less resistance to this energy than the surrounding medium through which it passes would have a greater amount of energy channeled through it.

Keeping all of this in mind and knowing that the Great Pyramid is a mathematical integer of the earth, it may not be so outlandish to propose that the pyramid is capable of vibrating at a harmonic frequency of the earth's fundamental frequency.

In *The Giza Power Plant: Technologies of Ancient Egypt,* I have amassed a plethora of facts and deductions based on sober consideration of the design of the Great Pyramid and nearly every artifact found within it. When taken together, these all support my premise that the Great Pyramid was a power plant and the King's Chamber its power center. Facilitated by the element that fuels our Sun (hydrogen), and uniting the energy of the universe with that of the earth, the ancient Egyptians converted vibrational energy into microwave energy. For the power plant to function, the designers and operators had to induce vibration in the Great Pyramid that was in tune with the harmonic resonant vibrations of Earth.

Once the pyramid was vibrating in tune with Earth's pulse, it became a coupled oscillator and could sustain the transfer of energy from the earth with little or no feedback. The three smaller pyramids on the east side of the Great Pyramid may have been used to assist the Great Pyramid in achieving resonance, much like today we use smaller gasoline engines to start large diesel engines. So let us now turn the key on this amazing power plant to see how it operated.

THE GIZA POWER PLANT

The Queen's Chamber, located in the center of the pyramid and directly below the King's Chamber, contains peculiarities entirely different from those observed in the King's Chamber. The characteristics of the Queen's Chamber indicate that its specific purpose was to produce fuel, which is of paramount importance for any power plant. Although it would be difficult to pinpoint exactly what process took place inside the Queen's Chamber, it appears that a chemical reaction repeatedly took place there.

The residual substance the process left behind (the salts on the chamber wall) and what can be deduced from artifacts (grapnel hook and cedarlike wood) and structural details (Gantenbrink's "door," for example) are too prominent to be ignored. They all indicate that the energy created in the King's Chamber was the result of the efficient operation of the hydrogen-generating Queen's Chamber.

The equipment that provided the priming pulses was most likely housed in the subterranean pit. Before or at the time the "key was turned" to start the priming pulses, a supply of chemicals was pumped into the northern and southern shafts of the Queen's Chamber, filling them until contact was made between the grapnel hook and the electrodes that were sticking out of the door. Seeping through the "lefts" in the Queen's Chamber, these chemicals combined to produce hydrogen gas, which filled the interior passageways and chambers of the pyramid. The waste from the spent chemicals flowed along the horizontal passage and down the well shaft.

Induced by priming pulses of vibration—tuned to the resonant frequency of the entire structure—the vibration of the pyramid gradually increased in amplitude and oscillated in harmony with the vibrations of the earth. Harmonically coupled with the earth, vibrational energy then flowed in abundance from the earth through the pyramid and influenced a series of tuned, Helmholtz-type resonators housed in the grand gallery, where the vibration was converted into airborne sound. By virtue of the acoustical design of the grand gallery, the sound was focused through the passage leading to the King's Chamber. Only frequencies in harmony with the resonant frequency of the King's Chamber were allowed to pass through an acoustic filter, which was housed in the antechamber.

The King's Chamber was the heart of the Giza power plant, an impressive power center comprising thousands of tons of granite containing 55 percent silicon-quartz crystal. The chamber was designed to minimize any damping of vibration, and its dimensions created a resonant cavity that was in harmony with the incoming acoustical energy. As the granite vibrated in sympathy with the sound, it stressed the quartz in the rock and stimulated electrons to flow by what is known as the piezoelectric effect.

The energy that filled the King's Chamber at that point became a combination of acoustical energy and electromagnetic energy. Both forms of energy covered a broad spectrum of harmonic frequencies, from the fundamental infrasonic frequencies of the earth to the ultrasonic and higher electromagnetic microwave frequencies.

The hydrogen freely absorbed this energy, for the designers of the Giza power plant had made sure that the frequencies at which the King's Chamber resonated were harmonics of the frequency at which hydrogen resonates. As a result, the hydrogen atom, which consists of one proton and one electron, efficiently absorbed this energy, and its electron was "pumped" to a higher energy state.

The northern shaft served as a conduit, or a waveguide, and its original metal lining—which passed with extreme precision through the pyramid from the outside—served to channel a microwave signal into the King's Chamber. The microwave signal that flowed through this waveguide may have been the same signal that we know today is created by the atomic hydrogen that fills the universe and that is constantly bombarding Earth. This microwave signal probably was reflected off the outside face of the pyramid, then focused down the northern shaft.

Traveling through the King's Chamber and passing through a crystal box amplifier located in its path, the input signal increased in power as it interacted with the highly energized hydrogen atoms inside the resonating box amplifier and chamber. This interaction forced the electrons back to their natural "ground state." In turn, hydrogen atoms released a packet of energy of the same type and frequency as the input signal. This "stimulated emission" was entrained with the input signal and followed the same path.

The process built exponentially—occurring trillions of times over. What entered the chamber as a low energy signal became a collimated (parallel) beam of immense power as it was collected in a microwave receiver housed in the south wall of the King's Chamber and was then directed through the metal-lined southern shaft to the outside of the pyramid. This tightly collimated beam was the reason for all the science, technology, craftsmanship, and untold hours of work that went into designing, testing, and building the Giza power plant.

The ancient Egyptians had a need for this energy: It was most likely used for the same reasons we would use it today—to power machines and appliances. We know from examining Egyptian stone artifacts that ancient craftspeople must have created them using machinery and tools that needed electricity to run. However, the means by which they distributed the energy produced by the Giza power plant may have been a process very different from today's.

I would like to join the architect James Hagan and other engineers and technologists in extending my utmost respect to the builders of the Great Pyramid. Though some academics may not recognize it, the precision and knowledge that went into its creation are—by modern standards—undeniable and a marvel to behold.

The evidence presented in *The Giza Power Plant,* for the most part, was recorded many years ago by men of integrity who worked in the fields of archeology and Egyptology. That much of this evidence was misunderstood only reveals the pressing need for an interdisciplinary approach to fields that have, until recently, been closed to nonacademics and others outside the fold of formal archeology and Egyptology.

Much of our ignorance of ancient cultures can be placed at the feet of closed-minded theorists who ignore evidence that does not fit their theories or fall within the province of their expertise. Sometimes it takes a machinist to recognize machined parts or machines! As a result, much of the evidence that supports a purpose for the Great Pyramid as anything other than a tomb has been ignored, discounted without serious consideration, or simply explained away as purely coincidental.

The technology that was used inside the Great Pyramid may be quite simple to understand but difficult to execute, even for our technologically "advanced" civilization. However, if anyone is inspired to pursue the theory presented here, his or her vision may be enhanced by the knowledge that re-creating this power source would be ecologically pleasing to those who have concern about the welfare of the environment and the future of the human race.

Blending science and music, the ancient Egyptians had tuned their power plant to a natural harmonic of the earth's vibration (predominantly a function of the tidal energy induced by the gravitational effect that the Moon has on Earth). Resonating to the life force of Mother Earth, the Great Pyramid of Giza quickened and focused her pulse, and transduced it into clean, plentiful energy.

We know very little about the pyramid builders and the period of time wherein they erected these giant monuments, yet it seems obvious that the entire civilization underwent a drastic change, one so great that its technology was destroyed, with no hope of its being rebuilt. Hence a cloud of mystery has denied us a clear view of the nature of these people and their technological knowledge.

Considering the theory presented in *The Giza Power Plant,* I am com-pelled to envision a fantastic society that developed a power system thou-sands of years ago that we can barely imagine today. This society takes shape as we ask the logical questions: "How was the energy transmitted? How was it used?" These questions cannot be fully answered by examining the arti-facts left behind. However, these artifacts can stimulate our imaginations fur-ther; then we are left to speculate on the causes for the demise of the great and intelligent civilization that built the Giza power plant.

32 Return to the Giza Power Plant

Technologist Chris Dunn
Finds New Fuel for His Thesis

Christopher Dunn

*T*he *Giza Power Plant: Technologies of Ancient Egypt* was published in August 1998, and an article summarizing its theory appeared the same year in *Atlantis Rising*. Since then I have been overwhelmed by the response to the theory. The reviews have been nothing short of incredible! I have received letters and e-mails from all over the world supporting the argument that high levels of technology existed in prehistory and that the Great Pyramid represents the pinnacle of that technology.

Though the power plant theory may explain every characteristic and noted phenomenon found within the Great Pyramid, without actually replicating its function (which is way beyond my own personal resources), the theory could be ignored or dismissed as being too fantastic by those who feel more secure with conventional views of prehistory. Not so with the hard evidence of machining!

There is a section in the book that is increasingly being seen as the "smoking gun" that proves, beyond a doubt, that the pyramid builders used advanced technology. It is not a simple matter to dismiss the physical constraints imposed on those who would attempt to replicate accurately the granite artifacts found in abundance all over this ancient land. Those who try to dismiss it do so from inexperience and do not understand the subtleties of the work, or they cling desperately to the belief that Western civilization is the first civilization to develop science and to translate that science into products that require advanced methods of manufacturing.

My article, *Advanced Machining in Ancient Egypt* (later expanded to become my book *The Giza Power Plant*), has been under public scrutiny for around fifteen years. With the level of support that it has received from those who, today, would be charged with performing the same kind of work performed by the ancient Egyptians, along with additional proof, it is rising from the rank of theory to fact. Since its original publication, in 1984, this tentative, controversial thorn in the side of Egyptologists has been reinforced time and time again by my own on-site inspections and by others who have had the opportunity to see these incredible artifacts for themselves. The weight of evidence and the educated opinions of those who understand are creating a consensus that is overturning our understanding of prehistory.

The most awesome implication may be that civilizations are mortal!

Civilizations such as ours can rise to great heights only to be dashed by natural or engineered effects. In a blink of an eye, we can lose it all! Whether as one or as multiple blinks of an eye, our distant ancestors in prehistoric Egypt received a mortal blow to the industry capable of creating the artifacts we see there today. Whether that blow came from extraterrestrial forces, a comet, geophysical disturbances, or even a nuclear war is open to speculation. The fact remains that their industries did exist and somehow became extinct!

The purpose here is not to belabor the obvious or to restate what others have stated more eloquently (I know I'm "preaching to the choir" for the most part), but rather to provide an update on what has happened since the book was published. On a recent trip to Egypt, as a participant in the conference Egypt in the New Millennium, I was able to perform additional on-site inspection of some of the artifacts I described in my articles and book.

I was also blessed to discover startling evidence that supports and confirms a unique and important aspect of the Giza power plant theory. This was evidence that made chills run down my spine, for it came about in a rather unexpected manner. This evidence was inside the Great Pyramid in the grand gallery, and I am still amazed by what I found. I will elaborate on this later.

It is with great appreciation for the organizers, attendees, and speakers at this conference that this article is written. Their spirit, diversity, and camaraderie buoyed my spirit and gave me strength. But more than that, through their support and patronage (which was sometimes accompanied with frustrating and arduous conditions, with our blessed guide Hakim almost being thrown in jail), further evidence to support the power plant theory has now been captured on video and becomes part of the historical record.

A large part of my presentation at Gouda Fayed's conference center in Nazlet El Samman was to be an on-site inspection and demonstration of the precision of several artifacts. Gouda's place overlooked the Sphinx, with the Giza plateau and the pyramid complex forming an awe-inspiring backdrop.

Though I can say with great confidence that I have proved that the ancient pyramid builders used advanced methods for machining granite, the full scope of the work has not yet been determined or documented. For my trip to Egypt in 1995, I had taken some instruments with me to inspect the flatness of artifacts that, just by simple observation, appeared extremely precise.

An example of precise machined art from ancient Egypt
(PHOTOGRAPH BY CHRISTOPHER DUNN)

Mere looking, however, is not a sufficient means to determine the true characteristics of the artifacts. I needed some kind of known reference with which I could compare the precision. I also needed something simple and transportable. The precision-ground straightedge I used in 1995 allowed me to determine a higher order of precision in many different artifacts than what has been described in any previous literature.

This year, in my backpack, I carried a precision-ground twelve-inch-long parallel, or straightedge, precise to within .0001 inch. I also had a precision toolmaker's solid square. I knew exactly the artifacts I wanted to use it on—the inside corners of the granite boxes at the temple of the Serapeum at Saqqara and inside the pyramids. Also in my tool kit was a set of precision Starrett radius gauges for inspecting the machined radius that makes the transition from one surface or contour of an artifact to another. These instruments are critical to our understanding of the basic attributes of the artifacts.

The Serapeum
(PHOTOGRAPH BY CHRISTOPHER DUNN)

Unfortunately, I was unable to access the rock tunnel at the temple of the Serapeum, where more than twenty huge black granite and basalt boxes weighing over seventy tons reside. We pleaded with the officials at the site, and I even discussed it with a local businessman who claimed to have considerable power and influence in such matters. Nevertheless, I was told that the Serapeum was closed because it was a danger to the public. "What kind of danger?" I asked, and was told in reply that dripping water threatened to collapse the roof. I chose not to ask the obvious question about where the water came from in such an arid country. There was enough other work to do.

Following my morning presentation on the advanced machining methods of the ancient Egyptians, the entire conference group and the film crew proceeded to the Giza plateau and into the bedrock chamber of the second largest pyramid on the plateau: Khafre's pyramid. In this chamber in 1995 I had discovered the perfect flatness on the inside surfaces of the black granite box (commonly and mistakenly, in my opinion, known as the sarcophagus). At that time I had uttered the words "Space-age precision!" to a group of Spanish tourists who were looking on as I beamed my flashlight behind the precise edge of a steel parallel and revealed the stunning precision of the surface.

Although I confidently wrote articles citing this as additional proof of the level of technology practiced by the pyramid builders, in the back of my mind was the nagging need to go back to Egypt with additional instruments and do more tests. Each time I go to Egypt I approach these relics with eager anticipation and some trepidation. Will I find them the same? Will the next range of instruments confirm or deny what was gleaned on the previous visit?

The cool confines of the passageway leading to the bedrock chamber of Khafre's pyramid were a welcome relief from the burning Egyptian sun. It felt familiar and right to be there. I was excited to share the discovery I had made four years earlier with the wonderful people who attended the conference, as well as being able to document the event on video. But still there was that twinge of doubt. Had I made a mistake in the past? Would the new instruments reveal anything significant?

Climbing into the black granite box set into the floor of the chamber, I placed my twelve-inch straightedge on the inside surface. The "edge" used this time had been prepared differently from the one I had used in 1995, as it had a chamfer on both corners. For those interested, I slid this edge along the smooth interior of the granite box with my flashlight shining behind it and demonstrated its exact precision. But I was anxious to perform other tests.

The squareness of the corners was of critical importance to me. Modern machine axes are aligned orthogonally, or exactly perpendicular, to each other to ensure accuracy. This state ensures that the corners cut into an object on the machine are square and true.

The requirements for producing this condition go beyond coincidental simplicity. I wasn't expecting the corners of the sarcophagus to be perfectly square, for perfection is extremely difficult to achieve. I was flabbergasted as I slid my precision square along the top of the parallel (I used the top of the parallel to raise the square above the corner radius), and it fit perfectly on the adjacent surface.

"Bloody hell!" I exclaimed as the significance of this find came over me. I pointed it out to others

Dunn measures the precision of the surfaces in the Serapeum sarcophagus.
(Photograph by Tim Hunkler)

in the group. (Alan Alford would spend the next few days mimicking me with a good-natured "Bloody hell!") The film crew was busy capturing my exploration on video as I went to each corner and found the same condition. On three corners, the square sat flush against both surfaces. One corner had a gap that was detected by the light test, though it was probably only about .001 inch.

So not only did we have an artifact with perfectly flat surfaces, but the inside corners were also perfectly square. What else was significant about this so-called sarcophagus? The corners themselves! After conducting the test with the parallel and the square, I pulled out my radius gauges to check the corner radius. As I checked the corner, I chuckled to myself with memories of a documentary I had seen earlier that year.

Those of you who saw the Fox special in September 2002 will remember the moment in it when the world's foremost Egyptologist and the director of the Giza plateau, Zahi Hawass, picked up a dolerite ball in the bedrock chamber under one of the satellite pyramids next to Khephren's pyramid. He was describing, to the Fox anchor Suzie Koppel, the Egyptologists' theory of the methods the ancient Egyptians used to create granite artifacts. This method involved bashing the granite with a round ball until the desired shape was achieved.

I'm not disputing that this is a viable means of creating a box and, indeed, there is evidence at Memphis near Saqqara that some boxes were created in this manner. These boxes had large corner radii, which were extremely rough and tapered toward the bottom—exactly what one would expect to produce using a stone ball. However, as Hawass was wielding his eight-inch-diameter ball in front of the cameras, my attention was focused on the shiny, black, so-called sarcophagus behind him, which sat in mute contradiction to his proposition.

The inside of this box had the same appearance as the box inside Khafre's pyramid. The surfaces appeared smooth and precise but, more important, the inside corners were equally as sharp as what I had witnessed in Khafre's pyramid. Just looking at it, one could see that to create such an artifact with an eight-inch-diameter ball would be impossible!

Likewise, creating the corner radius of the box inside Khafre's pyramid using such primitive methods would be impossible. Checking this corner radius with my radius gauges, I started with a half-inch radius gauge and kept working my way down in size until the correct one had inadvertently been selected. The inside corner radius of the box inside Khafre's pyramid checked $3/32$ inch. The radius at the bottom, where the floor of the box met the wall, checked $7/16$ inch. It should go without saying that one cannot fit an eight-inch ball into a corner with a $3/32$ radius, or even a one-inch radius.

THE GIZA POWER PLANT: THE PROOF

I don't think I have ever been as surprised as I was while filming inside the grand gallery. Filming inside the grand gallery had been especially rewarding, as I had had my doubts as to whether I would even get to go into the Great Pyramid. It had been closed to visitors, ostensibly for restoration, and we had spent almost a week of uncertainty over access. But after numerous calls and visits to officials, we finally got the go-ahead.

While most of the group meditated in the King's Chamber, the video crew and I went out into the grand gallery to do some filming. I was going to describe, on camera, my theory about the function of the grand gallery. This involved pointing out the slots in the gallery side ramps, the corbeled walls, and the ratchet-style ceiling. Equipped with a microphone, I stood just below the great step, the camera at the top. While the soundman adjusted his gear, I scanned the wall with my flashlight. It was then I noticed that the first cor-beled ledge had some scorch marks underneath it, and that some of the stone was broken away. Then, as the camera lights came on, things became really interesting.

In all the literature I had read, the grand gallery was described as being constructed of limestone. But here I was looking at *granite*! I noted a transi-tion point farther down the gallery where the rock changed from limestone to granite. I scanned the ceiling and saw, instead of the rough, crumbling lime-stone one sees when first entering the gallery, what appeared to be, from twenty-eight feet below, smooth, highly polished granite. This was of great significance to me. It made sense that the material closer to the power center would be constructed of a material that was more resistant to heat!

I then paid closer attention to the scorch marks on the walls. There was heavy heat damage underneath each of the corbeled layers, for a distance of about twelve inches, and it seemed as though the damage was concentrated in the center of the burn marks. Then, visually, I took a straight line through the center of each scorch mark and projected it down toward the gallery ramp. That was when chills ran down my spine and the hair stood out on my neck. The line extended in alignment with the slot in the ramp!

In *The Giza Power Plant,* I had theorized that harmonic resonators were housed in these slots and were oriented vertically toward the ceiling. I had also theorized that there was a hydrogen explosion inside the King's Chamber that had shut down the power plant's operation. This explosion explained many other unusual effects that have been noted inside the Great Pyramid in the past, and I had surmised that the explosion had also destroyed the resonators inside the grand gallery in a terrible fire.

Only with the powerful lights of the video camera did the evidence become clear, and illuminated before me, as at no other time before—the charred evidence to support my theory. This was evidence that I had not even been looking for!

Even as I conclude this article, I continue to receive confirmation that I'm on the right track. Others are stepping forward with their own research along the same lines. A more complete update on all of this, though, will have to wait for another time. Perhaps when the Egyptian government discloses what it finds behind Gantenbrink's door? I am most anxious to know what is dis-covered behind this so-called door. If my own prediction is correct, then yet another aspect of the power plant theory will be confirmed.

It has been an interesting year.

33 Petrie on Trial

Have Arguments for Advanced Ancient
Machining Made by the Great Nineteenth-
Century Egyptologist Sir William Flinders Petrie
Been Disproved? Christopher Dunn Takes On
the Debunkers

Christopher Dunn

If there is one area of research into ancient civilizations that proves the technological prowess of a superior prehistoric society, the study of the technical requirements necessary to produce many granite artifacts found in Egypt is it.

My own research into how many of these artifacts were produced started in 1977, and my article *Advanced Machining in Ancient Egypt* was first published in *Analog* magazine in 1984. It was later expanded to fill two chapters in my book *The Giza Power Plant: Technologies of Ancient Egypt.*

As this body of work became more popular and well known, it was only a matter of time before the orthodox camp attempted to diminish the significance of the artifacts and thereby discredit my work.

Albeit ineffectual, this they have done in both subtle and obvious ways:

1. Documentaries have been produced that attempt to reinforce Egyptologists' views that bashing granite with hard stone balls produced fabulous granite artifacts.
2. A stonemason named Denys Stocks was taken to Egypt to demonstrate how the use of copper and sand, along with a tremendous amount of manual effort, can produce holes and slots in granite. This he succeeded in doing, much to the satisfaction of orthodox believers.
3. Two authors who claimed to be onetime supporters of alternate ideas such as mine switched camps and wrote a book entitled *Giza: The Truth.* Though unschooled in the mechanical arts, Ian Lawton and Chris Ogilvie-Herald were determined to take an antagonistic approach to the ideas I have presented and to support the orthodox view.

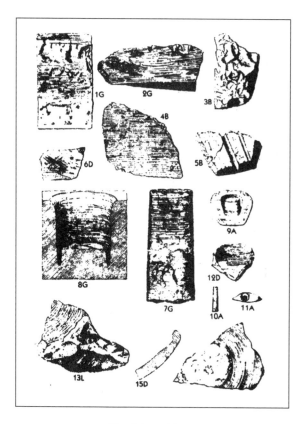

Petrie's artifacts

In each of the above cases, the limited perspective and incomplete analysis of all the evidence, though probably passing muster with their own peer reviews, do not pass muster with my own peers, who consist of technologists involved in such work today. In fact, the consensus among the latter group is that the former are dead wrong. However, none of us is perfect, and everyone has his Achilles' heel.

In retrospect, I will admit to having probably taken my analysis too far when I proposed that ultrasonic machining produced the artifact known as Core #7. My theory of ultrasonic machining was based on Sir William Flinders Petrie's book *Pyramids and Temples of Gizeh*. In this book, Petrie described an artifact with marks of a drilling process that left a spiral groove in granite indicating that the drill sank into the granite at .100 inch per revolution of the drill.

My conviction was shaken when I read, in *Giza: The Truth*, that two researchers, John Reid and Harry Brownlee, had effectively dismissed my

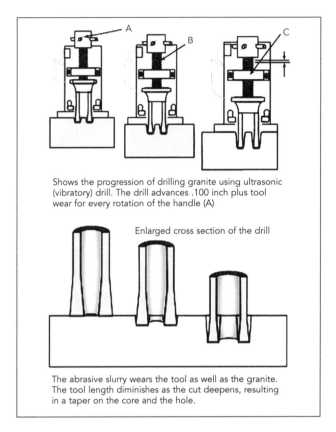

Shows the progression of drilling granite using ultrasonic (vibratory) drill. The drill advances .100 inch plus tool wear for every rotation of the handle (A)

Enlarged cross section of the drill

The abrasive slurry wears the tool as well as the granite. The tool length diminishes as the cut deepens, resulting in a taper on the core and the hole.

Ultrasonic drilling technology
(DRAWING BY CHRISTOPHER DUNN)

theories of how the ancient Egyptians had drilled granite. After a physical examination of this artifact, they testified that the grooves were not spiral grooves but individual rings, and were common to cores found in any modern quarry in England. A photograph of this core in *Giza: The Truth* was positioned in a way that seemed to support their contention; however, I was unable to disprove them because I had not even been in the same room as the core, let alone physically examined it.

Until I had the opportunity to perform a detailed inspection of the piece, which requires more than mere visual scrutiny, I was forced to defer to the observations of Reid and Brownlee. Nevertheless, even in so doing, if they were basing their observations on the photograph in *Giza: The Truth,* I had questions about those observations. What we have is a photograph that shows the frustrum of a cone (Core #7) with grooves cut into it. After reading this report, I immediately posted, to my Web site, a statement to the effect that I suspended any assertions I have made about ultrasonic machining of these holes and cores and I also asserted that I was prepared to examine the core for myself.

On November 10, 1999, I flew out of Indianapolis heading for England. My Webmaster, Nick Annies, had arranged, with the Petrie Museum, for the inspection of the core while the museum was closed for academic research. Nick and I took the train to King's Cross on Monday, November 15, 1999. A short walk to the University College, London, found us, at 10:30 A.M., standing on the bottom step of the Petrie Museum, looking up at a gregarious doorman who advised us to have a cup of tea while we waited for the museum to open and then pointed us in the direction of a cafeteria. Not only a cuppa did we find there, but a wonderful English breakfast as well!

Then it came time to inspect the infamous Core #7. Although I had talked and written about this core for more than fifteen years, this was not the reverent visit to a holy relic that one might expect. I was not especially breathless with excitement to take the artifact into my latex-gloved hands. Nor was I impressed with its size or character. To tell the truth, I was profoundly unmoved and disappointed. With the old Peggy Lee song "Is That All There Is?" bouncing around in my head, I peered at this insignificant-looking piece of rock that had fueled such a heated debate on the Internet and in living rooms and pubs across the globe.

I was thinking to myself as I looked at the rough grooves on its surface, "How do I make sense of this?" And, "What was Petrie thinking about?" I looked up at Nick Annies standing over me. He had a look on his face that reminded me of my mother, within whose face I sought comfort when, at the age of eight, I was lying on the operating table having a wart burned out of my palm by a long, hot needle.

Not a word passed between us as I formulated my ultimate confession to the world. I had made a huge mistake in trusting Petrie's writings! The core appeared to be exactly as Reid and Brownlee had described it! The grooves did *not* appear to have any remote resemblance to what Petrie had described. With the truth resting where a wart once grew, I was frozen in time.

With resignation I proceeded to check the width between the grooves using a 50X handheld microscope with .001 gradated reticle to .100 inch. At this point, I was certain that Petrie had been totally wrong in his evaluation of the piece. The distance between the grooves, which are scoured into the core along the entire length, was .040–.080 inch. I was devastated that Petrie had even gotten the distance between the grooves wrong! Any further measurements, I thought, would just be perfunctory. I couldn't support any theory of advanced machining if Petrie's dimensions of .100 inch feed-rate could not be verified! Nevertheless, I continued with my examination.

The crystalline structure of the core under microscope was beyond my ability to evaluate. I could not determine, as surely as Petrie had, that the groove ran deeper through the quartz than through the feldspar. I did notice that there were some regions, very few, where the biotite (black mica) appeared to be ripped from the felspar in a way that is similar to other artifacts found in Egypt. However, the groove passed through other areas quite cleanly without any such ripping effect, though again I support Brownlee's assertions that a cutting force against the material could rip the crystals from the felspar substrate.

William Flinders Petrie

I then measured the depth of the groove. To accomplish this I used an indicator depth gauge with a fine point to enable it to reach into a narrow space. The gauge operated so as to allow a zero setting when the gauge was set on a flat surface without any deviations. When the gauge passed over a depression (or groove) in a surface, the spring-loaded indicator point pushed into the groove, causing the needle to move on the gauge dial, indicating the precise depth.

The depths of the grooves were .002 and .005 inch. (Actually, because there were clearly discontinuities in the groove at some locations around the core, the actual measurement would be between .000 and .005 inch.)

Then came the great question. Was the groove a helix or a horizontal ring around the core? I had deferred to Reid and Brownlee's assertions that they were horizontal and I was, at this juncture, painfully assured that it was the correct thing to do. It was Petrie's description of the helical groove that made Core #7 stand apart from modern cores. It was one of the principal characteristics upon which I had based my theory of ultrasonic machining. But what I held in my hand seemed to support Reid and Brownlee's objections to this theory, for they said that the core had an appearance similar to any other core one may produce in a quarry.

White cotton thread was the perfect tool to use when inspecting for a helical groove. Why not use a thread to check a thread! I carefully placed one end of the thread in a groove while Nick secured it with a piece of Scotch tape. While I peered through my 10X Optivisor, I rotated the core in my left hand, making sure the thread stayed in the groove with my right. The groove varied in depth as it circled the core, and at some points there was just a faint scratch that I would probably not have detected with my naked eye. As the other end of the thread came into view, I could see that what Petrie had described about this core was not quite correct.

Petrie had described a single helical groove that had a pitch of .100 inch. What I was looking at was *not* a single helical groove, but *two* helical grooves. The thread wound around the core following the groove until it lay approximately .110 inch above the start of the thread. Amazingly, though, there was *another* groove that nestled neatly in between!

I repeated the test at six or seven different locations on the core, with the same results. The grooves were cut clockwise, looking down the small end to the large—which would be from top to bottom. In uniformity, the grooves were as deep at the top of the core as they were at the bottom. They were also as uniform in pitch at the top and bottom, with sections of the groove clearly seen right to the point where the core granite was broken out of the hole.

These are *not* horizontal striations or rings as trumpeted in *Giza: The Truth*, but rather helical grooves that spiraled down the core like a double-start thread.

To replicate this core, therefore, the drilling method should produce the following:

- A clockwise double helical groove from top to bottom with a .110 to .120-inch pitch.
- A groove between .000 and .005 inch deep.
- A taper from top to bottom. Some ripping of the quartz is acceptable.

I was quite impressed with the deepness of the groove, so after returning home I walked out to the tool room and talked to toolmaker Don Reynolds, who was working on a surface grinder. I asked him if he had a sharp diamond wheel dresser. (These are used to dress carborundum and other types of grinding wheels.) He did in fact have one; it had been barely used, and had a nice sharp point. (These industrial diamonds are set into a steel shank, which is then fixtured so as to sit on a magnetic chuck.) I asked him how deep a groove he thought he could scratch into a piece of granite with the diamond.

He said, "Let's find out!"

We walked over to a granite surface plate while I jokingly admonished him not to try it on the work surface. He pressed the diamond point into the side of the plate. Bearing down with all the weight he could throw behind it, he scoured the side of the plate with a scratch about four inches long.

We both felt the scratch. "How deep would you say that is?" I asked.

"Oh, between .003 and .005 inch," he said.

"Let's check it out then!" I said.

Don fixtured an indicator gauge in a surface gauge and zeroed the fine needle point on the surface. As he passed it over the groove, the point dropped into the groove and the dial read only .001 inch!

The reason I bring this up is that it has been suggested that if the core *did* have a spiral groove, it would have been created by the lateral pressure of a spinning drill as it was being rapidly withdrawn from the hole. Bringing all my thirty-eight years of experience to bear, for the following reasons I cannot imagine that this is remotely possible:

1. This idea relies on centrifugal force to cut the groove, as the drill is being withdrawn and passing over a widening gap, and to achieve greater centrifugal force, the drill would need to spin faster.
2. There wouldn't be sufficient lateral force to cut a groove in granite to a depth of .001 inch, let alone .005 inch. It is as simple as that.
3. With a spinning drill shank that has the freedom to roam inside an oversized bearing, the drill will seek the path of least resistance, which is *away from* the granite.
4. Petrie's observations were valid when he claimed that this was not a viable means of creating the groove, because of a buildup of dust between the tube and the granite.

Why such a commotion regarding a small, insignificant core? Because it was seen as the weakest area of my work, and therefore easily disputed. It also served to obscure and divert attention from other, more significant artifacts that I have described. Thus, I would challenge the orthodox camp to forget about Petrie's Core #7 for now and provide explanations for all of the other artifacts I describe in my book. I would challenge them to demonstrate, with the tools they have educated us with for centuries, how the ancient Egyptians created such awesome precision and geometry in hard granite, diorite, basalt, and schist.

They can't.

For these, my friends, are the products of a highly advanced civilization.

34 How Did the Pyramid Builders Spell Relief?

Do We Really Know Why the Ancients Used Such Giant Stones in the Pyramid's So-Called Relieving Chambers?

Christopher Dunn

While conducting explorations in the Great Pyramid in 1836, the British military man Colonel William Richard Howard-Vyse was in a crouched space above the King's Chamber examining a mysterious layer of granite beams that were similar to the granite beams that formed the ceiling of the King's Chamber beneath him. The crouched space is named Davison's Chamber, after Nathaniel Davison, who had discovered it in 1765.

Howard-Vyse, who reportedly had received £10,000 from his family for this exploration and, more important, to liberate themselves from his presence, was intent on making a significant discovery and thus far was not having any luck. The granite layer over his head posed a tantalizing clue that something might be lying behind it. Noticing a crack between the beams of the ceiling, Howard-Vyse mulled over the possibility of yet another chamber existing above. Being able to push a three-foot-long reed into the crack, without obstruction, seemed an indication that there must be some other space beyond.

Howard-Vyse and his helpers made an attempt to cut through the granite to find out if there was another chamber above. Discovering in short order that their hammers and hardened steel chisels were no match for the red granite, they resorted to gunpowder. A local worker, his senses dulled by a supply of alcohol and hashish, set the charges and blasted away the rock until another chamber was revealed.

Similar to Davison's Chamber, a ceiling of monolithic granite beams spanned the newly discovered chamber, indicating to Howard-Vyse the possible existence of yet *another* chamber above. After blasting upward for three and a half months and to a height of forty feet, they discovered three more chambers, making a total of five.

The topmost chamber had a gabled ceiling made of giant limestone

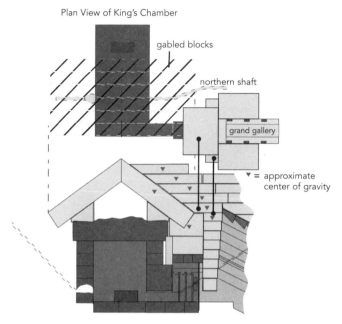

Plan View of King's Chamber

gabled blocks

northern shaft

grand gallery

▼ = approximate center of gravity

View showing possible construction of King's Chamber without "relieving chamber"

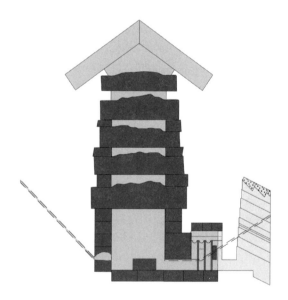

King's Chamber and the so-called "relieving chamber"
(DRAWINGS BY CHRISTOPHER DUNN)

blocks. To construct these five chambers, the ancient Egyptians had found it necessary to use forty-three pieces of granite weighing up to seventy tons each. The red-granite beams were cut square and parallel on three sides, but were left seemingly untouched on the top surface, which was rough and uneven. Some of them even had holes gouged into their topsides.

In this article we will look at the evidence and attempt to explore reasons for this phenomenal expenditure of resources from both the conventional perspective and the alternative perspective. Considering the enormous effort that must have gone into delivering to the Giza plateau these enormous monoliths, we will ask, "Within the framework of the established hypothesis on the Great Pyramid, was all of this work really necessary?"

By today's standards, quarrying and hauling five hundred miles for just *one* of the forty-three granite beams that are placed above the King's Chamber would not be a simple task. Yet the ancient Egyptians accomplished this task not just once, but many times. The seveny-ton weight, however, is not the limit of what the ancient Egyptians were capable of. Large obelisks of up to four hundred tons were also quarried, hauled, and erected. Howard-Vyse surmised that the reason for the five superimposed chambers was to relieve the flat ceiling of the King's Chamber from the weight of thousands of tons of masonry above.

Although most researchers after Howard-Vyse have generally accepted this speculation, there are others, including the world's first Egyptologist, Sir William Flinders Petrie, who have not. Important considerations cast doubt on this theory and prove it to be incorrect.

What needs to be considered is that there is a more efficient and less complicated technique in chamber construction elsewhere inside the Great Pyramid. The Queen's Chamber negates the argument that the King's Chamber's overlying "chambers of construction" were designed to allow a flat ceiling. The load of masonry bearing down on the Queen's Chamber is greater than that above the King's Chamber, due to the fact that this chamber is situated below the King's Chamber.

If a flat ceiling had been needed for the Queen's Chamber, it would have been quite safe to span this room with the kind of beams that are above the King's Chamber. The construction of the Queen's Chamber employed cantilevered limestone blocks that transferred the weight of the masonry above to the outside of the walls. A ceiling similar to the one in the King's Chamber could have been added to this design and, as with the beams above the King's Chamber, the beams would be holding up nothing more than their own weight.

When the builders of the Great Pyramid constructed the King's Chamber,

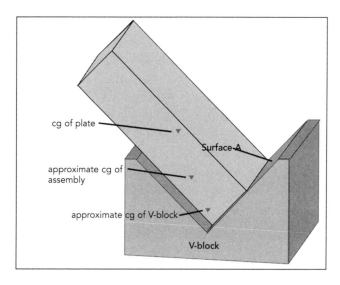

King's Chamber and the "relieving chamber."
Weight-bearing arrangement above the
King's Chamber in the Great Pyramid.
(DRAWING BY CHRISTOPHER DUNN)

they were obviously aware of a simpler method of creating a flat ceiling. The design of the King's Chamber complex, therefore, must have been prompted by other considerations. What were these considerations? Why are there five superimposed layers of monolithic seventy-ton granite beams? Imagine the sheer will and energy that went in to raising one of the granite blocks 175 feet in the air! There must have been a far greater purpose for investing so much time and energy.

I made the above argument in my book, *The Giza Power Plant.* Since its publication, the contrary opinion that I had articulated had evidently become a point of discussion on a message board because I received an e-mail from Egyptology student Mikey Brass, within which was a link to a translation of a German magazine article. The question was posed to Frank Dörnenburg, a participant in the discussion: Why so many layers? He writes:

> I have been debating elsewhere, the Kings Chamber, and the question of why five 'Relieving' Chambers were needed to be used to spread the massive weight above the King's Chamber. My answer to this was I simply did not know. A good answer to this question can be found in *Göttinger Miszellen 173*: "The old method of corbelling channeled the weight force directly to the walls of a chamber. The new, and here

for the first time used, gable-roof redirects the force down AND sideways. If the Egyptians had put the gable roof in the King's Chamber
directly on the ceiling like in the Queen's Chamber, the sideways force
would have damaged the great gallery. So they had to put the gable
above the upper layer of the gallery's construction. The easiest way to
do this was to stack small chambers. And if you look at a cross section you will see that now the sideways force of the roof goes well
over the roof of the gallery."

Superficially, what is proposed in the above hypothesis may seem plausible. It is, however, a construct founded on flawed assumptions and an incomplete analysis of the entire King's Chamber complex. Before accepting it as
factual, we need to consider the following.

The hypothesis assumes that dynamic lateral forces would follow the
direction of the angled blocks and that these lateral forces would accumulate
as more stone was piled on top of the gabled blocks. According to the hypothesis, the consequence of each block added above the King's Chamber causes
additional lateral thrust to push against the southern end of the grand gallery.

The drawing on page 253 represents a mechanical setup with which many
manufacturing technologists are intimately familiar. It is a steel plate resting
in a V-block. If we allow that the above hypothesis *is* correct, the plate would
push on surface A, causing lateral movement.

At rest, the plate will put more pressure on the opposite surface due to the
center of gravity of the piece. Except for gravity, there are no dynamic forces
at work. There is only dead weight, which is distributed according to each
member's center of gravity. When an object is placed on an inclined plane, it
has the potential to move down that plane by gravitational forces acting upon
it. This movement continues until an obstruction is encountered, at which
time the kinetic energy that causes lateral motion ceases.

The gabled ceiling blocks above the King's Chamber are situated on an
inclined plane cut into the core blocks. Assuming that, like the Queen's
Chamber, the center of gravity of these blocks lies outside the chamber walls,
the blocks may be described as cantilevered, whereas there is no archthrust at
the apex where two opposing blocks meet. The entire weight of the block is
borne by the blocks that form the inclined plane, with some weight being carried by the block that holds the lower end.

Without knowing for sure what design features were employed, I can
envision a design that would be sound and not damage the grand gallery. The
rough measurement between the ends of the gabled blocks and the grand

gallery south wall is about nine feet. Considering the width of the gallery (between forty-two and eighty-two inches), it is reasonable to assume that the blocks that form the gallery south wall extend outside the inside surface—but to what distance? I don't know. However, considering that the King's Chamber's northern shaft bends around the grand gallery, it gives rise to the speculation that the blocks that form the gallery walls are deeper than four feet. (This is a significant point to make, and probably in itself worthy of a discussion. The northern shaft could have more easily been a straight shot to the sky, without the extra bends. It would have clearly missed the inside wall of the grand gallery by about four feet.)

With the grand gallery southern-wall blocks butted against the gallery east- and west-wall blocks, any lateral forces that might affect it from the King's Chamber's gabled ceiling blocks would give less cause for concern than, say, the forces acting on the roof of the horizontal passage from the pressure of the Queen's Chamber's gabled ceiling blocks—or the pressure of the blocks bearing down on the roof of the grand gallery.

Moreover, building on top of gabled ceiling blocks does not necessarily mean that they must bear a tremendous accumulation of weight. As described in the drawing above, the distribution of load does not necessarily have to bear down on the gable.

Perhaps the most significant argument against what has been proposed in *Göttinger Miszellen,* and the simplest to understand, can be made by pointing to a plan view of the Great Pyramid. As we can see, the King's Chamber is thirty-four feet in length. The grand gallery is forty-two to eighty-two inches wide—barely the width of one gabled ceiling block.

Therefore, when looking at a side view of the chambers, the hypothesis may appear plausible, but it falls apart under scrutiny, for even if we allow that there would be undue pressure on the south wall of the grand gallery, it would not necessitate five chambers being built across the entire thirty-four-foot length of the King's Chamber. Also, why five layers of beams? Why not a large open space with the gabled ceiling above?

In cutting these giant monoliths, the builders evidently found it necessary to craft the beams destined for the uppermost chamber with the same respect as those intended for the ceiling directly above the King's Chamber. Each beam was cut flat and square on three sides, with the topside seemingly untouched. This is significant, considering that those directly above the King's Chamber would be the only ones visible to those entering the pyramid.

Moreover, it is remarkable that the builders would exert the same amount of effort in finishing the thirty-four beams, which would not be seen once the pyramid was built, as they did the nine beams forming the ceiling of the King's Chamber, which *would* be seen. Even if these beams were imperative to the strength of the complex, deviations in accuracy would surely be allowed, making the cutting of the blocks less time-consuming—unless, of course, they were either using these upper beams for a specific purpose, and/or were using standardized machinery methods that produced these beams with little variation in their shape.

Why five layers of these beams? To include so many monolithic blocks of granite when constructing the King's Chamber is obviously redundant. To get an idea of the enormity of such a task today, my company, Danville Metal Stamping, recently acquired a hydroform press. The main body of the press weighs one hundred tons and had to be shipped more than one hundred miles to our plant. Because of weight distribution considerations, the Department of Transportation dictated that it be hauled on a special tractor-trailer with the weight distributed among nineteen axles. The length of this trailer approached two hundred feet and it required two additional drivers, positioned at key points along its length, to pivot it around corners.

The reason for describing this scenario is to point out that even using today's efficient, high-tech methods, there would have to be a damn good reason to move even one heavy load. The forty-three giant beams above the King's Chamber were not included in the structure to relieve the King's Chamber from excessive pressure from above, but rather to fulfill a more advanced purpose. Without a conventional explanation that makes sense, we must look for other answers to the mystery of these granite beams. When these granite beams are analyzed with a more utilitarian perspective, one can discern a simple yet refined technology operating at the heart of the Great Pyramid that makes more sense. The ancient Egyptians, or Khemitians, were brilliant in applying natural laws and using natural materials to enable this ancient power plant to function. The granite beams above the King's Chamber were an essential and integral part of making this pyramid machine hum.

35 Precision

Did the Ancients Have It? And If They Did,
Should It Matter to Us?

Christopher Dunn

The word *precision* comes from *precise*, which *Webster's* defines as "sharply or exactly limited or defined as to meaning; exact; definite, not loose, vague, or equivocal; exact in conduct; strict; formal; nice; punctilious." *Preciseness* is "exactness; rigid nicety; excessive regard to forms or rules; rigid formality." *Precision* is "the state of being precise as to meaning; preciseness; exactness; accuracy."

To many people, the application of precision in their lives is related to their words and actions. We have precise speech, precise timekeeping, and the precision of a military drill. We may have the good fortune to be invited to a dinner party by a "precision" and find the tableware in exact order, with nary a spoon or a goblet out of position.

The application of precision, as noted above, is part and parcel of being civilized. It is the discipline and order that is necessary for civilization to function successfully.

Beginning in the late 1800s, a different application of precision was gaining increased importance and seen to be necessary to ensure the successful outcome of human endeavors. The machines that were invented and used as laborsaving devices depended on precision components to function properly. In the 1800s, the cotton industry and steam power spawned the Industrial Revolution in the north of England. The demand for more-efficient spinning mills and looms gave rise to a greater emphasis on producing components that functioned precisely.

To make products that were consistent, variables in the manufacturing process had to be reduced or eliminated. To accomplish this, dimensional variables that were inherent in the manufacture of critical components needed to be reduced to acceptable levels. However, because of the inaccuracies of the machine tools of the day, skilled fitters were needed to scrape, chisel, and file components to close dimensions in order for them to fit properly.

Wars have accelerated the evolution of standardized measurements and the elimination of variables in the manufacturing process. Put yourself in the place of a soldier during the Civil War. His rifle was precision-crafted, but when replacing a component in the field, he had to hand-file the pieces to fit. Obviously, this was time-consuming, and in war, timing could make you a winner or a loser. Standards were necessarily instituted and suppliers had to meet these standards or lose business.

Anyone who has brought home a bicycle or piece of "ready-to-assemble" furniture can appreciate the precision that is required for these objects to go together easily. Have you ever found yourself trying to align a bolt in a pre-drilled hole that is off by an eighth of an inch? This is an example of the need for precision, and how the effort to produce precision products is actually an expensive, difficult endeavor.

In manufacturing today, components are made throughout the world and come together in an assembly plant. The exacting standards and precision of the product shipped from thousands of miles away ensure that when they go to the assembly line, the components fit together without additional work.

Most people will never actually create objects to a high precision. It is understandable, therefore, that most people overlook this important aspect of a civilization's infrastructure. To laypeople, precision is an abstract concept. This is not a criticism. If you have not had precision manufacturing experience, either professionally or as a hobby, an understanding of the concept of precision is academic.

We are end users of powerful precision technologies that fuel our civilization and make our lives easier. Without manufacturing precision, cars would not run, planes would not fly, and CDs would not play. The precision we create is born out of necessity. We do not create it without good reason, because the costs of producing artifacts today go up exponentially if the demand for accuracy is greater.

An example of close accuracy and precision is the twelve-inch straight-edge that I took to Egypt in 1999 and 2001. The edge was finished on a precision grinder. Its deviation from a perfect, straight line was a mere .0001 inch. For the reader who cannot relate to what that means in real terms, take a hair out of your head and split it equally along its length into twenty parts. One part is approximately equal to .0001 inch. (The average hair is .0025 inch.) Or, to compare it to our "some-assembly-required" example above, this straightedge is 1,250 times *more* precise than the predrilled hole that was off by an eighth of an inch.

If we were to miraculously uncover an unidentified artifact in the Sahara Desert that had been buried for thousands of years, how would we determine its purpose? If the speculation arises that it may have had some technological purpose, the challenge would be to prove it, which would require us to reverse-engineer its design to determine its function. Reverse engineering has been a part of industrial competitiveness for years. Engineers would buy a competitor's product and by studying its design and components would understand the science and engineering behind its function. This is why the recovery of a potential or real enemy's weapons of war is important.

If, after a cursory examination of this unidentified prehistoric artifact, we determine that it may have been a machine that functions as a tool to create artifacts, how would we know that it was a *precision* machine tool? In order to prove the case for our prehistoric precision machine tool, it would need to be measured for accuracy. Certain components associated with precision machine tools are manufactured to a high accuracy.

Flat surfaces necessary for the machine to function properly would be finished to within .0002 inch. This kind of accuracy separates primitive tools and those that are the result of need and development. The discovery of this precision would elevate the artifact to a higher purpose. If these components were not precise, the arguments against it being the product of an advanced society would be strengthened.

The critical evidence, therefore, is the accuracy of the surfaces being measured. Artisans do not create surfaces with such accuracy unless the artifact they are creating needs to function to exact specifications. Unless there is a need, precision isn't even a consideration.

When looking for prehistoric machines, though, we tend to look for artifacts that are made of iron or steel, not granite, primarily because we use iron and steel to construct our machines. We see things as *we* are, not how *they* are. Nevertheless, the critical proof that would be demanded to support the conclusion that a steel artifact was a precision machine *is* its precision and the product of the machine. This precision can be found in Egypt—crafted into many artifacts made of stable igneous rock that would survive tens of thousands of years and still retain their precision.

We may not have the iron and steel used to create the artifact, but we have the products in abundance. Many of these artifacts, I believe, may have been misidentified and assigned to a time that doesn't support the hypothesis, that the tools used to create them may have eroded over a much longer period of time than established dates would allow. There is support for such a speculation if we look at artifacts purely from an engineering perspective. It has been said that to understand the ancient Egyptian culture, you have to think like an

Egyptian. To understand its technological accomplishments, however, you have to think like an engineer.

THE SERAPEUM

The granite box inside Khafre's pyramid has the same characteristics as the boxes inside the Serapeum. Yet the boxes in the Serapeum were ascribed to the eighteenth dynasty, more than eleven hundred years later, when stoneworking was in decline. Considering that this dating was based on pottery items that were found and not the boxes themselves, it would be reasonable to speculate that the boxes have not been dated accurately.

Their characteristics show that their creators used the same tools and were blessed with the same skill and knowledge as those who created Khafre's pyramid. Moreover, the boxes in both locations are evidence of a much higher purpose than mere burial sarcophagi.

They are finished to a high degree of accuracy; their corners are perfectly square, and their inside corners are astoundingly sharp. All of these features are extremely difficult to accomplish, and none of them is necessary for a mere burial box.

Dunn shows a crude sarcophagus at Memphis that could possibly have been made with tools such as the stone balls postulated by Egyptologists.
(PHOTOGRAPH BY TIM HUNKLER)

In 1995 I inspected the inside and outside surfaces of two boxes in the Serapeum with a six-inch precision straightedge that was accurate to .0002 inch. My report on what I discovered has been published in my book *The Giza Power Plant* and published on my Web site.

The artifacts I have measured in Egypt have the marks of careful and remarkable manufacturing methods. They are unmistakable and irrefutable *in their precision,* but origin or intent will always be open to speculation. The accompanying photograph was taken inside the Serapeum on August 27, 2001. Those taken of me inside one of these huge boxes show me inspecting the squareness between a twenty-seven-ton lid and the inside surface of the granite box on which it sits. The precision square I am using was calibrated to .00005 inch (that is, 5/100,000 of an inch) using a Jones & Lamson comparitor.

The underside of the lid and the inside wall of the box are incredibly square. Finding that the squareness was achieved not just on one side of the box but on both raises the level of difficulty in accomplishing this feat.

Think of this as a geometric reality. In order for the lid to be perfectly square with the two inside walls, the inside walls would have to be perfectly parallel. Moreover, the topside of the

Christopher Dunn in the Khafre "sarcophagus"
(PHOTOGRAPH BY TIM HUNKLER)

box would need to establish a plane that is square to the sides. That makes finishing the inside exponentially more difficult. The manufacturers of these boxes in the Serapeum not only created inside surfaces that were flat when measured vertically and horizontally, but they also made sure that the surfaces they were creating were square and parallel to each other, with one surface, the top, having sides that are five feet and ten feet apart from each other. But without such parallelism and squareness of the top surface, the squareness noted on both sides would not exist.

As an engineer and craftsman who has worked in manufacturing for more than forty years and who has created precision artifacts in our modern world, in my opinion this accomplishment in prehistory is *nothing short of amazing.* Nobody does this kind of work unless there is a very high purpose for the artifact. Even the *concept* of this kind of precision does not occur to an artisan unless there is no other means of accomplishing what the artifact is intended to do. The only other reason that such precision would be created in an object is that the tools that are used to create it are so precise that they are incapable of producing anything less than precision. With either scenario, we are looking at a higher civilization in prehistory than what is currently accepted. The implications are staggering.

This is why I believe that these artifacts that I have measured in Egypt are the smoking gun that *proves,* without a shadow of a doubt, that a higher civilization existed in ancient Egypt than what we have been taught. The evidence is cut into the stone.

The boxes that are off the beaten tourist's path in the rock tunnels of the Serapeum would be extremely difficult to produce today. Their smooth, flat surfaces, orthogonal perfection, and incredibly small inside corner radii that I have inspected with modern precision straightedges, squares, and radius gauges leave me in awe. Even though after contacting four precision granite manufacturers I could not find one who could replicate their perfection, I would not say that it would be impossible to make one today—if we had a good reason to do so.

But what would that reason be? For what purpose would we quarry an eighty-ton block of granite, hollow its inside, and proceed to craft it to such a high level of accuracy? Why would we find it necessary to craft the top surface of this box so that a lid with an equally flat underside surface would sit square with the inside walls?

There may be arguments against the claims of advanced societies in prehistory. Some may argue that the lack of machinery refutes such claims, but a *lack* of evidence is *not evidence*. It is fallacious to deny or ignore what exists by arguing for what does not exist. When we ponder the purpose for creating such precision, we inexorably move beyond the simple reasons espoused by historians and are forced to consider that there was a civilization in prehistory that was far more advanced and vastly different from what was previously thought. We do not need to look for secret chambers or halls of records to know that this civilization existed. It is crafted into some of the hardiest materials with which they worked—igneous rock.

36 The Obelisk Quarry Mystery

Do Egyptologists Really Know
How These Monuments Were Created?

Christopher Dunn

In my articles and book, I have injected a distinct bias when I have viewed ancient Egyptian artifacts. In this article I will explain where my bias came from and I will answer the following questions: "Isn't it possible to create all these wonderful artifacts in ancient Egypt with primitive tools? Because there are volumes of work that describe how these tools were capable of such work, we don't need to resort to fantastic inventions that don't exist in the archeological record, so why do you?"

My biased opinion of the level of technology used by the ancient Egyptians comes from many years of work in manufacturing. For six years (over 12,480 hours) I operated hand tools and machine tools of many varieties, both large and small, in the production of artifacts that were crafted to engineering specifications. At the end of this six years I had completed my apprenticeship and was presented with journeyman documents, to benefit from as I saw fit.

The opportunities that followed spanned more than three decades. During this time, I must admit that my bias was further reinforced by exposure to the environment in which I had chosen to make a living. The effect this environment has had on my brain, I fear, is irreversible. By the time I had been rescued and promoted to the sterile confines of a senior manager's office, more than 62,400 hours of environmental exposure in engineering and manufacturing had left deeply embedded scars in my critical thinking skills regarding how things are made.

These scars describe a path of struggle: the struggle to convert ideas into physical reality. The struggle is to sketch an idea onto paper and then proceed to pour, cut, shape, and mold that idea, with precision, into a functioning device. The struggle is to employ every intellectual and physical tool available, within those disciplines of science, engineering, manufacturing, and metrology that embrace function, form, and precision.

However, these scars also describe a path of disappointment when ideas do not work and a path of elation when, having learned from mistakes, there is success. Associated with both, the higher forces of humility etch a little deeper.

Perhaps I was too hasty in exclaiming space-age precision after discovering an accuracy of .0002 inch on the inside of a large, prehistoric, granite box. Perhaps the lathe marks were not really lathe marks. Perhaps I am overconfident when I look at tool marks on an artifact and can identify the tool that made them. I have considered that a part of my bias could be related to a time in my career when I had to think like an American, rather than an Englishman.

But, then, I don't remember any drastic changes there, except the revelation that engineers are forced to think in similar ways regardless of what country they are in. That's the price of living in a physical world with natural laws. Of course, the other environmental effect of living in a culture different from the one in which you spent your formative years is the stripping away of preconceived chauvinistic views of your natal culture as it relates to other cultures. This leads to a greater tolerance and acceptance of the views of others.

The reason I am telling you this is to give you some idea of the mistake I made in presenting my work. Much of what I have taken for granted when looking at artifacts in Egypt needed to be more fully explained. I realized that I had been putting the cart before the horse. In studying ancient Egyptian artifacts, I looked at the final product and wrote about the geometry and the precision. For the most part, I neglected to discuss all of the methods that are required and by which these artifacts were created. To me it seemed obvious that they were the products of technologies of which there is no surviving evidence.

What I have been faced with, though, are arguments that cling to the notion that the use of primitive tools, such as stone hammers and pounders, copper chisels, and abrasive materials such as sand, is sufficient to explain the existence of *all* the stoneware created in ancient Egypt. It is argued that these tools, in the hands of a large, skillful workforce with plenty of time at its disposal, are capable of creating all of these artifacts. It is argued that the ancient Egyptians did not consider time in the same way we do. To the ancient Egyptians (a civilization that covered several millennia), a decade was but a drop in the ocean of time, a century a mere goblet. So when an Egyptologist is asked to explain how a particularly difficult-to-create object is made, the main ingredient is time, and lots of it.

For a culture that spanned so many centuries, the ancient Egyptians were building for eternity. By their architecture and building materials, they were quite obviously concerned about the continuity of their Ka, or spirit, and the continuity of their civilization. It all sounds very logical and complete, and I found myself nodding my head in agreement. I cannot deny that handwork can produce many beautiful and precise objects in extremely difficult-to-work materials.

Yet even as I found myself agreeing, I still had a nagging concern that something was not quite right. There had to be a more cogent argument to which orthodox Egyptologists would listen. It has become quite obvious that ringing my bell next to artifacts that are incredibly precise was falling on deaf ears.

Following the publication of my previous article, entitled "Precision," I engaged in some discussions on Internet message boards. This is not the first time I have participated in such discussions. Since I discovered these aerobic exercises for the fingers, as far back as 1995, my enthusiasm for such discourse has been tempered by the reality that in most cases Internet debates are time-wasting and futile. I have been advised to avoid them like the plague— mostly by those who are closest to me, my family (particularly my wife).

Nevertheless, out of this masochistic exercise came some insight as to how I can redress my mistakes. What I noticed is that I found myself discussing my work with people who did not agree with my conclusions. Because they did not agree with my conclusions, they quickly adopted the findings of scholars who have published their own studies and who articulated conclusions that are more consistent with what is believed about the history of the ancient Egyptians.

The foremost authority on ancient Egyptian stoneworking today is Denys Stocks, of Manchester University. Stocks's work effectively trumps any prior commentary on the subject and is invaluable in analyzing the techniques of the ancient stonemasons. Stocks's opinions on the subject carry more weight because they are based on experimental data gathered in Egypt using materials that are a part of the archeological record. The opinions of Sir William Flinders Petrie in his book *Pyramids and Temple of Gizeh* (which was published in 1893) and Lucas and Harris in their *Ancient Egyptian Materials and Industries* are preempted by Stocks's field studies and considerable effort. The most recent work by Stocks was the Aswan project funded by "NOVA" during the creation of its "Obelisk" documentaries.

For this reason, I will focus on the working of granite, for in the course of his credible and scientific research at Aswan, Stocks produced some hard data on material removal rates that enables us to perform a reasonably accurate time study. The analysis is quite simple and is used by estimating engineers in manufacturing to provide estimated costs for producing modern-day artifacts.

What follows are calculations based on Stocks's research on the amount of time necessary to quarry one granite obelisk. The time will not include

An obelisk at Karnak

the time necessary for pulling its 440-ton mass out of the quarry. Nor do the calculations address the finishing of the block to its smooth, flat surface, or the numerous deeply etched, incredible glyphs. Last, they do not take into account the time it would take to transport and erect the obelisk in front of Pylon V at Karnak.

We will start at the Aswan granite quarries, where we will select a suitable area for our stone. Based on the finished dimensions, the raw piece of stone will be tall. The method used by the ancient Egyptians to separate a large, important stone from the bedrock was to cut a channel all the way around the piece and then undercut it, leaving pillars supporting its weight. This hypothesis seems most reasonable and sensible. When looking at the unfinished obelisk at Aswan, we see that a trench was cut all around the obelisk, and if work had continued, an undercut would have been necessary to separate the granite from the bedrock.

The channel has scoop-shaped quarry marks, which led the Egyptologist Dieter Arnold to claim that each worker "sent to the granite" was assigned an area of "75 centimeters (10 palms) wide and divided into working sections 60 centimeters long, the minimum space for a squatting or kneeling worker." This would be a somewhat cramped area barely two feet by two and a half feet wide for a worker swinging a heavy stone ball, and considering that there would have needed to be a line of workers, each one equally aggressive in wielding his stone ball, the risk of injury does not go unnoticed.

Nevertheless, for the sake of argument, I will use these figures in my calculations. Mark Lehner, in the "Obelisk" documentary, concurred that this method was probably the one used by the ancient Egyptians, and he even performed some experimental work himself.

Based on the material removal rate information, therefore, a quick analysis of the time necessary to quarry an obelisk can be made, though we might believe that, with a sufficient amount of labor, the time it takes to accomplish a given project could be reduced. This is not necessarily true. Within any project are constraints or bottlenecks. So while we may command a workforce of one thousand, a bottleneck will effectively reduce the number engaged in a given project significantly. The constraint in the obelisk-quarrying project is the number of workers able to work on a two-foot by two-and-a-half-foot patch of granite.

 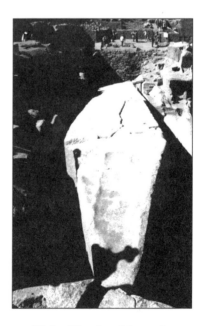

Left: The unfinished obelisk at Aswan. Right: The tip of Aswan's unfinished obelisk (PHOTOGRAPHS BY GREG HEDGECOCK)

Obviously, this is only one at a time. The time it would take to quarry the block, therefore, is based on the cubic mass of material to be removed, divided by the material removal rate. The mass of material is the width, multiplied by the length, multiplied by the depth. (The results follow the metric dimensions presented by Stocks, which are given in cubic centimeters [cu.cm]. Meters, feet, and inches are also given.) The depth of the channel is open to question. Looking at the photographs, there is a considerable amount of bedrock removed, down to the top of the block.

It could be argued that other blocks might have been quarried away from its top for other purposes and, therefore, this distance could not be considered part of the project. I will estimate, therefore, that the depth of the channel had to have sunk into the bedrock nine feet for the obelisk and another two feet for the undercut. The depth has to include quarrying deep enough that a worker may quarry a channel underneath the block that is wide enough for him to crawl under to chisel away the rock.

In the following table, it is assumed that a worker is pounding the granite using a dolerite ball. Stocks estimates that the material removal rate for a dolerite ball is thirty cubic cm per hour. While there was no mention of the removal of waste or the replacement of pounders as they became ineffective, it is assumed that the material removal rate continues unabated, according to Stocks's experimental data.

Patch	Feet	Inches	Meters	Centimeters
Width	2.46	29.53	0.75	75.00
Length	1.97	23.63	0.60	60.00
Depth	11.00	132.00	33.52	335.24
Cubic mass	53.29	92,093.20	15.09	1,508,571.43
Material removal rate/hour per Stocks (cu.cm)			30.00	
Number of hours for one worker			50,285.71	
Number of days (assuming 10-hr. day)			5,028.57	
Number of years (assuming 320-day year)			15.71	

Now let us analyze the length of time it would take to create an undercut. For the calculation on the undercut, we will use Stocks's removal rate using a hammer and flint chisel. I have switched to this rate on the basis of a reasonable assumption that efficiencies will go down as the worker has to lie on his side without the aid of gravity to impact the surface. Stocks's material removal rate for a hammer and flint chisel was 5 cu. cm. per hour.

Although it challenges the imagination to believe that anyone other than a diminutive person/worker can effectively chisel a two-foot by two-and-a-half-foot tunnel underneath the granite, for the sake of argument I will base my calculations on such an assumption. I will also base my calculations on the assumption that there are workers on both sides of the granite chiseling toward each other, thus halving the distance necessary to create the full undercut.

Patch	Feet	Inches	Meters	Centimeters
Width	2.46	29.53	7.50	75.00
Length	1.97	23.63	6.00	60.00
Depth	4.00	48.04	12.20	122.00
(half box width)				
Cubic mass	19.40	33,514.60	549.00	549,000.00
Material removal rate/hour (cu.cm)			5.00	
Number of hours for one worker			109,800.00	
Number of days (assuming 10-hr. day)			10,980.00	
Number of years (assuming 320-day year)			34.31	

Using constraint analysis, the *minimum* amount of time just to quarry the stone is *fifty years!* It is physically impossible to assign more workers to accomplish the task in less time. Workers may come and go to replace tired and sick workers, but at any given time, only one worker can labor away at that patch of granite. The 30-cu. cm. per hour removal rate does *not* continue unabated until we have a perfectly flat surface with sharp and square corners, either. We are still left with the task of *finishing* the product, which, in my estimation, would conservatively take another decade using the tools that Egyptologists allow the ancient Egyptians to have in their tool kit.

On the base of Hatshepshut's pair of obelisks are inscriptions that tell us that the pair were quarried and raised into position in a seven-month period. To merely quarry the raw block in such a time would mean that the cutting rate would need to be increased at least *thirty-seven times*. Tools capable of such efficiency are not a part of the archeological record. Along with all previous considerations and claims of geometry and precision, and now using the Egyptologists' own data, this confirms that the assertions of the Egyptologists are incorrect and that the ancient Egyptians were much more advanced than what we have allowed in the past.

37 Behind the Pyramid's Secret Doors

What Does Astonishing New Evidence Reveal about the Great Pyramid's True Purpose?

Christopher Dunn

On Monday, September 16, 2002, at 8:00 P.M. Eastern Standard time, Fox television in the United States broadcast live from the Giza plateau in Egypt an exploration of the southern shaft in the Queen's Chamber in the Great Pyramid. Since 1993, when German robotics engineer Rudolph Gantenbrink made his initial exploration of this 8-eight-inch-square, 220-foot long shaft, millions of Egypt-watchers around the world have been waiting for the day when additional explorations would take place and another tantalizing barrier to greater knowledge might be removed.

The two-hour Fox/National Geographic extravaganza provided a torturous prelude to the moment when iRobot's masonry drill bit finally broke through into the space beyond and the endoscopic camera was inserted into the hole to take a peek at what lay beyond Gantenbrink's door.

The buildup to the production explored several ideas on what lies behind this so-called door.

Before the show aired, Dr. Zahi Hawass, chairman of Egypt's Supreme Council of the Antiquities (SCA), expressed a belief that a book about Khufu would be discovered: "What this door might hide is very important to know, that Khufu wrote a sacred book and maybe this book is hidden behind this door, or maybe a papyrus roll telling us about building the pyramids."

Hawass's comments were taken further by the Egyptian State Information Service: "Hawass stated that such doors were constructed for religious purposes due to the books found there, such as the gateways, the cavities, and the road which guided the dead to the hereafter and warned them against the dangers they might face."

The German Egyptologist Ranier Stadelman, who directed the work of Rudolph Gantenbrink in 1993, expressed a belief that the so-called door was a false door for the king's soul to pass through on its way to Osiris, represented

Gantenbrink's door

by the star Sirius. He believed that the copper fittings were handles that the king would use to lift the door.

Robert Bauval, author with Adrian Gilbert of *The Orion Mystery: Unlocking the Secrets of the Pyramids,* predicted that a statue would be discovered and that the end of the shaft served as a serdab (a narrow chamber commemorating the dead) from which the ancient Egyptians viewed the stars.

John Anthony West, the author of *Serpent in the Sky,* thought there would be nothing but core masonry behind this door. A caller to the Art Bell show during an interview I had with George Noory on September 15 identified herself as an Egyptologist and claimed to *know* what was behind the door. Dismissing my hypothesis on what would be behind the door, she claimed that they would find a space thirty feet long that contained sacred sand.

My own hypothesis, which we will discuss in a moment, has changed little since the publication of my book, *The Giza Power Plant,* in 1998. I resurrected it on my Web site and discussed it in interviews both prior to and after September 16.

The confidence in Chairman Hawass became noticeably muted as the program drew to a close. He cautioned the viewers that there might be nothing behind the door at all. His prophetic comments became a sickening reality to all of us as the endoscopic camera with its fish-eye lens pushed through the hole and a distorted image came into view. There appeared to be nothing there but a rough-looking block a short distance away.

With inimitable style and gusto, Dr. Hawass could hardly contain his excitement at the dismal image sent back by the camera. "It's another door!" he said with glowing enthusiasm. "With a crack!" (The old Peggy Lee song played with melancholy in my head . . . "Is That All There Is?")

Hawass's pre-broadcast predictions were downgraded a week later to "Everything now needs a careful look. We will ask the National Geographic Society to cooperate to reveal more mysteries. After this broadcast, can we expect them to reveal anything but mysteries? After all, it's the mysteries that keep the viewers coming back for more."

On September 23, 2002, news came out of Egypt that the Pyramid Rover team had successfully explored the northern shaft in the Great Pyramid. This shaft, opposite the southern shaft, posed problems for Gantenbrink in 1993. Upuaut II was unable to navigate around earlier explorers' rods that were jammed in the passage as they attempted to push the rods around a bend in the shaft.

The iRobot team had a cunning but simple solution to the problem that Gantenbrink was faced with. They turned the robot 90 degrees and sent it up the shaft gripping the walls, instead of the ceiling and floor. In this manner,

Shaft on the east side of the Great Pyramid
(PHOTOGRAPH BY AMARGI HILLIER)

it was able to ride over the top of the obstacles. Of the northern shaft, Hawass had an opinion that was beyond all reasonable demands of any craftsman living in any era.

Subject to the scrutiny and attention of the world press, the information coming from the chief of the SCA became increasingly unusual. It is an unfortunate position to be in to be considered an expert and explorer in residence for the National Geographic Society and not have any well-thought-out answers for a hungry press: ". . . the passage had bends and turns in an apparent attempt by builders to avoid the main chamber."

This could indicate the unexplained passageways were built after the pyramids were completed and were not part of the original design. Hawass speculated that the passages could be connected to an attempt by Cheops to promote himself as Egypt's sun god. Belief at the time said kings became the god in death. Hawass believes the shafts, which have been chiseled out of the pyramid's stone structure, are passages the king will face before he travels to the afterlife.

Then, one week after going before the cameras in his Indiana Jones hat and predicting the discovery of a royal diary of Khufu, Dr. Hawass was again before the press:

"This find in the northern shaft, coupled with last week's discovery . . . in the southern shaft, represents the first major, new information about the Great Pyramid in more than a century," said Zahi Hawass, director of Egypt's Supreme Council of Antiquities. "This is not *Raiders of the Lost Ark*," Hawass said, scoffing at the idea that hidden treasure would be found.

Hawass proceeded to predict unabashedly that behind the stone block at the end of the northern shaft would be another door. (Cue Peggy Lee.) Actually, I believe Hawass is correct. Behind the block at the end of the northern shaft they will discover another space similar to the one at the end of the southern shaft. This time, I believe, they will find a shaft that is on the right side of the cavity, perhaps in the floor, but more than likely in the right wall.

Compared to Dr. Hawass as quoted above, I have used more of the Great Pyramid's *entire* inner design to arrive at my prediction. I have discussed this subject with knowledgeable and staunch believers of the tomb theory, and they insist that it doesn't matter what is found behind the door; it will still support the tomb theory. One conversant commented that even a vertical shaft that goes down into the bedrock would be incorporated into the tomb theory because if the Pharaoh wanted a vertical shaft, he could have one. His reason was that Egyptology is not a hard science and does not need to conform to the same standard.

In *The Giza Power Plant* theory, every architectural element in the Great Pyramid is integrally linked. Some features can be analyzed separately, but, for the most part, the Queen's Chamber, the King's Chamber, and the grand gallery are the principal features that work together in unison, and they cannot be separated from each other when considering a piece of evidence.

The features found in the King's Chamber led me to propose the use of diluted hydrochloric acid in the southern shaft and hydrated zinc in the northern shaft of the Queen's Chamber. The features in the grand gallery led me to understand the function of the King's Chamber. The features in the Queen's Chamber indicate that a chemical reaction was taking place there. The hypothesis rises or falls on the evidence found in these areas.

For the theory to hold, evidence that is discovered in the future has to support it. Some evidence, such as what will be found behind Gantenbrink's door, can be predicted by what is found in the chamber, the southern shaft, and the northern shaft. The power plant will either be vindicated, severely challenged, or even dismissed, based on what is revealed.

Before the Pyramid Rover exploration, I went on record as being fully prepared to admit that I was wrong if a search of the southern shaft did not reveal another shaft, or shafts, that will be redirected and eventually lead to a point underneath the pyramid. I also predicted that, on the back side of the door, the copper fittings would have connections or would continue away from the door to a point underneath the Great Pyramid.

Unfortunately, as of now, there have not been any clear images of the back side of the so-called door, so this part of the prediction has not been ver-

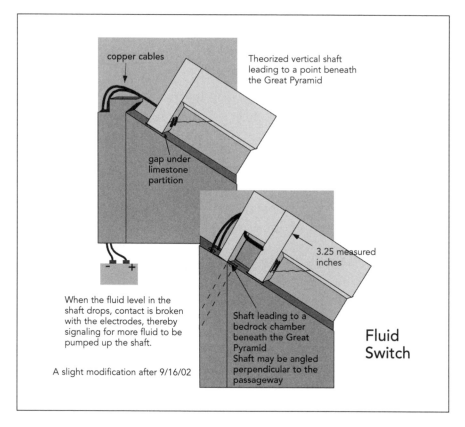

The operation of a fluid switch
(DRAWING BY CHRISTOPHER DUNN)

ified. However, the illustration in my book predicted one of the attributes of the door and the evidence vindicated this prediction. In my illustration, the thickness of the block is given, by scale, as three inches thick. My measure was arbitrary and based on nothing more than the proposed function of the block. The ultrasonic thickness tester on the Pyramid Rover measured the actual thickness and found it to be three inches thick (see schematic above).

Like everybody else in the United States, I was watching the video on Fox television. In the top left corner was LIVE and the bottom left carried the Fox symbol with Channel 27. There was really nothing for me to become excited about until a man in Germany uploaded to the Maat message board a high-resolution image that he had taken of the National Geographic program broadcast on Sky Television in Europe. This image seemed to indicate that there was more to be seen in the area that was occluded by the Fox logo.

I copied the image into a graphics program and auto-adjusted the levels, which lightened the dark areas. I stared at the screen—for what seemed to be eternity—at what was revealed.

I know that if you stare at something long enough, you might be able to see a face or some other shape, but the rectangular shape in the left corner of the new block became immediately apparent. I then adjusted the levels, curves, and colors to bring more definition to the image and created construction lines (1 and 2) using the bottom corners as guides in order to create a vanishing point. It was my intention to see if the geometry of the rectangular shape on the left side was indeed a true rectangle and parallel with the wall.

Striking a line from the vanishing point (3) and bringing it along the side of the rectangular shape, I became confident that I may have indeed discovered the vertical shaft that I had predicted would be there. Interestingly, the line in the floor (4) is also parallel to the walls, which indicates either that the floor is made of two blocks or that a groove is cut in the floor. In this enhanced image, the signs of staining on the floor lead from the vertical shaft end, which is also square with the walls. It appears that the second door is also notched in this area.

Because the chemical flowing into the Queen's Chamber did not need to be a great torrent or even of the volume that a normal faucet would produce, replenishing the shaft with fluid would not require a large orifice. The notched corner as seen in the bottom right corner of the block would be all that was needed to maintain the fluid level. Moreover, if we look at the size of the vertical shaft behind the door by scale, it is only about one and a half inches wide and four inches long.

The exploration of the northern shaft and what was discovered at the end was predictable and, without any shadow of a doubt, vindicates the purpose for these shafts as outlined in *The Giza Power Plant*. The image of another door with copper fittings and the subtle difference between these fittings and those at the end of the northern shaft support the hypothesis regarding the chemicals used. The electrodes are affected by different chemicals a different way.

In the southern shaft, the action of the dilute hydrochloric acid eroded the copper over time. Because the upper part of the copper was covered with chemical for a shorter period of time than the lower part, as the fluid was always falling, the lower part of the copper was eroded more than the upper part. This resulted in a taper of the copper and the ultimate failure of the left electrode.

In the northern shaft we see a different effect. Because this shaft contained a hydrated metal, such as hydrated zinc, what we see is an electroplating of the left electrode. This is normal and predictable; considering that electricity flows from cathode (+) to anode (-), there would be a deposit of zinc on the anode. What we see in the photograph taken by the Pyramid Rover is a white substance on the left electrode only. There is no erosion on these electrodes, and the thickness of the metal is considerably less than on those in the southern shaft. The stained limestone is on the left and on top of the electrode. Studies on what causes this effect are still being made.

Plug in the northern shaft, Queen's Chamber

Though Egyptology is not considered to be a hard science, scientific standards should be employed when trying to explain this edifice. Arguments should follow the rules of evidence and conform to scientific principles. While Egyptologists may say the tomb theory is unassailable, my view has been that if the tomb theory cannot follow logical scientific arguments, and be subject to radical revision when new data emerges, then it fails.

These are the standards applied to alternate theorists, such as Hancock, Bauval, and myself, so we should expect no less from those who teach and support the accepted view. Moreover, the theory should be predictable. What was discovered behind Gantenbrink's door, though not yet brought into full view, was not predicted by Egyptologists and does nothing to support the theory that this edifice was originally a tomb.

Scientific and social progress demands that we all be skeptics and question the accepted mores and theories that have been handed to us. Alternative views need to be discussed. Indeed, they should be welcomed by anyone who is serious about learning what flaws may exist with his or her own ideas. Egyptology should not be immune to these scientific precepts, though its orthodox protectors' awkward attempt to force contradictory data to fit an unsupportable hypothesis gives little hope for change.

38 The Case for Advanced Technology in the Great Pyramid

What Does the Evidence Really Show about the Advancement of Its Builders?

Marshall Payn

*One of the tragedies of life is the murder of a
beautiful theory by a brutal gang of facts.*

LA ROCHEFOUCAULD

The Khufu (Cheops) pyramid defies how we depict ancient technology. Over two million limestone blocks rise to the height of a forty-story building. Each baseline exceeds two and a half football fields. Standing on top, an archer cannot clear the base with an arrow. All this comes from what was supposedly an agrarian society, forty-five hundred years ago.

And that's not all. The precision and craftsmanship surpass our modern understanding. Occupying an area of thirteen acres, the entire bedrock base has been carved to less than an inch out of level. It is oriented within a tiny fraction of a degree from the cardinal points. Outer casing stones and inner granite blocks fit with such precision that a razor blade cannot be inserted between them. Blocks weighing as much as seventy tons (about what a railroad locomotive weighs) have been lifted to the height of a ten-story building and mated to the next block with wondrous precision.

How did they do these things? We don't know. Just a few generations before Khufu, there *were* no pyramids. Where did the technology come from? We have no answers. Any method of construction suggested, to date, for this pyramid does not satisfy the accepted standards of technology. But the reality is that the pyramid is real, and regardless of how they built it, they built it. Egyptians built pyramids for another thousand years, but today most of those are unrecognizable rubble. Only the older ones are intact, which argues against the assumption of accrued knowledge. By whatever technological means these older ones were built, the Egyptians themselves somehow lost that technology.

More intriguing is why they were built in the first place. In spite of the fact that *no* body or funerary object—dating to the same time that the fourth-dynasty pyramids were built—has ever been found in any of them, orthodox Egyptology vehemently asserts that *all* pyramids are tombs and *only* tombs, built to house the bodies of pharaohs. Later pyramids had funerary connotations, but no bodies.

Egyptology's explanation of grave robbers does not address the absence of any evidence of robbers and fails to explain how purported robbers could bypass the barriers constructed to prohibit intrusion. Perhaps funerary considerations introduced after the fourth dynasty

The Great Pyramid of Giza

were connected to the marked degeneration in construction quality. So let's test the "tombs-only" conviction with just one of the pyramid's unique design features.

The descending passage is roughly 350 feet long, of which about 150 feet is through masonry and another 200 feet is through bedrock. A century ago Sir Flinders Petrie, known as the granddaddy of Near East archeology, measured the descending passage. To show his adeptness for precision, he measured the pyramid's perimeter by triangulation, as the base was covered with rubble. He calculated it to be 3,022.93 feet. Twenty-five years later the Egyptian government hired a professional surveyor after the rubble had been cleared away, and by traditional surveying techniques found it to be 3,023.14 feet. Petrie was off by 2.5 inches in 3,000 feet—off by 0.007%.

The straightness of the passage and the flatness of its ceiling and sides intrigued his penchant for precision. Because the floor had been so damaged, he didn't consider it. The passage is about four feet high by three and a half feet wide and descends at an angle of 26 degrees. It is oriented due north, and today is aligned to Polaris. Petrie determined that "[t]he average error of straightness in the built part of the passage is only $1/50$ inch, an amazingly minute amount in a length of 150 feet. Including the whole passage, the error is under ⅛ inch on the sides, and ³/₁₀ inch on the roof, in the whole length of 350 feet." How on earth did they construct this straightness, this optical precision on the scale of a football field? They didn't have lasers. Walk through the steps of possible construction methods. How could such precision have been derived?

Answer: We don't know. They used some sort of technology and/or tools we simply don't know about. But what we do know, using our own technology, is that they could not have done this by accident.

And obviously, no matter how they *did* do it, it required a huge effort. Thus, one thing now is absolutely clear: They didn't go through such extreme effort for precision in the passage to carry a body through one time. By any kind of rationale, this should put the tomb-only notion to rest.

This information has been available for a century. It is suggested that the tomb-only theory has persisted because the curriculum for Egyptology has not included fundamental sciences and mathematics, and therefore does not provide the foundation to evaluate such elementary technical matters.

So what, then, could be the pyramid's purpose? There may be several, but a good bet for at least one use for the descending passage is as an observatory. Astronomy is the oldest discipline of science and the ancients are known to have been astute astronomers. Great deeds by the ancients were motivated by their respective religions, and their religions were derived from astronomy. To them, studying the heavens was not merely a scientific effort; their immortality depended on it.

Along with the measurable movements of the Sun, Moon, planets, and stars, many scholars recognize that the ancients knew about the precession of the equinoxes. Like a top that circles slowly while spinning rapidly around its central axis, Earth makes the slow circle of precession at about one degree every seventy-two years, or a complete circle once every 26,000 years, while spinning around its axis once every twenty-four hours. Usually attributed to Hipparchus, 150 B.C.E., the knowledge of this moving of the vault of the heavens is demonstrated by ancients far older than Hipparchus, and their religions reflected this knowledge.

Sighting from the bottom of the descending passage, the upper opening subtends an angle of just over half a degree. It would take a span of thirty-six years for an observer to follow any star close to the true pole (i.e., today's Polaris) as it enters the opening from the left and continues to the right until it disappears. Thus, seventy-two years would equal one degree of precession and 360 times that would yield a precession cycle of just under 26,000 years.

It is well known that Egypt's ancients had the ability to deal with such mathematics. So considering religion and astronomy, the precision in design of the descending chamber as an observatory seems more credible than the idea that it had been designed to carry a body through it once, and attributing such precision to happenstance.

Another purpose for the Khufu pyramid (it is the largest and thereby might well epitomize the ancients' technology) could be to serve as a monument to preserve knowledge—something of a time capsule. A large number of scholars outside of Egyptology believe it preserves dimensions of our planet, whereby the base perimeter is equal to one half of a degree of equatorial longitude. Does it?

Perimeter 3,023.14 ft. = ½ minute
6,046.28 ft. = 1 minute
362,776.8 ft. = 1 degree
so 68.7077 miles = 1 degree
360 degrees = 24,734.78 miles

If you stand on the equator and walk due north for 3,023.14 feet, the theory is that you've walked one half of one minute of longitude. The earth's longitude would then equal 24,735 miles. Satellite measurement is 24,860 miles, or a difference of 125 miles. This is accuracy of 99.5 percent. Egyptology calls this coincidence, and that is certainly possible. But if the theory has merit, then the only other dimension of a sphere, its radius, would have, as its counterpart, the pyramid's height. If such proves out, the theory would indeed have merit. But does it?

The height of the Khufu pyramid was 480.7 feet. Various measurements differ minutely, but not enough to affect the theory. Using the formula above, $480.7 \text{ feet} \times 2 \times 60 \times 360 = 3,933$ miles. This computes to a polar radius of the earth of 3,933 miles, which, compared to the satellite's measure of 3,960 miles, yields a difference of 27 miles or an accuracy of 99.3 percent. Ninety-nine point five percent . . . 99.3%. The mathematics of engineering does not allow such accuracy to be dismissed as coincidence.

How could the ancient Egyptians have derived these measurements? Again, look to astronomy (*The Secrets of the Great Pyramid*, Peter Tompkins). There are many other features of the pyramid for which we have no explanations, so this knowledge is but one example of what they knew and what we've only known for a few hundred years. But there stands the pyramid.

Then comes the question of the pyramid as a scale of the earth's dimensions:

Why such a big scale? Why not a pyramid half the size—a dramatic reduction of work to attain and preserve the same information?

A hint comes from an unexpected discipline—mythology. The highly esteemed scholar Joseph Campbell, writing about myths of disparate cultures (Icelandic, Babylonian, Sumerian, Egyptian, and others, including biblical scripture) in his book *The Masks of God—Occidental Mythology,* found the number 43,200 or its direct multiple or derivative. In fact, he traced this number back to Neolithic times. This engendered in him what he called "ecstatic panic" in that the supposed independent reoccurrence of this number, he reasoned, represented some relationship to cosmic rhythm, perhaps even a universal constant. Remember the Khufu pyramid's scale: $2 \times 60 \times 360 = 43,200$! Professor Campbell's ecstatic panic might have been too much for him had he known this. Could this number in some way have been used by the builders to determine the pyramid's dimensions?

Bottom line: (1) The notion that the pyramids were only tombs is disproved. That they were tombs at all has *never* been proved, even though the younger ones, not the older ones, had funerary characteristics. (2) The ancients demonstrated technology far exceeding what's been credited to them, far exceeding a simple mausoleum, reaching out with accuracy and methodology unexplained today.

Where did this technology come from? We don't know. But they had it and then they lost it. And rising above the Giza plateau is the most massive monument to that loss, the great Khufu pyramid, the oldest and only survivor of the Seven Wonders of the Ancient World.

PART SIX

NEW MODELS TO PONDER

39 Visitors from Beyond

Our Civilization Is a Legacy from Space Travelers,
Says Zecharia Sitchin, and His New Book Offers to
Unveil New Secrets of Divine Encounters

J. Douglas Kenyon

From a Human Potentials conference in Washington, D.C., to a Whole Life Exposition in Seattle, from campus bull sessions in Berkeley to cocktail party discussions in Boston, no talk of the hot alternative explorations into the mysterious wellsprings of civilization gets very far these days without at least a passing reference to the work of Zecharia Sitchin. And there are no signs that interest in the author of the five volumes of *The Earth Chronicles* and *Divine Encounters: A Guide to Visions, Angels and Other Emissaries* is cooling.

In fact, "Sitchinites," as his true believers unabashedly call themselves, have managed to proclaim, in nearly every available forum from talk shows to the Internet, their gospel according to Sitchin—namely, that mankind owes most of its ancient legacy to visiting extraterrestrials. Moreover, Sitchinist "evangelism" has—with some help from the movie *Stargate*—achieved a not insignificant foothold in the public imagination. And while many may quarrel with Sitchin's conclusions, very few will dispute that the Russian-born Israeli resident and ancient language expert has indeed come up with some very intriguing, if not compelling, data.

Indeed, few can match Sitchin's scholarly credentials. One of a handful of linguists who can read Sumerian cuneiform text, he is also a recognized authority on ancient Hebrew as well as Egyptian hieroglyphics. Not a little controversy, though, surrounds his unusual method of interpreting the ancient texts. Whether biblical, Sumerian, Egyptian, or otherwise, Sitchin insists they should be read not as myths but rather quite literally, essentially as journalism.

Forget about Jungian archetypes and metaphysical/spiritual analysis. "If somebody says a group of fifty people splashed down in the Persian Gulf," he argues, "under the leadership of Enki and waded ashore and established a settlement, why should I say that this never happened, and this is a metaphor, and this is a myth, and this is imagination, and somebody just made it all up, and not say [instead] this tells us what happened."

Beginning with *The 12th Planet,* Sitchin has expanded his unique explanation of the ancient texts into a vast and detailed history of what he believes were the actual events surrounding mankind's origins. Presented is extensive six-thousand-year-old evidence that there is one more planet in the solar system from which "astronauts"—the biblical "giants," or Annunaki—came to Earth in antiquity.

Subsequent titles in *The Earth Chronicles* series are *The Stairway to Heaven, The Wars of Gods and Men, The Lost Realms,* and *When Time Began.* (A companion book to the series, *Genesis Revisited,* was also published.) Sitchin describes in detail the evolving love-hate relationship between men and

Sitchin at Karnak, next to the statue of Amenhotep II, whom he believes to be the Pharaoh of the Exodus
(COPYRIGHT ZECHARIA SITCHIN)

the "gods" and his belief that this relationship shaped the early days of man on Earth.

Whatever the Annunaki may have thought of their new creation, the literary critics have found Sitchin's work impressive. "A dazzling performance," raved *Kirkus Reviews.* The *Library Journal* found it "exciting . . . credible."

Divine Encounters relates many stories from biblical, Sumerian, and Egyptian sources. From the Garden of Eden to Gilgamesh, Sitchin believes all references to deity, or deities, are actually indicating the Annunaki, but he does distinguish between the current so-called UFO abduction experience as studied by the Harvard professor John Mack and the ancient encounters. Stressing that he personally has never been abducted, he points out that whereas the current experience is usually viewed as a negative phenomenon with needles and other forms of unwelcome intrusion, "in ancient times, to join the deities was a great and unique privilege. Only a few were entitled to such an encounter."

Many of the encounters were sexual. The Bible clearly states, he points out, "that they [the Anunnaki] 'chose as wives the daughters of men and had children by them, men of renown,' et cetera, the so-called demi-gods regarding which there are more explicit tales both in Mesopotamian literature and Egyptian so-called mythology, and Greek to some extent—Alexander the Great believed that these sons of the gods were mated with his mother."

The Epic of Gilgamesh tells how one goddess tried to entice the hero into her bed and how he suspected that if she succeeded, he would end up dead. Other encounters involved "virtual reality" and experiences "akin to the *Twilight Zone.*" Also up for analysis are the experiences of the prophets Jeremiah, Ezekiel, and Isaiah. Finally, Sitchin claims to have unraveled the secret identity of the being named YHWH, and to have come to a "conclusion that is mind-boggling even for me." Nothing further could be elicited on the subject. "Buy the book," he suggests.

In the nearly twenty years since *The 12th Planet* first appeared, Sitchin has seen a considerable change in attitudes toward his work. Still, unlike von Dannikin's and others', Sitchin's study has not been lambasted by other scientists, a fact that he attributes to the soundness of his research. "The only difference between me and the scientific community—I'm talking about Asyriologists, Sumeriaologists, et cetera—is that they refer to all these texts which I read [literally] as mythology." Today, he says many researchers have come to follow his line of reasoning. By his latest reckoning, there are nearly thirty books by other writers that have "been spawned," he says, by his writings.

While Sitchin's "facts" may be beyond challenge, many of his conclusions are another matter, even among today's most avant-garde thinkers. The Mars researcher Richard Hoagland complains that Sitchin is trying to "treat the Sumerian cuneiform text like some kind of ancient *New York Times,*" while others, like the symbolist scholar John Anthony West, believe subtleties in the high wisdom of the ancients have eluded Sitchin.

For those, his views are essentially simplistic and materialistic. He is a mechanistic reductionist and a throwback to nineteenth-century positivism. Still others are reminded of the efforts of fundamentalist preachers to pin the mystical visions of Saint John the Revelator on specific historical personages (e.g., Napoleon, or Hitler, or Saddam Hussein as the anti-Christ).

Sitchin, though, remains unrepentant, with little use for what he calls "the established view," which he says is that "the texts deal with mythology and that it all is imagination, and—whether metaphor or not—that these things never happened. Someone just imagined them." In contrast, he has "no doubt that these things really happened."

The argument that the Sumerian and Egyptian civilizations got their impetus from extraterrestrials, nevertheless, does not rule out the notion that there could have been earlier and perhaps even more-advanced civi-

Sitchin with an Olmec stone head in Mesoamerica
(COPYRIGHT ZECHARIA SITCHIN)

lizations on Earth. "There's no denial of that," he says, citing Sumerian and Assyrian writings. Ashurbanipal, for instance, said he could read writing from before the flood, and describes cities and civilizations that existed before the deluge, but which were wiped out by it. So, on any question of whether there could have been an earlier civilization before the Sumerians or even before the flood—which Sitchin places at seven thousand to eight thousand years prior, "the answer is absolutely yes." No matter how far back he goes, though, Sitchin sees behind human achievement only the hand of Annunaki.

Plato should be taken literally too, though Sitchin says he has some difficulty placing the location of Atlantis, "whether it was in the middle of the Atlantic Ocean, whether it was in the Pacific in what was known later as Mu, or whether it was in Antarctica, I don't know what actually [Plato] was talking about, but the notion that once upon a time there was a civilization that was destroyed or came to an end through a major catastrophe, a great flood or something similar, I have absolutely no problem with that."

Sitchin is among those who believe that the Great Pyramid is much older than is maintained by orthodox Egyptology. In his second book, *The Stairway to Heaven,* he took considerable pains to establish that the famous cartouche cited as evidence that the structure was built by Khufu was, in fact, a forgery. Sitchin meticulously makes the case that Colonel Howard-Vyse actually faked the marks in the spaces above the King's Chamber where he claimed to have

*Sitchin says the "spacecraft" in the center is passing Mars
on the right, Earth on the left.*
(COPYRIGHT ZECHARIA SITCHIN)

discovered them. Since publication, additional corroboration has come from
the great-grandson of the master mason who assisted Howard-Vyse. It seems
that Colonel Howard-Vyse was seen entering the pyramid on the night in
question with brush and paint pot in hand and was heard to say that he
intended to reinforce some of the marks he had found, ostensibly to render
them more legible. Upon failing to dissuade Howard-Vyse from his plan, the
mason quit. The story, however, was kept alive and handed down through the
family until it eventually came to Sitchin, further reinforcing his unshakable
conviction of the true antiquity of the Great Pyramid.

Regarding the "Face on Mars," Sitchin is ambivalent. Whether or not the
"face" is real or a product of light and sand, he is more impressed by other
photographed structures. Citing his own training at Jerusalem's Hebrew
University in the 1940s, he argues, "One of the rules you learn [in archeology]
is if you see a straight line, it means an artificial structure, because there are
no straight lines in nature. Yet there are quite a number of such structures
recorded by the cameras."

According to Sitchin, it all corroborates the Sumerian statement to be
found in his first book. "Mars served as a way station," he says, citing a five-
thousand-year-old Sumerian depiction and other texts. "They say that the turn
was made at Mars." He believes an ancient Mars base may have been recently
reactivated, which could account for the disappearance of the Russian Phobos
Mars Mission as well as the U.S. Mars Observer two years ago. He also speculates that such a site may prove to be where many UFOs are now originating.

When the reporter inquired as to just what Sitchin might think of
*Hamlet's Mill: An Essay Investigating the Origins of Human Knowledge and
Its Transmission through Myth,* the work of Giorgio de Santillana and Hertha
von Dechend, Sitchin offered to kiss him on both cheeks. It seems that the two

M.I.T. professors, in their great investigation of the origins of human knowledge and its transmission through myth, had raised the question: "But now, is Nibiru as important as all that?" and had gone on to answer it, "We think so. Or, to say it the other way around: once this astronomical term and two or three more are reliably settled, one can begin in earnest to get wise to and to translate Mesopotamian code."

Sitchin does not hesitate to stake his claim: "I think that I achieved it." For him it is clear, Nibiru is and remains the twelfth planet.

40 Artifacts in Space

For Author Richard Hoagland,
the Trail of Ancient ETs Is Getting Much Warmer

J. Douglas Kenyon

Since its discovery in 1981, a gigantic and enigmatic face gazing upward from the Cydonia region of Mars has held out the tantalizing promise of scientific proof that intelligent life in the universe is not unique to Earth. Though photographed from a satellite five years earlier, the face had gone officially unnoticed, so the space expert Richard Hoagland (author of *The Monuments of Mars*) and his associates, including many top scientists and engineers who felt anything but optimistic about the chances for an effective official follow-up, proceeded to launch their own investigation.

The photos of the "Face on Mars" and an apparent complex of ruins nearby were subjected to years of exhaustive research. Utilizing the most advanced tools of scientific analysis, The Mars Mission, as the group terms itself, has produced more than enough evidence to argue plausibly that the objects of Cydonia are the remains not only of an ancient civilization, but also of one possessed of a science and technology well beyond our own.

Richard Hoagland
(PHOTOGRAPH BY TOM MILLER)

The startling possibility that such artifacts exist has created considerable public pressure to return to the Red Planet and was cause for more than a little consternation in the summer of 1993, when NASA lost contact with its Mars Observer probe just as it was about to begin a detailed photographic survey that could have proved the issue, one way or the other.

How long must we now wait until the argument can be tested? Well, perhaps not too long after all. As it turns out, the cherished, concrete evidence

282

that man is not alone in the universe may well exist in our own backyard—relatively speaking, as the Hoagland group claims to have discovered, in numerous NASA photographs, evidence of an ancient civilization on our closest neighbor, the Moon. And in this case, if NASA isn't up to the verification job, Hoagland insists that he and his backers are. The result could be the first privately funded mission to the Moon.

If anybody can pull it off, Hoagland may be the man. For more than twenty-five years a recognized authority on astronomy and space exploration, Hoagland has served as a consultant for all of the major broadcast networks. Among his many valued contributions to history and science, the best remembered is probably his conception, along with Eric Burgess, of Mankind's First Interstellar Message in 1971: an engraved plaque carried beyond the solar system by the first man-made object to escape from the Sun's influence, Pioneer 10.

Hoagland and Burgess originally took the idea to Carl Sagan, who successfully executed it aboard the spacecraft, and subsequently acknowledged their creation in the prestigious journal *Science*. It was Hoagland who proposed the Apollo 15 experiment in which astronaut David Scott, before a worldwide TV audience, simultaneously dropped a hammer and a falcon feather to see if it was true—as Galileo had predicted—that both would land at the same time. Once again, Galileo was vindicated. Since the 1981 discovery of the Face on Mars, Hoagland had devoted most of his time to the pursuit of scientific evidence for extraterrestrial intelligence.

Atlantis Rising spoke with Hoagland the day after Hollywood's latest space epic, *Stargate,* opened nationwide to enormous audiences. Because the film deals with the idea of extraterrestrial intervention in Earth's history, we wanted to know what portents, if any, he saw. "The problem with the movie," Hoagland said, "is that the vehicle for anything interesting isn't there after the first half hour. It disintegrated into a kind of shoot-'em-up with an awful lot of ends totally unfulfilled." But the film's quality—or lack of it—notwithstanding, Hoagland is encouraged by the public reception. "The fact that people are rushing to see this indicates to me there is almost an archetypal compulsion to know more, and if we put together the right vehicle, which we are attempting to do, we may have a ready audience."

Hoagland was alluding to a couple of film projects, now in the talking stages, based on the Mars and Moon work. The outcome, hopefully, will be both a scientific documentary and a fictionalized treatment presenting some of the more speculative aspects of the research. Such matters, though, are not his primary concern.

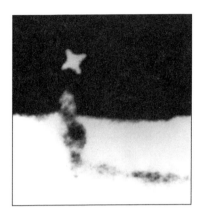

A structure called the Shard, whose vertical structure casts a long shadow. This NASA photograph is from the Lunal Orbiter III. (The starlike object to the upper left is a camera registration mark.)

An image from NASA, Apollo taken from a lunar orbit near the craters Ukert and Triesnecker. This structure has been dubbed the Castle.

Uppermost in Hoagland's mind and in those of his associates are recent discoveries on the Moon. In clear NASA photos, some nearly thirty years old—from both manned and unmanned missions, from orbiters and landers—can be seen giant structures unexplainable by any known geology—what Hoagland calls "architectural stuff."

"In sharp contrast to the Mars data, where we have been constrained to look at two or three pictures of the Cydonia region with increasingly better technology—3D tools, color, polarametric, and geometric measurements—with the Moon we are data-rich. We have literally thousands, if not millions, of photographs."

Yet with pictures taken from many directions and many different lighting conditions, angles, and circumstances, Hoagland's team has produced "stunning corroboration" that all the photos are of the "same highly geometric, highly structural, architectural stuff." In fact, he says, "in many cases, the architects on our team now are able to recognize the standard Buckminster Fuller tetrahedal truss, a hexagonal [six-sided] design, with cross bars for bracing. I mean, we're looking at standard engineering, though obviously not created by human beings."

The structure appears to be very ancient, "battered to hell by meteors . . . it looks like it had gone through termite school. It's been moth-eaten and shattered and smashed by countless bombardments," he says. "The edges are soft and fuzzy because of micro-meteorite abrasions like sand blasting."

Hoagland explains that on an airless world, there's nothing to impede a meteor from reaching the surface or reaching a structure on the ground.

Nevertheless, he says, "we're seeing a prodigious amount of structural material." Spread over a wide area, the material is turning up at several locations. "It looks as if we're seeing fragments of vast, contained enclosures—domes—although they are not inverted salad bowls. They are much more geometric, more like the step pyramids of the Biosphere II in Arizona. We're looking at something that is extraordinarily ancient, left by someone not of this Earth, not of this solar system, but from some-place else."

One of the most interesting structures appears to be an enormous freestanding tower, "a crystalline glasslike, partially pre-served structure—a kind of a megacube—standing on the remnants of a supporting structure roughly seven miles over the south-west corner of a central part of the Moon called the Sinus Medii region."

Artist Tom Miller's conjectural image of what a Shard site on the Moon might look like

If all of this exists, one of the most important questions may be: Why didn't NASA notice? If Hoagland is right, he says, "Something funny has been going on." Indeed.

Recently Hoagland presented the lunar material at Ohio State University. In the months since, discussions have raged on the Internet, Prodigy, CompuServe, and other online computer services. Many questions now being put to him are coming from scientists and engineers within NASA, many of whom have had direct experience with the lunar program, yet have been kept in the dark regarding any ET evidence. Hoagland has passed on the present state of the research and asked for input, and he's left with the inescapable impression that, as he puts it, "something incredible has been missed."

As Hoagland sees it, there are only two possible explanations: "Either we're dealing with incredible dumbness, in which case we spent twenty billion dollars for nothing because we went there, took photographs, came home and didn't realize what we were seeing, or we're dealing with the careful manipu-lation of the many by the few."

The latter may not be as implausible as it might at first sound. "If you're in a system that is cornerstoned on honesty, integrity, openness, full disclosure," he explains, "and there are folks in there who are operating contrary to those precepts, they won't get caught because no one is suspicious."

Actually, Hoagland has moved beyond suspicion to belief, and he says he can prove his point. The "smoking gun" is a report by the Brookings Institution, commissioned by NASA at its inception in 1959. Entitled "Proposed Studies on the Implications of Peaceful Space Activities for Human Affairs," the study "examines the impact of NASA discoveries on American society ten, twenty, thirty years down the road," Hoagland says. "On page 215 it discusses the impact of the discovery of evidence of either extraterrestrial intelligence—i.e., radio signals—or artifacts left by that intelligence, on some other body in the solar system.

"The report names three places that NASA might expect to find such artifacts—the Moon, Mars, and Venus. It then goes on to discuss the anthropology, the sociology, and the geopolitics of such a discovery. And it makes the astounding recommendation that, for fear of social dislocation and the disintegration of society, NASA might wish to consider *not* telling the American people. It's right there in black and white. It recommends censorship. Now that's what they've been doing," Hoagland says.

Hoagland believes that the anthropologist Margaret Mead, one of the authors of the report, was responsible for the recommendation, which he believes came out of her experience in American Samoa. In the 1940s, Mead witnessed the devastation of primitive societies exposed for the first time to sophisticated Western civilization. "That experience so moved her," says Hoagland, "so changed her perspectives that when she examined the whole ET possibility, she projected and mapped on that experience. She basically felt that if we even learned of the existence of extraterrestrials, it could destroy us; therefore people can't be told."

Believing as he does that NASA, and perhaps even higher levels of government, has been committed to keeping people in the dark regarding the realities of extraterrestrial intelligence, Hoagland is not very sanguine about the chances of success for such high-profile programs as SETI (Search for Extraterrestrial Intelligence). "They are a complete, absolute farce. They are a false-front Western town," he says. "They do not mean what they purport to mean. They are a red herring. They are a bone to the *Star Trek* generation."

In fact, Hoagland has become so dubious of government intentions on such matters that he suspects the entire alien abduction phenomenon is a misinformation campaign calculated to scare people off the subject. "If there has been a policy to obfuscate and confuse people on behalf of the objective data," he reasons, "what would that policy do and how far would it extend to the idea of ET contact? If you had a few real contacts with someone who was trying to give us messages and trying to lead us to new insights and the fear on the part of government structure had been that this will destroy civilization itself, would not that government also put in place a program to misinform, to confuse, to politically spin in the wrong direction those few real contacts, by submerging them in a sea of misinformation about contacts?"

Hoagland sees in the crop circle phenomenon part of the evidence for benign extraterrestrial contact. "The thing that makes them different from the monuments of Mars or the ancient cities on the Moon," he reasons, "is that they are occurring in the crop field here on Earth and they are occurring in the present time." He sees little doubt that the circles are not of this world. "We simply do not have the technology, let alone the knowledge base, to construct the multileveled communication symbols that the crop circles represent. So that once you eliminated the hoaxers . . . " He chuckles. "If Doug and Dave hoaxed the circles, they deserve a Nobel Prize."

Hoagland resumes his thought: "The level of sophistication of the information encoded in these symbols is so vast and so congruent with the lunar and Mars work that you're forced to conclude that whoever the artists are, they know a bit more than contemporary science, and/or the media, or, for that matter, the government."

At any rate, Hoagland's group is now planning an end run around the government's monopoly on ET-related space exploration information. The time has come, he believes, for a privately funded mission to the Moon. Already investors have expressed interest. "We're talking a few tens of millions of dollars," he says, "not really the price for the special effects in one major motion picture. We could go to the Moon and get stunning live CCD-quality color television images of the things we're seeing in these thirty-year-old NASA still pictures—still frames."

Such a mission, if funded, could be launched within fifteen months. Using new technology and a solid-fueled rocket, a five hundred- to six hundred-pound payload could be delivered into lunar orbit, where it could provide "stunning camera and telescopic live transmission capabilities," he says. The mission could even do more science. One group has expressed interest in sending a gamma ray spectrometer designed to survey the Moon for water, which, in Hoagland's scenario, there now has to be.

The mere possibility of such a mission may already be forcing NASA to be more open. Hoagland and other members of his group have recently received a front-door invitation to view extensive previously unreleased film archives. The bureaucracy, he feels, is already moving to cover itself and forestall the eventual embarrassment of being proved out of touch, to say the least.

41 The Pulsar Mystery

Could the Enigmatic Phenomenon Be the Work
of an Ancient ET Civilization? A New Scientific
Study Makes the Astonishing Case

Len Kasten

Logic would dictate that there must be some type of connection among all the worlds in our galaxy, the so-called Milky Way. Viewed from afar, it appears to be a single, spiral-shaped unit with a luminous center. What forces operate to cause so many "billions and billions" of stars to cohere to this unit? They must be vast and incredibly powerful. Now, as we enter the twenty-first century, discovery of these forces is clearly the next frontier in physics and astronomy. It is the next step in the logical progression that began only five hundred years ago with Columbus's discovery of the spherical shape of the planet.

This logical progression continued with Galileo's "heresy" that the earth revolves around the Sun, Kepler's discovery of elliptical orbits around the Sun, and then, triumphantly completing the "Copernican Revolution," Newton's deduction, in 1687, of the Second Law of Mechanics and the Law of Universal Gravitation, which elegantly proved Kepler's three laws of planetary motion. Then, it wasn't until Sir William Herschel developed a powerful telescope in 1781 that we began to peer out into the cosmos and to comprehend its complexity and immensity and to understand that what we thought were clouds of cosmic dust were actually countless other stars like our Sun.

Herschel, his son John, and his daughter Caroline eventually cataloged over 4,200 star clusters, nebulae, and galaxies, thus setting the stage for the modern era of astronomy. Then, with the orbital placement of the Hubble Telescope in 1990, we finally began to understand our stellar neighborhood. What has become known as the "local group" is dominated by our Milky Way and the giant spiral galaxy Andromeda, but also includes some minor galaxies. But even now, with all that we do know, we still know almost nothing about the implications of "membership" in our galaxy. Has our solar system simply been fortuitously "captured" by the immense centrifugal force of the galactic hub, or does the entire galaxy somehow act as an organic whole?

GALACTIC EXPLOSIONS

Thanks to the author Paul LaViolette, Ph.D., we can begin to appreciate that certain galactic "events" have a very profound physical effect on our little Sun and planet way out here in the outer reaches of a spiral arm. LaViolette, a physicist with a doctorate in systems theory, has postulated the existence of something called a "galactic superwave." In his book *Earth*

Dr. Paul LaViolette

Under Fire: Humanity's Survival of the Apocalypse, he claims that astronomical and geological evidence suggests that a "protracted global climatic disaster" occurred on this planet about 15,000 years ago.

One piece of this evidence derives from a new technique developed by scientists in the late 1970s measuring the concentration of the element beryllium-10 in ice-core samples drilled at Vostok, East Antarctica. Minute quantities of this rare isotope are produced when high-energy cosmic rays collide with nitrogen and oxygen atoms in our stratosphere.

Since a time frame can be associated with each layer of the ice-core sample by measuring the Be-10 concentrations at various levels, the fluctuations of cosmic bombardments of Earth can be precisely determined. The Vostok samples clearly showed a peak of cosmic radiation between 17,500 and 14,150 years ago, associated with a sharp increase in the ambient air temperature from -10 C to about 0 C. This, claims LaViolette, caused the end of the ice age and ushered in the era of moderate temperatures that made modern civilization possible.

This concept of the galactic superwave, apparently caused by massive "explosions" at the galactic core, is not entirely new to astronomers. However, they view them as relatively rare events, occurring perhaps every ten million to one hundred million years and having no particular effect on our solar system because they believe that the galactic magnetic lines of force prevent cosmic radiation from propagating very far from the core.

But LaViolette has amassed an impressive profusion of evidence, from many different sources, that these events are much more frequent and that they are really massive bombardments of cosmic ray particles (electrons, positrons, and protons) with the power of five to ten million "highly-charged" supernova explosions that reach, in full strength, to the farthest limits of the galaxy!

The theories of Paul LaViolette are highly controversial in astronomy circles even though he makes his case with careful and thorough research. Perhaps it is because he is not afraid to boldly go where other scientists fear to tread—into the realm of myth and legend to find supporting evidence for his theories.

His book *The Talk of the Galaxy: An ET Message for Us?* puts forth another daring proposition. He argues that pulsars are high-tech galactic "beacons" very likely created by highly developed extraterrestrial civilizations, and are being used to signal the advent of galactic events, especially the superwaves. These books, taken together, sketch out a fantastic scenario that radically changes the status quo of the astronomical, anthropological, and archeological landscapes, and opens up a new universe of potential research and investigation.

LaViolette may well be just the pivotal researcher to lift science out of stale, inbred stagnation into invigorating, human-oriented realms and new directions for the twenty-first century. In view of the importance of his theories, we set up an interview for the purposes of this article. When we spoke with him, we were surprised at how deftly he was able to shift back and forth from science to mythology to support his ideas.

CONTINUOUS CREATION VS. BIG BANG

Perhaps one of LaViolette's most heretical theories relates to the purpose of these galactic core explosions. His explanation resurrects that bête noire of modern science, the concept of the ether. LaViolette is convinced that these tremendous energy discharges are nothing less than an ongoing process of the creation of matter itself from the etheric flux, which invisibly pervades the entire universe.

This idea of "continuous creation" is in direct opposition to the now generally accepted "Big Bang theory," which most esotericists have never really been comfortable with, but which does seem to satisfy those religious groups who believe that "creation" was literally a single primordial act by God. A complete discussion of this subject can be found in LaViolette's book, *Genesis of the Cosmos: The Ancient Science of Continuous Creation*, and also in his follow-up book, *Subquantum Kinetics: The Alchemy of Creation*.

The concept of the all-pervasive etheric substratum from which matter is created was really originally derived from ancient Hindu metaphysics, but had gained considerable scientific credence up until the late nineteenth century, when it was supposedly "put to bed" by the famous Michelson-Morley experiment in 1887. However, this experiment was seriously flawed because it assumed the ether to be another physical dimension rather than a precursor to energy itself. Today, although orthodox science may not have granted respectability to etheric theory, it certainly doesn't mind using it every day to explain the propagation of radio and television waves.

FIRE AND FLOOD

According to LaViolette, these galactic explosive phases occur about every 10,000 to 20,000 years and last anywhere from several hundred to several thousand years. Evidence of this frequency began emerging in 1977, but scientists considered it an aberration. The electrons and positrons travel radially outward from the core at near light speed, but the protons travel much more slowly because they are about two thousand times heavier.

They disperse and are then captured by the magnetic fields in the galactic nucleus. The superwave itself would not normally have much of an effect on the Sun or Earth, since the energy would be about one-thousandth of that radiated by the Sun. But the solar system is surrounded by a cloud of dust and frozen cometary debris that remains on the periphery because of the solar wind, which has an expelling action and cleanses the entire solar system.

However, the superwave, when it arrives, would push back this dust cloud into the interplanetary medium and would block out the light of the Sun, Moon, and stars, and the Sun would appear to go dark. Also, the superwave and dust particles would energize the Sun and increase flaring activity so much that dry grasslands and forests would spontaneously catch fire. This heat would also melt the glaciers, releasing tremendous quantities of water, causing extensive flooding all over the planet.

A whole panoply of cascading catastrophes would then ensue, including earthquakes and increased seismic activity, high winds, failed crops, and destroyed vegetation, along with high, ultraviolet radiation, causing skin cancers and increased mutation rates. In short, it would be a time of cataclysmic destruction that would probably snuff out much of the human and animal life on the planet.

LaViolette, in *Earth Under Fire*, cites all the legends and myths relating to cataclysmic events, all of which appear to have occurred during the time of the last galactic superwave—that is, about 15,000 years ago. The Greek myth of Phaeton, for example, the semi-mortal son of Helios, the sun god, who was given the reins of the sun chariot and caused it to crash into the earth thereby setting off a tremendous worldwide conflagration, is claimed to be a metaphor for that era when the superwave caused an extraordinary increase in infrared and ultraviolet emissions from the Sun, along with ultra-high flaring activity.

This could easily have caused a "scorched-earth" phenomenon, according to LaViolette. The Greek writer Ovid says of this event, "Great cities perish, together with their fortifications, and the flames turn whole nations into ashes." Then, as the glaciers melted and the ocean levels rose all over the world, large landmasses would have become submerged.

This might easily account for the flood legends in just about every ancient civilization. LaViolette compiled a list of about eighty societies with some sort of flood myth. He has no doubt that the deluge that sank Atlantis was caused by glacial meltwater. He says, "The . . . 'sinking' of Atlantis simply refers to the melting and ultimate wasting of the continental ice sheets," which "spawned a foray of destructive glacier wave floods." Interestingly, the Phaeton myth concludes with massive flooding sent by Zeus to quell the flames. According to Plato's *Timaeus,* this would have occurred about 11,550 years ago, right around the time of the last stage of the superwave.

LITTLE GREEN MEN

In *The Talk of the Galaxy,* LaViolette turns his attention to those puzzling anomalies of astronomy, the pulsars. Having established, in his earlier books, a very convincing case for galactic events that affect all the worlds therein, it was natural to question whether or not pulsars have any connection with these events. The fact that they emitted such consistently regular pulsations suggested to him that they were of intelligent origin.

This was not a new theory. Several scientists involved in the SETI project have speculated on this subject. LaViolette tells us that Professor Alan Barrett, a radio astronomer, theorized in a *New York Post* article in the early 1970s that pulsar signals "might be part of a vast interstellar communications network which we have stumbled upon."

It was, in fact, the first thought that occurred to the two astronomers who discovered the first pulsar signal, in July 1967 at Cambridge University in England. Graduate student Jocelyn Bell and her astronomy professor, Anthony Hewish, named the source of the signal LGM 1, an acronym for Little Green Men. By the time they published their astonishing discovery in *Nature* magazine in February 1968, having discovered a second pulsar, they were afraid to suggest an ETI (extraterrestrial intelligence) thesis because

A radio telescope listens for signals from the Crab Nebula
(ART BY TOM MILLER)

they feared ridicule from colleagues, and were afraid that the discovery would not be taken seriously by scientists. But nevertheless, they continued with this naming convention up to LGM 4!

Of the many theories advanced to explain pulsars, the one that had prevailed by 1968, and is still accepted today by default, is known as the Neutron Star Lighthouse Model. Proposed by Thomas Gold, it postulates that the signal comes from a rapidly rotating burned-out star that has gone through a supernova explosion that transformed it into a bunch of tightly packed neutrons. This would have made it incredibly dense and much smaller, reduced from about three times the size of the Sun to no more than thirty kilometers. Gold theorized that as it rotates, it emits a synchotron beam, much like a lighthouse beacon, which is picked up on Earth as a brief radio pulse. To match the pulsar frequencies, these stars would have to spin at rates up to hundreds of times per second.

SIGNAL COMPLEXITY

LaViolette has compiled a very impressive and convincing set of reasons why the pulsars are very likely of intelligent rather than natural origin and why they cannot possibly fit the Neutron Star model. They all relate to the fact that the signal is totally unlike any other ever encountered in terms of both precision and complexity. Of major importance is the fact that the pulses are timed not precisely from pulse to pulse, but only when time-averaged over two thousand pulses.

Then the time-averaged pulse is exceedingly accurate and regular. Furthermore, in some pulsars the pulse drifts at a constant rate, adding another layer of complexity to the signal. Another factor has to do with amplitude modulation. Some of the pulses increase in amplitude in varied yet regular patterns. Then many of the pulses exhibit something called "mode switching," wherein the pulse suddenly exhibits an entirely new set of characteristics that persist for a time, and then it reverts to its original mode.

In some cases, this switch is frequency dependent and in others the switching conforms to regular patterns. LaViolette argues that an ET civilization would expect us to understand that such a complex signal must necessarily be intelligently designed. Perhaps they assume that we have the computer power necessary to comprehend the logic behind all the variability. The Neutron Star model has to be continually "stretched" to encompass these characteristics as they are discovered. At this point, it has been contorted beyond recognition in order to explain this complexity, but astronomers are reluctant to abandon "the sizable mental investment involved."

In terms of precision, some stars do show periodic, regular variations in color and luminosity. Several binary X-ray stars pulse with periods accurate to six or seven significant digits. Pulsars, on the other hand, are from a million to one hundred billion times more precise! LaViolette speculates that if Bell and Hewish "had known then what we know now, perhaps they would not have rejected the ETI communication scenario as readily as they did."

MARKER BEACONS

Perhaps the most striking of all pulsar characteristics is their placement in the galaxy. When their positions are plotted within the galactic "globe," which is a projection of the galaxy similar to the Mercator for Earth, they all seem to congregate in certain key locations. The densest concentration is found on or near the galactic equator, not the galactic center as one would have expected if they were created out of supernova explosions as theorized.

Then they seem to clump around two points along the equator. These two points are precisely at the one-radian marks measured from the earth. A radian is a universally understood geometric measurement of an angle that marks off an arc around the circumference equal in length to the circle's radius, and is always 57.296 degrees. Using the earth as the center of the circle and placing the galactic center on the equator, perhaps the most significant pulsar in the galaxy falls precisely at a one-radian mark!

The so-called Millisecond Pulsar is the fastest out of all 1,100 discovered to date. It "beats" at 642 pulses per second. It is also the most precise in timing, being accurate to seventeen significant digits, which surpasses the best atomic clocks on Earth, and it emits optically visible, high-intensity pulses.

LaViolette believes that the Millisecond Pulsar was deliberately placed there by ETs to function as a marker beacon expressly for our solar system, as they knew we would understand the significance of the one-radian point.

LaViolette's main thesis is that all of the pulsars "visible" to Earth were put in place in order to convey a message to us relative to the galactic superwave. This, he says, explains why two unique (too complex to explain here) pulsars that LaViolette calls the "King and Queen of Pulsars" were positioned in the Crab and Vela nebulae, both of which were the sites of supernova explosions.

He estimates that after reaching the Earth about 14,130 years ago, the last superwave would have reached the Vela complex about one hundred years later and detonated a supernova there by heating up the unstable stars to the explosion point. Then, about 6,300 years later it would have reached the Crab nebula and triggered a supernova there. These very large supernovas would have become visible on Earth at 11,250 B.C.E. and C.E. 1,054, respectively. By placing marker beacons at these points, LaViolette believes the ETs were giving us information about that superwave that we could use to predict future waves, along with their associated cataclysmic effects.

LaViolette believes that we already have the technology to build our own Force Field Beaming Technology. Therefore, the day may not be far off when Earthlings can join the galactic community and help to inform some other unfortunate planet of the approach of a fearsome galactic superwave.

42 The Physicist as Mystic

David Lewis

A child staring at the clear night sky beholds the wonder of the universe and its mystery. How, after all, to such a simple mind, to any mind, can the starry expanse go on and on, never ending? For if it were to end, we imagine, there would always be something beyond. And then what about the beginning, and before that, and so on? The two apparent extremes describe what the French philosopher and mathematician, Blaise Pascal called *les deux infinis,* the two infinities.

As science probes this mystery, subatomically and cosmically, it searches within the domain of finite understanding for its answer. Since Darwin, Western scientists have told us that matter gave birth to reality, to life, that reality is concrete, which is to say finite, the wonder of infinity as observed on a starry night notwithstanding. But in its attempt to define reality, to put it into an intellectual box, materialistic science finds itself in the land of mystics, the realm it sought to avoid all along.

Delving deeply, relentlessly, into any subatomic particle in the universe, cutting-edge physicists find that nothing is as it appears to be. Indeed, they find that the physical universe is but a ripple in an ocean of infinite energy, even as hangers-on, such as Paul Kurtz and his Committee for Scientific Investigation of Claims of the Paranormal and so many others in the material sciences, assert that nothing exists beyond matter. They assert, in fact, that matter is ultimate reality. Unfortunately for the absolute materialists, though, the tide turned some time ago.

Early in the twentieth century, Albert Einstein amazed the world with his discoveries in the world of astrophysics. With his general theory of relativity, he opened the doors of science to the M-word—Mysticism. He told us that space and time are intertwined, relative coordinates in reality that make up the space-time continuum. He also suggested that matter is inseparable from an ever-present quantum energy field, that it is a condensation of that field, and that this ineffable field is the sole reality underlying all appearances.

The implications brought into question the Western world's most basic assumptions about the universe, about matter, and about our perceptions as human beings. Einstein, though, only opened the door to the mystical realm. Much more followed.

Quantum theory evolved beyond Einstein's landmark discoveries. Physicists, in their quest to define matter's essential properties, found that the most minute particles in the universe, protons, electrons, photons, and so on—the very fabric of the material universe—transcend three-dimensional reality. Electrons, they discovered, are not matter in any standard sense. The diameter of an electron, for instance, cannot be measured: An electron can be shown to be two things at once, both a wave and a particle, each with differing characteristics that should exclude the other's existence from a purely material viewpoint.

As particles, they behave like a larger visible object, a baseball, or a rock. As waves, though, electrons mysteriously shape-shift into vast energy clouds. They display magical properties, stretching across space with the apparent ability to bilocate. Physicists have discovered, moreover, that these magical abilities characterize the entire subatomic universe, adding a mind-boggling dimension, and a mystical one, to the nature of the universe itself.

Even more astounding revelations waited in the world of physics. The observer, modern physicists found, actually *determines* the nature of a subatomic particle. When physicists *observe* particles as particles, they find them, understandably, to be particles. But when observing the same particles *as waves,* they find them to be waves, the implication being that matter is defined by conscious perspective rather than being fixed or finite.

A MORE PROFOUND UNDERSTANDING

The physicist David Bohm, one of Einstein's protégés, delved more deeply into this mystery; he took the implications of the new physics even further. He discerned that if the nature of subatomic particles depends on an observer's perspective, then it is futile to search for a particle's actual properties, as was science's goal, or to think that subatomic particles, the essence of matter, even exist before someone observes them. In his plasma experiments at the Berkeley Radiation Laboratory, Bohm found that individual electrons act as part of an interconnected whole.

In plasma, a gas composed of electrons and positive ions in high concentration, electrons more or less assume the nature of a self-regulating organism, as if they were inherently intelligent. Bohm found, to his amazement, that the subatomic sea he created was conscious. By extension, the vast subatomic reality that is material creation may also be said to be conscious.

To those who foresaw the implications, Bohm shattered the useful but limiting premise that led science to its many achievements in modern times, crossing a new barrier beyond which lurked the unknown, a scientific twilight zone. Intellectual observation, it turned out, the fulcrum of the scientific method since Francis Bacon, could take an observer only so far. As with any dogma, what was once a useful guideline became a stifling limitation. Negating the ability of the human intellect alone to fathom ultimate reality, Bohm, then, challenged the scientific world to adopt a more profound understanding.

Reality, Bohm's work suggests, has a more subtle nature than that which can be defined by linear, human thinking, the province of modern science and the intellect. Within the fabric of reality, Bohm found not just the wave/particle duality phenomenon as described above, but also an interconnectedness, a Non-Space or Non-Local reality where only the *appearance* of waves also being particles exists. He saw, perhaps intuitively, that it is ultimately meaningless to see the universe as composed of parts, or disconnected, as everything is joined, space and time being composed of the same essence as matter.

A subatomic particle, then, does not suddenly change into a wave (at velocities that would have to be beyond the speed of light, as Bohm's mentor Einstein suggested); it already is a wave sharing the same Non-Space as the particle. Reality, then, is not material in any common sense of the word. It is something far more ineffable. Physicists call this "Non-Locality." Mystics call it "oneness."

In spite of those who disagreed, Bohm evolved a yet more profound understanding, that of an interconnected whole with a conscious essence, where all matter and events interact with one another, because time, space, and distance are an illusion relative to perspective. He developed, in fact, a holographic model of the universe, in which the whole can be found in the most minute part—in a blade of grass or an atom—and where matter, circumstance, and dimension result from holographic projections of subtle but powerful conscious energy.

Actual location and, by extension, the shape-shifting of particles both manifest reality; in fact, they exist only in the context of relative appearances. Bohm discovered that everything is connected to everything else, past, present, and future, as well as time, space, and distance, because it all occupies the same Non-Space and Non-Time.

David Bohm brought to physics and the scientific world the understanding that has propelled mystics and sages since the dawn of time. Rejecting the idea that particles do not exist until they are observed, he, like the Nobel exists, they say, contrary to Einstein's belief that appreciation of the mysterious lies at the center of all true science.

In letters to a friend, Darwin himself argued strenuously in favor of gradualism, the theory that all life evolved slowly and inexorably from primitive matter without sudden changes, in order to avoid supporting any possible supernatural or biblical creation theories. That bias, we now find, remains fixed to such a degree that absolute materialism has become the established dogma of the scientific and academic worlds.

According to Allan Bloom, a professor at the University of Chicago, the suggestion of the existence of an Absolute, even of the philosophical variety, is looked on with derision in academic circles. He reveals in *Closing of the American Mind* that "Absolutism" of any sort has become taboo in university classrooms. No underlying order or intelligence can exist in the universe, the academics say. The avant-garde of theoretical physics, however, arrive with a new take on a very ancient philosophical and metaphysical Absolute.

ANCIENT WISDOM AND MODERN SCIENCE

Genesis of the Cosmos, Paul LaViolette's book about ancient myth and the "science of continuous creation," reveals an extraordinarily persistent message encoded throughout the ancient mythologies of the world, a message now echoed by quantum cosmologists such as Stanford's Andre Linde and even Cambridge's Steven Hawking.

Passed down to modern times from the mists of prehistory, these ancient myths repeatedly describe principles now pointed to in the newest of the new physics, that of a universal potential latent within all reality. "In all cases," LaViolette says, "the concept [the myths] convey effectively portrays how an initially uniform and featureless ether self-divides to produce a bi-polar . . . wave pattern."

LaViolette elaborates, telling us that an "ancient creation science" comes down to us through myth, which "conceives all physical form, animate or inanimate, to be sustained by an undercurrent of process, a flux of vital energy that is present in all regions of space . . . Thus the ancient creation science . . . infers the presence of lifelike consciences or spirits in all things, even in inanimate objects such as rocks and rivers or the Earth itself." While supporting his premise with the principles of quantum physics, LaViolette speaks to the materialists who inhabit the world of modern science: "This view of a vast, living beyond contrasts sharply with the sanitized mechanistic paradigm . . . which laureate and renowned physicist Brian Josephson, understood that physics must see the nature of subatomic reality in a new way. It is not simply that conscious perspective affects the nature of the subatomic quanta, Bohm revealed, but that the subatomic quanta *is* conscious, which means that *everything* is conscious, even inanimate objects and seemingly empty space, the very definition, if one were possible, of mystical or spiritual reality.

HALLOWED SPACE

Most physicists agree that a mere cubic centimeter of space brims with more energy than the sum of all the energy held in the entire material universe. One school of physics finds this calculation so incredible that it assumes it must be a mistake. But to those such as Bohm, the principle makes perfect sense. Matter, according to the avant-garde of subatomic physics, cannot ultimately be separated from what appears as empty space. It is, rather, a part of space, and part of a deeper, invisible order from which reality's unseen, conscious essence precipitates, as material form, and then returns to the invisible again. Space, then, is not empty, but instead filled with highly concentrated conscious energy, the source of everything in existence.

In *The Holographic Universe,* an elaboration upon the implication of Bohm's genius, Michael Talbott describes all of material creation as a "ripple . . . a pattern of excitation in the midst of an unimaginably vast ocean." Talbott goes on to say, paraphrasing Bohm, that, "despite its apparent materiality and enormous size, the universe does not exist in and of itself, but is the stepchild of something far vaster and more ineffable."

Talbott tells Bohm's story, capsulizing the implications of his revelations and of modern science's implicit nihilism. "Bohm," Talbott says, "believes that our almost universal tendency to fragment the world and ignore the dynamic interconnectedness of all things is responsible for many of our problems . . . we believe we can extract the valuable parts of the earth without affecting the whole . . . treat parts of our body and not be concerned with the whole . . . deal with . . . crime, poverty, and drug addiction without addressing . . . society as a whole." Bohm, Talbott says, believes that such a fragmented approach may even bring about our ultimate destruction.

The problem, then, in reconciling modern science, even modern physics, with the wonder a child feels while staring at a clear night sky, les deux infinis, remains the dogma of absolute materialism, of non-interconnectedness. Although the tide has turned in certain circles within the scientific community, matter, we are still told, is the source of all life. Nothing truly mysterious has denied the existence of an unseen supernatural realm and forged a wedge between science and religion."

High priests of physics such as the Nobel laureate Steven Weinberg and other notable physicists clearly leave the door open to LaViolette's Continuous Creation, syncretizing—according to the physicist Michio Kaku, of the City University of New York—Judeo-Christian, Buddhist, and scientific cosmologies. The high priests also express the likelihood of parallel universes, or a Multiverse, in which our reality is one of many that exist in Non-Time/Non-Space, a principle that sounds like the scientific version of transcendental existence.

Addressing the Big Bang theory's inability to account for what happened before the Big Bang, Kaku, in an article in the *London Daily Telegraph,* quotes Weinberg as saying, "An important implication is that there wasn't a beginning . . . the [multiverse] has been here all along." Grappling with how extremely unlikely it is that our reality, let alone another, ever presented conditions that would support biological life, Princeton's Freeman Dyson says, ominously for the materialists, "It's as if the universe knew we were coming."

BEYOND THE VEIL

The principles that science now begins to embrace, those of an inherently intelligent universe, have, of course, been espoused for thousands of years. Ancient Sanskrit texts describe the nature of *Purusha,* Supreme Consciousness, and *Chittam,* or mindstuff, as fundamental to the nature of reality. The mineral, vegetable, and animal kingdoms exist as grades of Supreme Consciousness, and man, being highly conscious, participates in this vast flow of subtle consciousness.

Here, the mind is a miniature universe, and the universe is the expansion of mind. And while the debate still rages in Western science, throughout history practitioners of the yogic science report, as actual conscious experience, what the high priests of physics relegate to abstract theory. In an exalted state of consciousness, for example, the great yogi Paramahansa Yogananda, who spent much of his life in the United States, experienced his own awareness merged with cosmic consciousness, having devoted himself to that goal for many years.

In his famous autobiography, Yogananda describes his experience: "My sense of identity was no longer confined to a body," he says, "but embraced the circumambient atoms . . . My ordinary frontal vision was now changed to a vast spherical sight, simultaneously all-perceptive . . . all melted into a luminescent sea. The unifying light alternated with materializations of form."

After describing a state of ecstatic joy, the renowned yogi goes on to say, "A swelling glory within me began to envelop towns, continents, the earth, solar and stellar systems, tenuous nebulae, and floating universes . . .The entire cosmos . . . glittered within the infinitude of my being." In the jargon of modern physics, this experience might be described as Non-Locality in the electron sea. In the jargon of Yoga, it is called Oneness with Supreme Consciousness, Ultimate Being, or God.

Like sages before him for thousands of years, Yogananda describes the universe beyond matter as being composed of indescribably subtle Light. He describes the material universe as being composed of the same essence but in a grosser form, a principle echoed throughout the world's mystical traditions and now in modern physics. Regarding the source of this Light, Yogananda says, "The divine dispersion of rays poured from an eternal source, blazing into galaxies transfigured with ineffable auras. Again and again I saw the creative beams condense into constellations, then resolve into sheets of transparent flame. By rhythmic reversion, sextillion worlds passed into diaphanous luster, then fire became firmament."

Perhaps more significant, the sage tells us that his experience of the center of all light and creation poured from a point of intuitive perception in his heart, not from his intellect, a point that emphasizes the limits of the Western scientific method. And while Western science may balk at such a subjective account, claiming it lacks scientific verification, those mystics who have devoted themselves to absolute perception throughout history report similar experiences. The yogic science, practiced within the laboratory of human consciousness, is, in fact, the science of consciousness, which physicists such as Bohm theorize as being inseparable from, and responsible for, all reality.

In his own way, our wonder-struck child beneath the stars probably draws the same conclusion.

Recommended Reading:
Selected Bibliography

Chapter 1 – Darwin's Demise

Behe, Michael. *Darwin's Black Box: The Biochemical Challenge to Evolution*. New York: Touchstone, 1998.

Darwin, Charles. *Origin of Species*. New York: New American Library, 1958.

Milton, Richard. *Facts of Life: Shattering the Myth of Darwinism*. Rochester, Vt.: Park Street Press, 1997.

Chapter 2 – Evolution vs. Creation

Capra, Fritjof. *The Tao of Physics*. Boston: Shambhala Publications, 1999.

Chalmers, David. "The Puzzle of Conscious Experience." *Scientific American* (December 1995).

Darwin, Charles. *Origin of Species*. New York: New American Library, 1958.

Flem-Ath, Rand, and Rose Flem-Ath. *When the Sky Fell: In Search of Atlantis*. New York: St. Martin's Press, 1997.

Hancock, Graham. *Fingerprints of the Gods: The Evidence of Earth's Lost Civilization*. New York: Three Rivers Press, 1995.

NBC TV Special, "The Mysterious Origins of Man," February 1996.

Santillana, Giorgio de and Hertha von Dechend. *Hamlet's Mill: An Essay Investigating the Origins of Human Knowledge and Its Transmission through Myth*. Jaffrey, N.H.: Godine Press, 1977.

Thompson, Richard, and Michael Cremo. *Forbidden Archeology*. Badger, Calif.: Torchlight Publishing, 1993. Condensed version: *Hidden History of the Human Race*. Badger, Calif.: Govardhan Hill Publishers, 1994.

Weinberg, Steven. *Dreams of a Final Theory*. New York: Vintage Books, 1994.

Chapter 3 – Exposing a Scientific Cover-Up

Cremo, Michael. *Human Devolution: A Vedic Alternative to Darwin's Theory*. Badger, Calif.: Torchlight Publications, 2003.

NBC-TV Special, "The Mysterious Origins of Man," February 1996.

Thompson, Richard, and Michael Cremo. *Forbidden Archeology.* Badger, Calif.: Torchlight Publishing, 1993. Condensed version: *Hidden History of the Human Race*, Badger, Calif.: Govardhan Hill Publishers, 1994.

Chapter 4 – In Defense of Catastrophes

NBC-TV Special, "The Mystery of the Sphinx," 1993.

Noone, Richard. *5/5/2000 Ice: The Ultimate Disaster.* New York: Harmony Books, 1986.

Plato. *The Timaeus and Critias of Plato.* Translated by Thomas Taylor. Whitefish, Mont.: Kessinger Publishing, 2003.

Schoch, Robert M., Ph.D., and Robert Aquinas McNally. *Voices of the Rocks: A Scientist Looks at Catastrophes and Ancient Civilizations.* New York: Harmony Books, 1999.

Settegast, Mary. *Plato Prehistorian: 10,000 to 5,000 BC in Myth and Archeology.* Cambridge, Mass.: Rotenberg Press, 1987.

Chapter 5 – Cataclysm 9500 B.C.E.

Allan, D. S., and J. B. Delair. *Cataclysm! Compelling Evidence of a Cosmic Catastrophe in 9500 BC.* Rochester, Vt.: Bear & Company, 1997.

Bauval, Robert. *The Orion Mystery: Unlocking the Secrets of the Pyramids.* New York: Three Rivers Press, 1995.

Hancock, Graham. *Fingerprints of the Gods: The Evidence of Earth's Lost Civilization.* New York: Three Rivers Press, 1995.

Hancock, Graham, and Robert Bauval. *The Message of the Sphinx: A Quest for the Hidden Legacy of Mankind.* New York: Three Rivers Press, 1996.

LaViolette, Paul, Ph.D. *Earth Under Fire: Humanity's Survival of the Apocalypse.* Schenectady, N.Y.: Starburst Publications, 1997.

Thompson, Richard and Michael Cremo. *Forbidden Archeology.* Badger, Calif.: Torchlight Publishing, 1993. Condensed version: *Hidden History of the Human Race*, Badger, Calif.: Govardhan Hill Publishers, 1994.

Chapter 6 – The Case for the Flood

Hancock, Graham. *Underworld: The Mysterious Origins of Civilization.* New York: Crown, 2002.

Plato. *The Timaeus and Critias of Plato.* Translated by Thomas Taylor. Whitefish, Mont.: Kessinger Publishing, 2003.

Schoch, Robert M., Ph.D. *Voyages of the Pyramid Builders: The True Origins of the Pyramids from Lost Egypt to Ancient America.* New York: Tarcher/Putnam, 2003.

Chapter 7 – The Martyrdom of Immanuel Velikovsky

Atlantis Rising #28. "The Fight for Alien Technology: Jack Shulman Remains Undaunted by Mounting Threats," Whitefish, Mont. July/August 2001.

Freud, Sigmund. *Imago.* Baltimore: Johns Hopkins University Press.

———. *Moses and Monotheism.* New York: Vintage, 1955.

Gardiner, Alan H., *The Admonitions of an Egyptian Sage from a Hieratic Papyrus* (the Papyrus Ipuwer). Lower Saxony, Germany. G. Olms Verlag, 1990.

Jones. London: The Hogarth Press and the Institute of Pschoanalysis, 1939.

Rose, Lynn, M.D. "The Censorship of Velikovsky's Interdisciplinary Synthesis" *Pensee Volume 2, Number 2: Velikovsky Reconsidered.* Portland, OR. Student Academic Freedom Forum, May 1972.

Velikovsky, Immanuel. *Ages in Chaos: From the Exodus to King Akhnaton.* Garden City, NY. Doubleday, 1952.

———. *Earth in Upheaval.* Garden City, N.Y.: Doubleday, 1955.

———. *Oedipus and Akhnaton.* Garden City, N.Y.: Doubleday, 1960.

———. *Worlds in Collision.* New York: Dell, 1965.

Chapter 8 – The Perils of Planetary Amnesia

New Scientist. London: June 1997.

"Remembering the End of the World," a documentary on Dave Talbott, available at www.kronia.com.

Thornhill, Wallace. CD. *The Electric Universe,* WholeMind, 8350 S.W. Greenway, #24, Beaverton, OR 97008, 1-800-230-9347, or www.kronia.com.

Velikovsky, Immanuel. *Worlds In Collision.* New York: Dell, 1965.

———. *Mankind in Amnesia.* London: Sidgwick & Jackson, 1982.

Chapter 9 – Thunderbolts of the Gods

Hesiod, *Theogony*. New York: Penguin Classics, 1973.

"Remembering the End of the World," a documentary on Dave Talbott, available at www.kronia.com.

Talbott, Dave. *The Saturn Myth*. New York: Doubleday, 1980.

Talbott, Dave, and Wallace Thornhill. "Thunderbolts of the Gods." Monograph/DVD sets. www.thunderbolts.info.

Thornhill, Wallace. CD. *The Electric Universe,* WholeMind, 8350 S.W. Greenway, #24, Beaverton, OR 97008, 1-800-230-9347, or www.kronia.com.

www.aeonjournal.com.

www.catastrophism.com.

www.holoscience.com.

Chapter 10 – The Enigma of India's Origins

Allan, D. S., and J. B. Delair. *Cataclysm! Compelling Evidence of a Cosmic Catastrophe in 9500 BC.* Rochester, Vt.: Bear & Company, 1997.

Doniger, Wendy, Wendy O'Flaherty, and Thomas Wyatt. *The Rig Veda: An Anthology: One Hundred and Eight Hymns, Selected, Translated and Annotated (Classic)*. New York: Penguin Classics, 1981.

Hancock, Graham. *Fingerprints of the Gods: The Evidence of Earth's Lost Civilization*. New York: Three Rivers Press, 1995.

Milton, Richard. *Facts of Life: Shattering the Myth of Darwinism.* Rochester, Vt.: Park Street Press, 1997.

The Ramayana: A Shortened Modern Prose Version of the Indian Epic, by R. K. Narayant Kampar Ramayanam. New York: Penguin Classics, 1972.

Chapter 11 – Pushing Back the Portals of Civilization

Atlantis Rising #1. "Getting Answers from the Sphinx." Whitefish, Mont.: November 1994.

Atlantis Rising #19. Review of *The Temple of Man.* Whitefish, Mont.: May 1999.

Bauval, Robert, and Adrian Gilbert. *The Orion Mystery: Unlocking the Secrets of the Pyramids.* New York: Crown, 1994.

Fox-TV/National Geographic Special, "Pyramids Live: Secret Chambers Revealed," Live broadcast of the Queen's Chamber in the Great Pyramid, Egypt. September 16, 2002.

Hancock, Graham. *Fingerprints of the Gods: The Evidence of Earth's Lost Civilization*. New York: Three Rivers Press, 1995.

Hancock, Graham, and Robert Bauval. *The Message of the Sphinx: A Quest for the Hidden Legacy of Mankind*. New York: Three Rivers Press, 1996.

Herodotus. *The Histories*, translated by James McConnell. London: Truebner Publishers, 1909.

Schwaller de Lubicz, R. A. *The Temple of Man*. Rochester, Vt.: Inner Traditions International, 1998.

West, John Anthony. *Serpent in the Sky: The High Wisdom of Ancient Egypt*. Wheaton, Ill.: Quest Books, 1993.

Chapter 12 – New Studies Confirm Very Old Sphinx

Baines, John, and Jaromír Málek. *Atlas of Ancient Egypt*. New York: Facts on File, 1980.

Coxill, David. "The Riddle of the Sphinx." *Inscription: Journal of Ancient Egypt.* Spring 1998.

Reader, C. D. "A Geomorphological Study of the Giza Necropolis, with Implications for the Development of the Site," *Archaeometry*, vol. 43, no. 1. Oxford: 2001.

Schoch, Robert M., Ph.D., and Robert Aquinas McNally. *Voices of the Rocks: A Scientist Looks at Catastrophes and Ancient Civilizations*. New York: Harmony Books, 1999.

Yamei, Hou, Richard Potts, Yuan Baoyin, Guo Zhengtang, Alan Deino, Wang Wei, Jennifer Clark, Xie Guangmao, and Huang Weiwen. "Mid-Pleistocene Acheulean-like Stone Technology of the Bose Basin, South China." *Science.* Washington, D.C. March 3, 2000.

Chapter 13 – R. A. Schwaller de Lubicz's Magnum Opus

Gurdjieff, G. I. *Beelzebub's Tales to His Grandson: An Objectively Impartial Criticism of the Life of Man*. New York: Arkana, 1992.

Schwaller de Lubicz, R. A. *Nature Word*. Rochester, Vt.: Inner Traditions International, 1990.

———. *The Temple in Man*. Rochester, Vt.: Inner Traditions International, 1977.

———. *The Temple of Man*. Rochester, Vt.: Inner Traditions International, 1998.

Swedenborg, Emanuel. *Essential Readings* (contains *"Correspondences"*) edited by Michael Stanley. Berkeley: North Atlantic Books, 2003.

———. *Heaven and Hell*. Translation by George F. Dole. West Chester, Pa.: Swedenborg Foundation and Chrysalis Books, 2001.

Chapter 14 – Fingerprinting the Gods

Flem-Ath, Rand, and Rose Flem-Ath. *When the Sky Fell: In Search of Atlantis*. New York: St. Martin's Press, 1997.

Hancock, Graham. *The Lords of Poverty*. New York: Atlantis Monthly Press, 1989.

———. *Ethiopia: The Challenge of Hunger*. London: Gollancz, 1985.

———. *Fingerprints of the Gods: The Evidence of Earth's Lost Civilization*. New York: Three Rivers Press, 1995.

———. *The Sign and the Seal, Quest for the Lost Ark of the Covenant*. New York: Touchstone, 1993.

Hancock, Graham, and Carol Beckwith, and Angela Fisher. *African Ark: People and Ancient Cultures of Ethiopia and the Horn of Africa*. New York: H. N. Abrams, 1990.

Santillana, Giorgio de, and Hertha von Dechend. *Hamlet's Mill: An Essay Investigating the Origins of Human Knowledge and Its Transmission through Myth*. Jaffrey, N. H.: Godine Press, 1977.

Chapter 15 – The Central American Mystery

Hart, Will. *The Genesis Race: Our Extraterrestrial DNA and the True Origins of the Species*. Rochester, Vt.: Bear & Company, 2003.

Chapter 16 – Destination Galactic Center

Jenkins, John Major. *Galactic Alignment: The Transformation of Consciousness According to Mayan, Egyptian, and Vedic Traditions*. Rochester, Vt.: Inner Traditions International, 2002.

———. *Mirror in the Sky*. Denver, Colo.: Four Ahau Press, 1991.

————. Web site: http://alignment2012.com.

Jenkins, John Major. *Maya Cosmogenesis 2012: The True Meaning of the Maya Calendar End Date.* Rochester, Vt.: Bear & Company, 1998.

The Secret of the Golden Flower, the Classic Chinese Book of Life. Translated by Thomas Cleary. New York: HarperCollins, 1991.

Waters, Frank. *Mexico Mystique.* Athens, Ohio: Swallow Press and Ohio University Press Books, 1989.

Chapter 17 – Megalithic England: The Atlantean Dimensions

Michell, John. *The Earth Spirit.* New York: Avon, 1975.

————. *The New View Over Atlantis.* London: Thames & Hudson, 2001.

————. *The View Over Atlantis,* New York: Ballantine, 1972.

Plato. *The Timaeus and Critias of Plato.* Translated by Thomas Taylor. Whitefish, Mont.: Kessinger Publishing, 2003.

Chapter 18 – Plato, the Truth

Blackett, William. *Lost History of the World.* London: Truebner & Sons, 1881.

Graves, Robert. *The Greek Myths.* New York: Penguin, 1992.

Herodotus. *The Histories,* translated by James McConnell. London: Truebner Publishers, 1909.

Kukal, Zadenk. *Atlantis.* Translated by Feodor Vasilliov-Smith. New York: Doubleday and Sons, 1970.

Lissner, Ivan. *Mysteries of the Ancient Past.* Chicago: Henry Regnery, 1969.

Plato. *The Republic.* New York: Penguin Books, 1955.

————. *The Timaeus and Critias of Plato.* Translated by Thomas Taylor. Whitefish, Mont.: Kessinger Publishing, 2003.

Robertson, Geoffrey. *The Sciences in Classical Civilization.* New York: Forestham Publishers, 1928.

Strabo. *The Geography.* H. L. Jones translation. 8 volumes. London: 1924.

Thucydides. *The Peloponesian War.* Translated by Max Adrian. London: Bridgetown Press, Ltd., 1904.

Chapter 19 – The Aegean Atlantis Deception

Haliburton, Arnold. *Ancient Crete.* Westport, Conn.: Praeger Press, 1963.

Plato. *The Timaeus and Critias of Plato.* Translated by Thomas Taylor. Whitefish, Mont.: Kessinger Publishing, 2003.

Chapter 20 – Atlantology: Psychotic or Inspired?

Bacon, Sir Francis. *The New Atlantis.* New York: Scribners & Sons, 1933.

Petraitis, Paul. *Athanasius Kircher, German Genius.* London: International House Publishers, Ltd., 1989.

Plato. *The Timaeus and Critias of Plato.* Translated by Thomas Taylor. Whitefish, Mont.: Kessinger Publishing, 2003.

Robertson, Geoffrey. *The Sciences in Classical Civilization.* New York: Forestham Publishers, 1928.

Spence, Lewis. *The History of Atlantis.* Kempton, Ill.: Adventures Unlimited Press, 1995.

———. *The Occult Sciences in Atlantis.* Boston: Red Wheel/Weiser, 1970.

———. *Popol Vuh (Book of Consul): The Mythic and Heroic Sagas of the Riches of Central America.* Whitefish, Mont.: Kessinger Publishing, 1942.

———. *The Problem of Atlantis.* Whitefish, Mont.: Kessinger Publishing, 1942.

———. *Will Europe Follow Atlantis?* Whitefish, Mont.: Kessinger Publishing, 1942.

Spence, Lewis, and Marian Edwards. *Dictionary of Non-Classical Mythology.* Whitefish, Mont.: Kessinger Publishing, 2003.

Spence, Lewis, and Paul Tice. *Atlantis in America.* Whitefish, Mont.: Kessinger Publishing, 1997.

———. *The Problem of Lemuria.* La Vergne, Tenn.: Lightning Source, Inc., 2002.

Steiner, Rudolf. *Cosmic Memory: Prehistory of Earth and Man.* New York: Rudolf Steiner Publications, 1959.

Chapter 21 – Atlantis in Antarctica

Flem-Ath, Rand, and Rose Flem-Ath. *When the Sky Fell: In Search of Atlantis.* New York: St. Martin's Press, 1997.

Hancock, Graham. *Fingerprints of the Gods: The Evidence of Earth's Lost Civilization*. New York: Three Rivers Press, 1995.

Hapgood, Charles. *Earth's Shifting Crust, A Key to Some Basic Problems of Earth Science*. New York: Pantheon Books, 1958.

————. *Maps of the Ancient Sea Kings: Evidence of Advanced Civilization in the Ice Age*. Kempton, Ill.: Adventures Unlimited Press, 1997.

NBC-TV Special, "The Mysterious Origins of Man," February 1996.

Plato. *The Timaeus and Critias of Plato*. Translated by Thomas Taylor. Whitefish, Mont.: Kessinger Publishing, 2003.

Chapter 22 – Blueprint from Atlantis

Aveni, Anthony F., Ph.D. *Archaeoastronomy in Pre-Columbian America*. Austin: University of Texas Press, 1975.

Bauval, Robert, and Adrian Gilbert. *The Orion Mystery: Unlocking the Secrets of the Pyramids*. New York: Crown, 1994.

Flem-Ath, Rand, and Rose Flem-Ath. *When the Sky Fell: In Search of Atlantis*. New York: St. Martin's Press, 1997.

Hancock, Graham, and Robert Bauval. *The Message of the Sphinx: A Quest for the Hidden Legacy of Mankind*. New York: Three Rivers Press, 1996.

Chapter 23 – Japan's Underwater Ruins

Nihon, Shoi, and W. G. Aston (translator). *Nihongi: Chronicles of Japan from the Earliest Times to A.D. 697*. Tokyo: Charles E. Tuttle, 1972.

Philippi, Donald L., *Kojiki*. New York: Columbia University Press, 1977.

Chapter 24 – West, Schoch, and Hancock Dive into Lemurian Waters

Hancock, Graham. *Fingerprints of the Gods: The Evidence of Earth's Lost Civilization*. New York: Three Rivers Press, 1995.

Hancock, Graham, and Robert Bauval. *The Message of the Sphinx: A Quest for the Hidden Legacy of Mankind*. New York: Three Rivers Press, 1996.

Schoch, Robert M., Ph.D. *Voyages of the Pyramid Builders: The True Origins of the Pyramids from Lost Egypt to Ancient America*. New York: Tarcher/Putnam, 2003.

Schoch, Robert M., Ph.D., and Robert Aquinas McNally. *Voices of the Rocks: A Scientist Looks at Catastrophes & Ancient Civilizations.* New York: Harmony Books, 1999.

West, John Anthony. *Serpent in the Sky: The High Wisdom of Ancient Egypt.* Wheaton, Ill.: Quest Books, 1993.

Chapter 25 – India 30,000 B.C.E.

Allan, D. S., and J. B. Delair. *Cataclysm! Compelling Evidence of a Cosmic Catastrophe in 9500 BC.* Rochester, Vt.: Bear & Company, 1997.

Atlantis Rising #12. "A Discussion by David Lewis of *Cataclysm! Compelling Evidence of a Cosmic Catastrophe in 9500 BC.*" Whitefish, Mont.: August 1997.

The Ramayana: A Shortened Modern Prose Version of the Indian Epic by R. K. Narayant Kampar Ramayanam. New York: Penguin Classics, 1972.

Chapter 26 – A Conversation with Peter Tompkins

Muck, Otto. The *Secret of Atlantis.* New York: Crown, 1978.

Tompkins, Peter. *Mysteries of the Mexican Pyramids.* London: Thames & Hudson, 1987.

Tompkins, Peter, and Christopher Bird. *The Secret Life of Plants.* New York: Harper and Row, 1973.

———. *Secrets of the Soil: New Solutions for Restoring our Planet.* Anchorage, Alaska: Earthpulse Press, 1998.

Tompkins, Peter and Livio Catullo Stecchini. *Secrets of the Great Pyramid.* BBS Publishing Corporation, 1997.

Chapter 27 – Ancient Agriculture, in Search of the Missing Links

Hart, Will. *The Genesis Race: Our Extraterrestrial DNA and the True Origins of the Species.* Rochester, Vt.: Bear & Company, 2003.

www.http://mysteriesunsealed.org.

Chapter 28 – Atlantean Technology: How Advanced?

Cayce, Edgar. *The Edgar Cayce Readings*, vol. 22. Virginia Beach, Va.: Association for Research and Enlightenment, 1988.

Cayce, Edgar, and Hugh Lynn Cayce. *Edgar Cayce on Atlantis.* New York: Warner Books, 1968.

Childress, David, and Ivan Sanderson. *Vimana Aircraft of Ancient India and Atlantis.* Kempton, Ill.: Adventures Unlimited Press, 1994.

Herodotus. *The Histories,* translated by James McConnell. London: Truebner Publishers, 1909.

Joseph, Frank. *Edgar Cayce's Atlantis and Lemuria: The Lost Civilizations in Light of Modern Discoveries.* Virginia Beach, Va.: A.R.E. Press (Association of Research and Enlightenment), 2001.

Plato. *The Timaeus and Critias of Plato.* Translated by Thomas Taylor. Whitefish, Mont.: Kessinger Publishing, 2003.

Robertson, Geoffrey. *The Sciences in Classical Civilization.* New York: Forestham Publishers, 1928.

Chapter 29 – Archeology and the Law of Gravity

Fox-TV/National Geographic Special, "Pyramids Live: Secret Chambers Revealed," Live broadcast of the Queen's Chamber in the Great Pyramid, Egypt. September 16, 2002.

"Secrets of Lost Empires: Obelisk" (#WG2405). *NOVA* documentary. WGBH Boston Video, 1997.

"Secrets of Lost Empires II: Pharaoh's Obelisk" (#WG900). *NOVA* documentary. WGBH Boston Video, 2000.

Chapter 30 – An Engineer In Egypt

Bauval, Robert, and Adrian Gilbert. *The Orion Mystery: Unlocking the Secrets of the Pyramids.* New York: Crown, 1994.

Dunn, Christopher. "Advanced Machining in Ancient Egypt" *Analog Science Fiction and Fact,* V104 #8, New York: August 1984.

Edwards, I. E. S., Ph.D. *Ancient Egypt.* Washington, D.C.: National Geographic Society, 1978.

"Genesis in Stone," a documentary featuring Christopher Dunn, Robert M. Schoch, Ph.D., and John Anthony West. Netherlands Television, Rooel Oostra Producer, 1995.

Hancock, Graham. *Fingerprints of the Gods: The Evidence of Earth's Lost Civilization.* New York: Three Rivers Press, 1995.

Petrie, Sir William Flinders. *Pyramids and Temples of Gizeh*. London: Keegan Paul International, 2002.

Chapter 31 – The Giza Power Plant, Technologies of Ancient Egypt

Dunn, Christopher. *The Giza Power Plant: Technologies of Ancient Egypt*. Rochester, Vt.: Bear & Company, August 1998.

Chapter 32 – Return to the Giza Power Plant

Dunn, Christopher. "Advanced Machining in Ancient Egypt." *Analog Science Fiction and Fact,* V104 #8, New York: August 1984.

———. *The Giza Power Plant: Technologies of Ancient Egypt*. Rochester, Vt.: Bear & Company, 1998.

Chapter 33 – Petrie on Trial

Dunn, Christopher. *The Giza Power Plant: Technologies of Ancient Egypt,* Rochester, Vt.: Bear & Company, 1998.

———. "Advanced Machining in Ancient Egypt." *Analog Science Fiction and Fact,* V104 #8, New York: August 1984.

Lawton, Ian, and Chris Ogilvie-Herald. *Giza: The Truth*. Montpelier, Vt.: Invisible Cities Press, 2001.

Petrie, Sir William Flinders. *Pyramids and Temples of Gizeh*. London: Keegan Paul International, 2002.

"Secrets of Lost Empires: Obelisk" (#WG2405). *NOVA* documentary. WGBH Boston Video, 1997.

"Secrets of Lost Empires II: Pharaoh's Obelisk" (#WG900). *NOVA* documentary. WGBH Boston Video, 2000.

Chapter 34 – How Did the Pyramid Builders Spell Relief?

Dunn, Christopher. *The Giza Power Plant: Technologies of Ancient Egypt*. Rochester, Vt.: Bear & Company, 1998.

Ludwig, Daniela. "Offene Fragestellungen in Zusammenhang mit der Cheopspyramide in Giza aus baukonstruktiver Sicht." *Göttinger Miszellen* 173/1999.

Petrie, Sir William Flinders. *Pyramids and Temples of Gizeh*. London: Keegan Paul International, 2002.

Chapter 35 – Precision

Dunn, Christopher. *The Giza Power Plant: Technologies of Ancient Egypt.* Rochester, Vt.: Bear & Company, 1998.

www.gizapower.com.

Chapter 36 – The Obelisk Quarry Mystery

Dunn, Christopher. "Precision." *Atlantis Rising* #32. Livingston, Mont.: March/April 2002.

Lucas, A., and J. R. Harris. *Ancient Egyptian Materials and Industries.* Mineola, N.Y.: Dover Publications, 1999.

Petrie, Sir William Flinders. *Pyramids and Temples of Gizeh.* London: Keegan Paul International, 2002.

"Secrets of Lost Empires: Obelisk" (#WG2405). *NOVA* documentary. WGBH Boston Video, 1997.

"Secrets of Lost Empires II: Pharaoh's Obelisk" (#WG900). *NOVA* documentary. WGBH Boston Video, 2000.

Chapter 37 – Behind the Pyramid's Secret Doors

Bauval, Robert, and Adrian Gilbert. *The Orion Mystery: Unlocking the Secrets of the Pyramids.* New York: Crown, 1994.

Dunn, Christopher. *The Giza Power Plant: Technologies of Ancient Egypt.* Rochester, Vt.: Bear & Company, 1998.

Fox-TV/National Geographic Special, "Pyramids Live: Secret Chambers Revealed." Live broadcast of the Queen's Chamber in the Great Pyramid, Egypt, September 16, 2002.

West, John Anthony. *Serpent in the Sky: The High Wisdom of Ancient Egypt.* Wheaton, Ill.: Quest Books, 1993.

www.gizapower.com.

Chapter 38 – The Case for Advanced Technology in the Great Pyramid

Campbell, Joseph. *The Masks of God—Occidental Mythology.* New York: Penguin Books, Rei Edition, 1991.

Petrie, Sir William Flinders. *Pyramids and Temples of Gizeh.* London: Keegan Paul International, 2002.

Tompkins, Peter. *Secrets of the Great Pyramid.* New York: Harper and Row, 1978.

Chapter 39 – Visitors from Beyond

Plato. *The Timaeus and Critias of Plato*. Translated by Thomas Taylor. Whitefish, Mont.: Kessinger Publishing, 2003.

Santillana, Giorgio de, and Hertha von Dechend. *Hamlet's Mill: An Essay Investigating the Origins of Human Knowledge and Its Transmission through Myth*. Jaffrey, N.H.: Godine Press, 1977.

Sitchin, Zecharia. *Divine Encounters: A Guide to Visions, Angels and Other Emissaries*. Rochester, Vt.: Bear & Company, 2002.

———. *The Earth Chronicles Expeditions: Journeys to the Mythical Past*. Rochester, Vt.: Bear & Company, 1994.

———. *The Epic of Gilgamesh*. New York: Penguin Books, 2003.

———. *Genesis Revisited*. Rochester, Vt.: Bear & Company, 2002.

———. *The Lost Realms*. Rochester, Vt.: Bear & Company, 2002.

———. *The Stairway to Heaven*. Rochester, Vt.: Bear & Company, 2002.

———. *The 12th Planet*. Rochester, Vt.: Bear & Company, 2002.

———. *The Wars of Gods and Men*. Rochester, Vt.: Bear & Company, 2002.

———. *When Time Began*. Rochester, Vt.: Bear & Company, 2002.

Chapter 40 – Artifacts in Space

Hoagland, Richard. *The Monuments of Mars: A City on the Edge of Forever*. Berkeley: North Atlantic Books, 2001.

"Proposed Studies on the Implications of Peaceful Space Activities for Human Affairs," a report by the Brookings Institution, commissioned by NASA. Washington, D.C.: November 30, 1960.

Chapter 41 – The Pulsar Mystery

Bell, Jocelyn. "Observation of a Rapidly Pulsating Radio Source." *Nature* 217: 709 (1968), with A. Hewish, J. D. H. Pilkington, P. F. Scott, and R. A. Collins. London.

———. "Observations of Some Further Pulsed Radio Source." *Nature* 218: 126 (1968), with J. D. H. Pilkington, A. Hewish, and T. W. Cole. London.

LaViolette, Paul, Ph.D. *Earth Under Fire: Humanity's Survival of the Apocalypse*. Fresno, Calif.: Starlane Publications, 1997.

————. *Genesis of the Cosmos: The Ancient Science of Continuous Creation.* Rochester, Vt.: Bear & Company, 2004.

————. *Subquantum Kinetics: The Alchemy of Creation.* Schenectady, N.Y.: Starburst Publications, 1994.

————. *The Talk of the Galaxy: An ET Message for Us?* Fresno, Calif.:. Starlane Publications, 2000.

Plato. *The Timaeus and Critias of Plato.* Translated by Thomas Taylor. Whitefish, Mont.: Kessinger Publishing, 2003.

Chapter 42 – The Physicist as Mystic

Bloom, Allan. *The Closing of the American Mind.* New York: Simon & Schuster, 1987.

LaViolette, Paul, Ph.D. *Genesis of the Cosmos: The Ancient Science of Continuous Creation.* Rochester, Vt.: Bear & Company, 2004.

Talbott, Michael. *The Holographic Universe,* New York: HarperCollins, 1991.

Contributors

Mel and Amy Acheson

Mel and Amy Acheson are freelance journalists and researchers who live in Oregon. They studied planetary catastrophism for forty years and for the past five years have collaborated with Wallace Thornhill and Dave Talbott on the Internet newsletter THOTH, which features the convergent theories of Thornhill and Talbott. The Achesons currently are working on a DVD/monograph series called "Thunderbolts of the Gods," available in 2005.

Peter Bros

Having disagreed at an early age with the accepted explanation that objects fall because it is a property of them to fall, Peter Bros challenged the current, splintered concepts of empirical science by taking an advanced science curriculum at Bullis Preparatory School, a degree in English at Maryland University, and a Doctor of Jurisprudence at Georgetown. The result is *The Copernican Series,* a multi-volume exposition that sets forth a consistent picture of physical reality and humanity's place in the universe.

Christopher Dunn

Christopher Dunn has spent more than four decades working at every level of high-tech manufacturing and is currently a senior manager at a Midwest aerospace company. His book, *The Giza Power Plant: Technologies of Ancient Egypt,* published by Bear & Company, Rochester, Vermont, continues to influence technologists and scientists across many disciplines.

William P. Eigles

William P. Eigles is the managing editor of *Aperture,* the quarterly publication of the International Remote Viewing Association, which promotes scientifically validated paranormal perception. A former attorney and professional engineer, he is a writer, advocate, and noetic adviser.

Rand Flem-Ath and Rose Flem-Ath

Rand Flem-Ath is a Canadian librarian and the author with his wife Rose Flem-Ath of *When the Sky Fell: In Search of Atlantis,* which originated the theory that Antarctica was Atlantis before a displacement of the Earth's crust occurred. He is also the author of *The Atlantis Blueprint,* a seminal scientific work on ancient sites across the globe. He and his wife live on Vancouver Island on Canada's beautiful west coast.

Will Hart

Will Hart is a veteran journalist and a regular contributor to *Atlantis Rising.* An independent researcher with a deep and abiding interest in history's mysteries, he is also a widely published outdoor photographer and the author of *The Genesis Race.*

Frank Joseph

Frank Joseph's books, published by Bear & Company, Rochester, Vermont, include *The Destruction of Atlantis; Survivors of Atlantis;* and *The Lost Treasure of King Juba.* He has been the editor in chief of *Ancient American* magazine since 1993, is a member of Ohio's Midwest Epigraphic Society, and was inducted into Japan's Savant Society in 2000.

Len Kasten

Len Kasten received a B.A. degree from Cornell University in psychology and literature. His interest in New Age subjects began when he was introduced to the Edgar Cayce material while living in Virginia. He studied theosophy with British author/teacher Cyril Benton who was the founder of the American Philosopher Society, and upon Mr. Benton's death, he became the president of the Society. Len Kasten was also the editor of the magazine *Metamorphosis,* which was one of the first New Age magazines in the country. He later became the editor of *Horizons,* published in Farmington, Connecticut.

J. Douglas Kenyon

J. Douglas Kenyon has spent the last forty years breaking down barriers to paradigm-challenging ideas. From hosting radio talk shows in the 1960s to narrating video documentaries in the 1990s, Doug has always pushed points of view largely ignored by the mainstream press. He founded *Atlantis Rising* magazine in 1994 and, since that time, it has become a "magazine of record" for ancient mysteries, alternative science, and unexplained anomalies. Doug Kenyon lives in Montana.

John Kettler

John Kettler is a frequent contributor to *Atlantis Rising* on alternative science as well as being a published poet. A military analyst for more than eleven years with Hughes and Rockwell, John Kettler is now a director for a marketing and graphics firm. He lives in Carson, California.

David Samuel Lewis

David Samuel Lewis is a journalist who has made a personal study of the issues of alternative science. He publishes *The Montana Pioneer,* a monthly news-and-human-interest journal distributed in southwest Montana. He also regularly contributes articles to *Atlantis Rising* that deal with alternative theories of history, science, human origins, and consciousness. Born and raised near Philadelphia, David Lewis now makes his home in Livingston, Montana.

Steven Parsons

Steven Parsons received a master's degree in journalism in 1989 from the University of Wisconsin, Madison, with a focus on science reporting. He has worked as a journalist and technical writer since then. His interest in the work of Immanuel Velikovsky began in the 1970s and was inspired by the continuing research of David Talbott and Wallace Thornhill.

Marshall Payn

Marshall Payn graduated with a degree in engineering from M.I.T. in 1956. He is experienced in both mechanical engineering and sales engineering and is presently the District Manager for an industrial valve company. He has done extensive research in archeology, specializing in the study of megalithic monuments, and is a frequent contributor to *Atlantis Rising.*

Joseph Ray

Joseph Ray studied at The Center for Brain Research at the University of Rochester, receiving his Ph.D. in 1965. Studying learning in various animal species, he published several "firsts," disputing the dominant but incorrect theory of behaviorism. Meditation and the writings of G. I. Gurdjieff led him to ancient Egyptian thought and an effort to deepen his understanding of the remarkable teachings of the ancient philosopher-scientist-priests.

Robert M. Schoch

Robert M. Schoch, a full-time faculty member at the College of General Studies at Boston University since 1984, earned his Ph.D. in geology and geophysics from Yale University. Dr. Schoch is known internationally as a specialist on ancient Egypt. His books include *Voices of the Rocks: A Scientist Looks at Catastrophes and Ancient Civilizations* (with R. A. McNally) and *Voyages of the Pyramid Builders: The True Origins of the Pyramids from Lost Egypt to Ancient America* (also with R. A. McNally).

Moira Timms

Moira Timms, M.S., is the author of the bestsellers *Prophecies and Predictions: Everyone's Guide to the Coming Changes, Beyond Prophecies and Predictions,* and *The Six O'clock Bus: A Guide to Armageddon and the New Age.* She is a researcher and "archaic futurist" specializing in the beginnings and endings of historical cycles. Her work encompasses a deep understanding of Egyptian Sacred Science (its symbolism, mythology, and mysteries), Jungian psychology, and prophecy.